Getting an Information Security Job

FOR DUMMIES®

A Wiley Brand

by Peter H. Gregory

Getting an Information Security Job For Dummies®

Published by: **John Wiley & Sons, Inc.,** 111 River Street, Hoboken, NJ 07030-5774, www.wiley.com

Copyright © 2015 by John Wiley & Sons, Inc., Hoboken, New Jersey

Media and software compilation copyright © 2015 by John Wiley & Sons, Inc. All rights reserved.

Published simultaneously in Canada.

For general information on our other products and services, please contact our Customer Care Department within the U.S. at 877-762-2974, outside the U.S. at 317-572-3993, or fax 317-572-4002. For technical support, please visit www.wiley.com/techsupport.

Wiley publishes in a variety of print and electronic formats and by print-on-demand. Some material included with standard print versions of this book may not be included in e-books or in print-on-demand. If this book refers to media such as a CD or DVD that is not included in the version you purchased, you may download this material at http://booksupport.wiley.com. For more information about Wiley products, visit www.wiley.com.

Library of Congress Control Number: 2014954662

ISBN 978-1-119-00281-9 (pbk) 978-1-119-00284-0 (ebk); ISBN 978-1-119-00262-8 (ebk)

Manufactured in the United States of America

10 9 8 7 6 5 4 3 2 1

Table of Contents

Introduction

The information security (InfoSec) profession got its start decades ago, but it consisted of few people, mostly in military and other secret organizations. With the appearance of the Internet in the 1990s, organizations started to put information online, and the InfoSec profession became a little more popular. Fast-forward to the mid 2010s, with its big security breaches as well as new laws and regulations, and information security is one of the hottest professions around the world.

About This Book

There are more than enough books on information security, but far too few professionals to do the work. Until now, there was no clear guide to getting into the profession. Delivered in the same rich tradition of the *Dummies* series, *Getting an Information Security Job For Dummies* is that clear guide on planning your entry in information security, no matter where you are in your career today:

- ✔ **If you're a student or recent graduate,** you'll get real-life information on what it's like in the information security profession.

- ✔ **If you're an experienced IT professional,** you'll understand how to make a lateral move into information security.

- ✔ **If you're already getting your start in information security,** you can chart your career path and decide what kind of an organization you may want to work in.

- ✔ **If you're in the information security job market,** you'll understand different types of information security jobs in different types of organizations.

- ✔ **If you need to hire an information security professional,** you'll find lots of information to help you focus on what kind of candidate you need and to better understand the people who are applying for your positions.

No matter why you're reading this book, you can use it as a security career reference. *Getting an Information Security Job For Dummies* is full of insight from real information security professionals, in their own voices. You'll begin to understand what the InfoSec profession is really like from professionals who have been going at it for years.

Foolish Assumptions

While writing this book, I've made some assumptions about you:

✔ **You are curious about technology and how things work.** Even if you're looking to get into the compliance or controls aspect of information security, it's still important to have a healthy appreciation for how technology supports an organization.

✔ **You dislike malware and the criminal organizations that create them.** Even if you don't yet understand how cybercriminals work, your conscience tells you that what they are doing is wrong, and you want to learn how to help organizations better defend themselves.

✔ **You enjoy learning.** My first clue: You are reading this book! Being in information security — or any branch of information technology — demands continuous learning. Security issues and technology itself change quite rapidly, and continuous learning is needed just to keep up!

✔ **You like Dr. Who** and his problem-solving capabilities, even if some of the scenarios he finds himself in are a little odd.

How am I doing so far? If all of my assumptions are right, you may be InfoSec material and ready to seriously consider a career in information security.

Icons Used in This Book

Throughout this book, you'll see icons in the left margin that call attention to information that's worth noting. No smiley faces winking at you or any other cute little emoticons, but you'll definitely want to take note! Here's what to look for and what to expect.

Throughout the book, you'll find stories and tips from information security professionals, in their own voices.

This icon identifies general information and core concepts that are well worth committing to your nonvolatile memory, your gray matter, or your noggin' — along with anniversaries, birthdays, and other important stuff!

Thank you for reading; we hope you enjoy the book; please take care of your writers! Seriously, this icon includes helpful suggestions and tidbits of useful information that may save you some time and headaches.

Whatever I'm warning you about is nothing *that* hazardous. These helpful alerts point out easily confused or difficult-to-understand terms and concepts.

Beyond the Book

In additional to the material in the print or ebook you're reading, this product also comes with more online goodies:

- ✔ **Cheat sheet:** The cheat sheet offers tips on interviewing for an information security job and building your personal brand. You can find the cheat sheet at www.dummies.com/cheatsheet/gettinganinformation-securityjob.

- ✔ **Web extras:** You'll find some great references that you can use, including a resume template, a sample resume, and a list of websites of value to information security professionals. Go to www.dummies.com/extras/gettinganinformationsecurityjob.

- ✔ Updates to this book, if we have any, are at www.dummies.com/go/gettinganinformationsecurityjobudupdates.

Where to Go from Here

If you're wondering what the information security profession is all about, go to Part I. If you want to dive into the education, training, and knowledge required in information security, start with Part II. If you're wondering what life is like in different types of organizations, Part III was written just for you. If you're ready to get out there in the InfoSec job market, go right to Part IV. If you love lists, head for Part V.

And for those who want to take an even deeper dive into the knowledge expected of information security professionals, get a copy of *CISSP For Dummies*, by Lawrence Miller and Peter H. Gregory.

Part I

So You Want to Be an InfoSec Professional

getting started
with

information

security

Visit www.dummies.com for great *For Dummies* content online.

In this part . . .

- ✔ Find out how industry conditions have led to today's high demand for skilled information security professionals.

- ✔ Understand typical job titles and their duties.

- ✔ Discover the security problems that governments and industries face today.

Chapter 1

Securing Your Future in Information Security

According to the *Cisco 2014 Annual Security Report*, the worldwide shortage of information security professionals exceeds *one million workers*. You have chosen a great time to learn more about this exciting and rapidly changing field!

This chapter takes a closer look at the changes in business and technology that have given rise to the high demand for information security workers. You also discover why information security is a great career field.

Why Does Information Security Matter?

Information security, or *InfoSec,* was once considered a technical discipline with little business relevance. Now, however, it is a topic of heated discussions in corporate boardrooms around the world. Information security matters because information technology matters — and because criminals are finding it easy to steal sensitive and private information from organizations' information systems.

Increased reliance on information systems

Organizations of every kind, as well as a growing number of private citizens, rely on information systems for conducting daily affairs more than ever before. We buy more and more Internet-connected products, partly for convenience and partly for the cool factor. Before long, it will be easier to count the things that *aren't* connected to the Internet.

You might have heard that data and information are the new currency. Although this statement might sound like a cliche, it's true for several reasons:

✔ Organizations can use software tools to examine electronic business records and gain valuable insights that help them find new opportunities. For instance, a grocery store can add new items to its inventory based on sales trends.

✔ Organizations can use information systems to make business processes more efficient. For example, if an organization puts sales details in an information system, the customer service department could electronically access those records and be far more efficient.

✔ For banks and other financial institutions, data actually *is* money, or at least the closest representation of money. For instance, transferring funds or paying bills online is mostly about making a number bigger in one place and smaller in another.

This increased reliance on Internet-connected systems and devices makes our businesses more efficient and our lives easier, but there is a dark side: Criminals are also turning to Internet-connected systems to disrupt businesses and steal valuable information.

Growth in cybercrime

Organizations of every kind are increasing their reliance on information systems for storing and processing valuable information. Meanwhile, cybercriminal organizations have grown, organized, and made vast improvements in the skills and tools they use to find and steal this information.

"Last year was the first year that proceeds from cybercrime were greater than proceeds from the sale of illegal drugs, and that was, I believe, over $105 billion," according to Valerie McNiven, who advises the U.S. Treasury on cybercrime. "Cybercrime is moving at such a high speed that law enforcement cannot catch up with it." Ms. McNiven made this claim in 2005; in the past ten years, cybercriminal organizations have made impressive gains in their capability to steal valuable data.

According to idtheftcenter.org, some of the largest security breaches in 2014 were as follows:

✔ Sony Pictures: 33 thousand documents and several unreleased films

✔ U.S. Weather System: breach to NOAA weather satellite network

✔ JP Morgan Chase: 76 million records

✔ Home Depot: 56 million records

✔ Community Health Systems/Tennova: 4.5 million records

✔ Michaels Stores: 2.6 million records

✔ Texas Health and Human Services: 2 million records

✔ Internal Revenue Service: 1.4 million records

✔ Staples: more than 1.1 million records

✔ Neiman Marcus: 1.1 million records

✔ State of Montana: more than 1 million records

✔ Viator: 880 thousand records

✔ Goodwill Industries: 868 thousand records

✔ Oregon Employment Department: 851 thousand records

✔ U.S. Postal Service: 800 thousand records

✔ Variable Annuity Life Insurance Company: 774 thousand records

✔ Spec: 550 thousand records

✔ Aaron Brothers: 400 thousand records

Although 2014 was not an encouraging year in information security, it is for businesses whose mission is the protection of critical information.

So many security breaches are occurring that several websites are devoted to listing them, including

✔ www.privacyrights.org

✔ www.idtheftcenter.org

✔ www.datalossdb.org

Improved defenses

This scourge of break-ins and breaches does not mean that governments and industries are going to turn tail and stop their expansion of information systems. Instead, organizations of every size and type are hiring security professionals to improve security measures that protect their systems. Security professionals are doing the following to protect critical data:

✔ Hardening systems and applications to make them more difficult to attack

✔ Adding layers of defense

- Performing security scans to find vulnerabilities
- Conducting internal audits of security controls
- Training personnel to recognize intrusion attempts
- Improving security in partner and supplier organizations
- Updating business processes to include security procedures

A Brief History of Cybercrime

As far back as recorded history goes, we know that whenever one party collects or creates anything of wealth, another party will do his or her best to steal or spoil the owner's wealth. It makes sense, then, that as individuals and organizations use information systems to create, store, or spend wealth, others will do whatever they can to take the wealth for themselves. As individuals and organizations become increasingly reliant on information systems, more valuable information is created. So news of security breaches in which these information hordes are stolen or vandalized should not come as a surprise.

It helps to wind the clock back a few years to see how security breaches all came about. Although the first security incidents weren't so much about stealing money, they provided the foundation for later incidents in which monetary theft *was* the object.

The history of cybercrime can be thought of as two different related trends on a collision course:

- Improvements in malware potency
- Increased use of computers, networks, and the Internet to manage and control just about everything

These trends have gradually moved toward each other, each gaining momentum. If you're imagining two locomotives barreling toward each other, that's not quite the right image. The collision of malware potency and increased computer dependence has been slower — like cold air from the north colliding with warm air from the south, wreaking unpredictable havoc in multiple locations.

Malware

Malware is a general term that encompasses many kinds of harmful programs or program fragments such as viruses, Trojan horses, worms, and bots (for a more detailed description of malware, see Chapter 3). Early forms of malware were simple, almost like experiments developed by computer hobbyists who thought, "I wonder what will happen if I build a piece of computer code that does this?"

These early versions of malware were crude and performed simple functions, such as displaying something on the computer screen or deleting files. The creators of malware made no attempt to hide themselves, because there was nothing to hide from.

Fast-forward to today, when malware has become so potent and stealthy that your life can become miserable if you depend on computers and networks.

Break-ins and breaches

Malware is not the only tool in an attacker's toolbox. Just as a lock-picking set is only one way to break into a building, other techniques are frequently used to break into computer systems, such as computer break-ins and breaches. Some of the techniques used include social engineering, phishing, and watering hole attacks. These attacks are occurring more often than before for a variety of reasons:

- ✔ More companies using information systems
- ✔ More companies are building interconnections
- ✔ Higher value information being stored on information systems
- ✔ Growing shortage of personnel who know how to implement good security
- ✔ Cybercriminal organizations building better intrusion tools
- ✔ Profitable cooperation among cybercriminal organizations

We are living in a perfect storm, where more companies are storing high-value information that they don't know how to protect from criminal organizations that are getting better at finding and stealing it. The situation is truly becoming dire, and we could use more help!

One of the biggest problems in computer security today is social engineering, which is any of several techniques of deception designed to take over computers or obtain sensitive information. When organizations do a good job of protecting their computers and networks, intruders turn to hacking people instead — too often with great success.

Fraud

Another form of cybercrime is online fraud. The definitions of *fraud*, according to Wiktionary, are

- ✔ Any act of deception carried out for the purpose of unfair, undeserved and/or unlawful gain.
- ✔ The assumption of a false identity to such deceptive end.
- ✔ A person who performs any such trick.

Fraud has been a problem since the beginning of history. And today, fraud has found a cozy home in the world of information systems and the Internet.

The most prevalent form of fraud is the *phishing scheme,* in which an adversary creates some ruse, identifies potential victims, and attempts to trick them into doing something they should not do. Here are some examples of email or other communications that the potential victim might receive:

- ✔ **Bank:** Your funds are low, or are being locked because of suspected fraud (this one's really ironic).
- ✔ **Taxes:** You owe taxes to the government and will be in trouble unless you pay right now.
- ✔ **Law enforcement:** You have overdue fines or there's a warrant for your arrest.
- ✔ **Sweepstakes:** You're the winner of a sweepstakes and must provide financial information to claim your prize.
- ✔ **Inheritance:** You have inherited money, and the organization that holds your funds needs help so that they can transfer your newfound wealth to you.
- ✔ **Friend in need:** A friend of yours is in trouble with law enforcement and needs you to send money to get out of jail.
- ✔ **Email account:** You need to confirm your identity and increase your storage to continue using your email account.

In these and virtually all others ruses, you think that you've been directed to the organization's website for the purpose stated, but you are actually sent to an imposter site. There, you might fill in your login credentials, which the fraudsters use to gain access to the real site and carry out their scheme, such as stealing your money or taking over your email account. Or the imposter site has a form that requests a credit card number, a bank account number, or other sensitive information that the fraudster can use to separate you from your money.

Today's online fraud schemes are nothing more than modern-day confidence tricks designed to convince you to trust an unknown party and then provide them with sensitive information.

Knowing Your Adversaries

Many technologists think that an information security program is all about technology: That technology is the root of the problem and technology will solve those problems. If this describes you, I appeal to you to open your mind to other ways of thinking about information security. Even if the aspect of information security that fascinates you the most is technology (and we need a lot more people like you), understanding the people behind technology-related issues can be helpful.

Information security involves a lot of technology but is at its root a people issue. Information security professionals are responsible for protecting assets against people: careless insiders, malicious outsiders, and many in between. Our vocabulary includes a lot of terms for things, including the different sorts of actors and their unique behaviors that we all eschew. I describe them in this section.

Hobbyists and enthusiasts

Because the term *hacker* has been maligned in recent years, I prefer to use the term *computer hobbyist* to describe computer enthusiasts who love to explore computers to understand more about how they work. Hackers, hobbyists, and enthusiasts — let's agree that they're all about the same.

Hobbyists are curious, peaceful folk who love technology, love to figure out how things work, and love to improve their electronic gadgets. Hobbyists and inventors are similar. Both enjoy making things better for themselves and others by taking things apart (logically or literally) to see how they work, and then modifying them to make them better. The world is full of people who like to tinker with their cars, motorcycles, radios, and computers. Think of early computer overclockers or musicians whose amps go up to 11.

Hobbyists with good judgment and discipline are our friends.

The fall of hackerdom

Before most people in the world were even born, the term *hacker* was generally a positive one. A hacker was a hobbyist who was curious about how electronic-ish things worked and would implement customizations to improve or enhance their performance. In the early days of computers, a *computer hacker* was one who sought to understand how computers worked and to employ changes to improve them.

Then as now, some hackers would explore computer systems — still seeking how they worked and ways of making modifications — but for malicious purposes.

The term *hacker* as a benevolent hobbyist has fallen into disuse and the dominant meaning of the term is a malicious person. And good hackers are generally known as computer hobbyists so they can distance themselves from the others.

Script kiddies

A deservedly maligned bunch, *script kiddies* are teenage troublemakers with too much time on their hands who use tools created by others to attack computers and networks. Typical script kiddies have little or no understanding of the inner workings of the tools they use.

Early in my career, script kiddies were typically the most significant problem for us — there were a lot of them and the tools they used could cause quite a bit of damage. But in retrospect, they were like gnats that swarmed around our faces, irritating and bothersome but usually not very harmful.

Like a lot of technologists, some script kiddies start as novices but build their knowledge and skills. They improve the tools they use and, eventually, write hacking tools of their own.

Hacktivists

Hacktivist is a blend of the words *hacker* and *activist* (think Greenpeace or PETA). Hacktivists are generally known for disrupting computers and networks belonging to organizations and governments with whom they disagree politically or ideologically.

It's a big crowded world, and the Internet is a never-ending fount of information about every sort of organization. For every organization, you'll likely find people who oppose what the organization does or stands for.

Some noteworthy examples of hacktivist activities follow:

- ✔ **PGP (pretty good privacy):** A popular email encryption program, PGP was thought to be released in response to a U.S. Senate bill that demanded government access to the plain text contents of voice, data, and other communications.

- ✔ **Website mirroring:** When an organization or a government blocks access to a particular website, a hacktivist will mirror (copy) the contents of the blocked site to another site, so that its contents can remain available.

- ✔ **Wikileaks:** This website publishes leaked industry and government documents.

Corporate spies

Companies spying on each other to obtain commercial secrets is nothing new. However, the migration of paper records to computers and the Internet has provided new opportunities and methods for companies to spy on each other. The Internet provides the means for spies to discover target systems and to steal their data for further analysis and exploitation.

The future is bright for information security jobs

There is a critical worldwide shortage of workers with information security skills. For the most part, these jobs pay well, with pretty good working conditions and a good standard of living.

In January 2014, the Ponemon Institute conducted a survey of information security managers and developed several key findings, including:

- ✔ 70 percent of respondents said that they don't have enough IT security staff.

- ✔ 58 percent of senior security staff positions and 36 percent of staff security positions went unfilled in 2013.

In 2014, Burning Glass Technologies market overview on information security jobs cited that job listings in cybersecurity have grown by 74 percent from 2007–2013, more than twice the growth rate for IT jobs overall.

Unlike the dot com bubble in the late 1990s, the growth rate in information security jobs is not a flash in the pan but a response to painful advances by cybercriminal organizations as well as increasing regulation on information security and privacy. Short of a miraculous discovery in data protection that cybercriminal organizations are unable to overcome (yeah, right!), the demand for information security jobs should remain strong for many years.

Malicious insiders

Take good care of your employees and they'll take good care of you. However, companies that don't treat employees so nicely sometimes pay a heavy price. Employees who are bored, angry, unhappy, or who think that they will soon be fired or laid off often use revenge to settle the score.

Now and then, we hear a tale in which an employee who believed that his or her job was about to end decided to exact revenge on the employer. The popular cult movie *Office Space* explores this theme in detail.

Careless insiders

A *careless insider* is a legitimate user in an organization but, well, careless. Perhaps the person lacks judgment, or is working too fast, or needs training, or is not paying attention.

Careless insiders can be especially damaging to an organization because they possess what intruders lack: issued login credentials.

Fraudsters

Fraudster is a broad label that includes people who deceive and steal. How they deceive and what they steal varies, but invariably they perform some kind of a trick to steal money.

Typical fraud cases in the broad category of cybercrime include the following:

- ✔ **Credit card fraud:** Fraudsters steal credit card numbers and use them to buy stuff they want. You might still get the frequent flyer miles or other rewards, but you're out the money, and that hurts.

- ✔ **Wire fraud:** Fraudsters employ malware that steals login credentials, and target a company with lots of money in the bank, in hopes that they can capture online banking and online wire transfer login codes. If they do, that giant sucking sound is the organization's money being transferred to an offshore account.

- ✔ **Identity theft:** These actors use a variety of ways to obtain enough personal information about people to permit the opening of credit cards and lines of credit in the name of the victim. (By the way, they aren't actually stealing your identity; they're borrowing it.)

Organized crime

Organized crime used to be known for sex and drug trafficking, illegal gambling, and protection rackets. Today, however, organized crime makes more money perpetrating online fraud and other Internet-based schemes. These organizations are in all corners of the world, but particularly in Eastern Europe, the Middle East, and Africa.

The sophistication of a lot of today's malware points to organizations with large, formal research and development budgets. Most of the easy hacks have been written; now more work (and bigger organizations) and better planning are required to build the tools necessary to break into systems and networks.

Rogue nation-states

The governments of several countries understand that state sponsorship is one way to develop malware and other techniques to break into networks and steal valuable information.

Nation-states sponsor cybercriminal activities for a number of reasons, such as to

✔ Steal political secrets

✔ Steal military secrets

✔ Aid local industries through industrial espionage

✔ Conduct industrial or military sabotage

If this sounds like traditional espionage — you're right! Today's spies have moved into cyberspace to do their work. If the information they want is online, many will use online means to try and steal it.

Cyberwarfare rules of engagement

If you're on the side of the white hats, cyberwarfare is not a lot of fun. If it seems like adversaries have the upper hand, it's because adversaries have the upper hand.

Cyberware is said to be asymmetric. In other words, a single individual can wield the same amount of attack effectiveness as the largest country in the world. With the right tools, an individual can cripple a large military organization.

The following lists some rules of engagement for attackers and defenders:

✔ Defenders must protect against all types of attacks, whereas an attacker can attack in any manner desired.

✔ Defenders must protect all systems against attack, whereas an attacker can attack any system of choice.

✔ Defenders must protect systems at all hours of the day and night, whereas an attacker can attack at a time of his or her choosing.

✔ Defenders must conform to policies and obey all applicable laws, whereas an attacker can break any law at any time.

Organizations Hiring InfoSec Professionals

These days it might be easier to ask, what types of organizations *don't* hire information security professionals? Every organization that uses computers and networks must employ people with security skills and knowledge. With the frequency of malware attacks, even a one-person IT department must be knowledgeable about basic security skills.

The following types of technology activities beg for security skills:

✔ Providing secure Internet connections

✔ Managing login credentials and access known as Identity Access Management

✔ Allowing secure remote access for valid users

✔ Providing supplier, partner, or customer access via Virtual Private Networks

✔ Maintaining secure email servers

✔ Managing and protecting the information on file servers

✔ Managing laptop computers for a mobile workforce

- ✔ Creating secure in-house written software
- ✔ Maintaining enterprise application access with user accounts

When an organization has one or more of the preceding in its technology environment, the organization's IT department had better have one or more of its IT people with some security skills. Otherwise, a lot is going to go wrong. I present the preceding list again, only this time I've added the consequences of poor security:

- ✔ **Internet connection:** Attacks from the Internet; malware from watering hole attacks.

- ✔ **Login credentials:** Attackers who stop at nothing to guess login credentials, including the use of automated tools that can perform brute-force attacks, in which thousands of different passwords per hour are guessed until the right one is found. Then it's "game over"!

- ✔ **Remote access:** Brute-force attacks against user accounts, eventually leading to successful break-ins.

- ✔ **Supplier, partner, or customer access:** Attacks from supplier, partner, or customer organizations. Misuse and abuse by personnel with poor judgment in those organizations.

- ✔ **Email server:** Incoming spam, malware, and phishing attacks.

- ✔ **File server:** Access management issues, data loss through lax access permissions; malware hosted on file server.

- ✔ **Laptop computers:** Stolen laptop computers with loss of data stored on them; attempts to break into organizations based on login information stored on stolen laptops.

- ✔ **In-house written software:** Exploitable vulnerabilities leading to data loss.

- ✔ **Enterprise applications:** Access management issues, people with excessive access privileges, terminated employees with still-active user accounts.

Now, look at the list one last time, to see what technology and security professionals need to do to protect systems and data:

- ✔ **Internet connection:** Network engineers need to understand how to make *edge devices* (the routers, firewalls, and other devices at an organization's outer boundary) resistant to attack. They also need to be able to install and manage firewalls and other protective devices with their complex rulesets to let the good guys in and keep the bad guys out, and to prevent malicious software from getting into the organization.

✔ **Login credentials:** User IDs, passwords, and security tokens are issued only to authorized personnel. In larger organizations, automated tools are used to reduce errors and watch for problems. Many systems can be configured to prevent brute-force attacks.

✔ **Remote access:** Some personnel must have access to an organization's internal network from any location. A remote access system must be built correctly so that only authorized personnel can get in.

✔ **Supplier, partner, or customer access:** Most organizations rely on other organizations for supplies, personnel, or services. In many such cases, people in those external organizations need access to internal resources. Every aspect of this process must be done right to prevent cybercriminals from exploiting external access and stealing data.

✔ **Email server:** Because email servers are connected to the Internet, systems engineers need to know how to correctly configure and "harden" email servers to prevent intruders from compromising the organization's email communications.

✔ **File server:** Internal and external file servers must be correctly configured and managed to protect all sensitive information stored on them and to prevent intruders from being able to access sensitive data.

✔ **Laptop computers:** Personnel who build and manage laptop computers (as well as tablets and other cool devices that we all want) must include the latest measures, such as whole-disk encryption and advanced malware prevention tools, to prevent the compromise of data stolen on laptops, as well as to protect the systems that laptops are permitted to connect to.

✔ **In-house written software:** Software developers need to understand how to write software that will be resistant to attacks such as buffer overflow, script injection, and authentication bypass.

✔ **Enterprise application with user accounts:** Personnel who manage user accounts for enterprise applications need to keep accurate records and use detailed procedures to make sure that no unauthorized personnel are given user accounts. Also, applications must be configured to track all user logins, and create alerts if any user accounts are under attack.

As you can see from this list, which is but a sampling of all the aspects that require security expertise in an organization, a wide set of skills is required for all IT workers, including specialized security personnel.

Chapter 2

Understanding InfoSec Roles: One Day in the Life

....

In This Chapter

▶ Understanding the paths to achieving a security job

▶ Exploring the array of security-related jobs

▶ Climbing to the heights of security management jobs

....

What is it like to have a security job?

Many people obtain security jobs after they've been in IT for a number of years. In many cases, the ability to get a security job is a matter of opportunity — being in the right place at the right time. However, a lot more than good luck is required; you need the desire and the aptitude for a security job.

Most people accumulated IT job experience and then move laterally into a security job. Others get a degree in computer science, management information systems, or information security and then get an entry-level InfoSec position. This chapter describes both job-hunting methods and also details the most common security jobs, from security analyst to CISO.

Getting Security Experience Where You Are Now

Workers early in their careers have the following complaint:

> ✔ *I want to get this new job, but it requires experience. How can I get experience if I don't have this job?*

Sounds like a chicken-or-egg problem, right? Not necessarily. Most security professionals didn't have a non-security-related job one day and a security job the next. Instead, they gained and built upon security skills in their current IT job.

In this section, you explore the following IT roles and discover how to build your information security knowledge and skills while in those roles:

- ✓ Service desk analyst
- ✓ Network administrator
- ✓ Systems administrator
- ✓ Database administrator
- ✓ Software developer
- ✓ Project manager
- ✓ Business analyst
- ✓ IT manager
- ✓ Human resources employee

All IT positions contain security-related skills and responsibilities. Everyone in IT should be aware of the security-related aspects of their jobs. IT workers are entrusted with a high level of privilege: they have access to sensitive data and the systems that control it.

Service desk analyst

A *service desk analyst* assists users how have problems with their computers, user accounts, or business applications. In some companies this position is the equivalent of a help desk technician or a PC fix-it dude (or dudette).

In many ways, service desk analysts have one of the most important non-security positions because they are in contact with users in all levels of the organization. For many employees, service desk analysts are the only IT people they will ever contact.

A service desk person must be able to recognize several types of security issues, such as the following:

- ✓ Forgotten passwords
- ✓ Requests to install software

✔ Phishing messages

✔ Unsafe practices, such as sharing passwords or visiting malicious web sites

Network administrator

The *network administrator* title can mean different things in different organizations. This role often includes the administration of the following:

✔ User accounts

✔ File server access

✔ Remote access

Network administrators are on the front lines of access control, and effective access control practices reduce the likelihood of a number of security-related problems, such as active user accounts for terminated personnel, granting excessive privileges, group accounts, and user accounts with non-expiring or non-complex passwords.

Systems administrator

A *systems administrator* (also called a systems engineer) configures and maintains server operating systems and, in some organizations, desktop operating systems.

A systems administrator — often shortened to sysadmin or SA — is usually responsible for all security-related configurations in operating systems, including the all-important *system hardening*, which is the practice of configuring a system to make it more resistant to attack.

A sysadmin may also manage user accounts, machine by machine or in a central directory such as Microsoft Active Directory or LDAP (lightweight directory access protocol). A sysadmin can learn and apply many security-related principles regarding user account management, such as the following:

✔ **High-quality passwords:** Systems should require long, complex passwords with reasonably short expirations (I suggest 90 days for users and 30 for administrators).

✔ **No shared user accounts:** SAs are usually close to their users, and as such should watch for various forms of abuse, including shared user accounts. That's *bad juju,* as I like to say.

✔ **Accounts with least privilege:** Users should have no higher privilege level than is required to accomplish their duties. If you give an ordinary user the local administrator privilege, you will be begging for security-related problems.

Database administrator

A *database administrator*, or *DBA*, is responsible for the care and feeding of databases that reside on servers as well as external storage systems.

A database management system is a sizeable piece of software in its own right, often with myriad configuration settings and its own user accounts and related settings. Like the system administrator, the database administrator must follow sound principles with regards to system hardening as well as user account management. Further, the DBA also controls access permissions to databases and their components.

Software developer

A *software developer* (also referred to as programmer, software development engineer, or programmer-analyst) develops systems software, application software, tools and utilities, and system interfaces. Some have a creative, free spirit and down-with-rules attitude that gives the whole lot a reputation for not wanting to work with security people.

Software development involves several significant security-related activities and aspects, including the following:

✔ **Secure coding:** Developers without training in secure coding are likely to introduce vulnerabilities such as buffer overflow and cross-site request forgery in their programs. Depending on the languages and tools they are using, developers will need to have a varying level of training and awareness, so that their programs will be free of security defects.

✔ **Security testing:** Developers often test the programs they write and maintain. Depending on the languages and tools they use, developers will need to perform security testing in addition to any functionality testing to ensure that their software is free of security-related defects.

✔ **Code reviews:** Developers should be checking each other's work, looking for security flaws that could permit their software to be compromised by an attacker.

My security career started in network support

Back in 1990, I was doing network support for a large dairy. They were having problems with their network and had been experiencing some unexpected financial reporting problems, so they had started to suspect fraud. The CFO approached me one Friday afternoon as I was working on the network and said something like, "So this system is secure, isn't it, and can't be the cause of our problems?"

Caught off-guard, I answered, "Yes, sure, it must be"

Driving home, I became increasingly concerned that I had answered without any evidence to back my words. This really worried me, so I went into the lab on the weekend and built an equivalent system that I proceeded to hack. I identified four or five issues and then devised controls to prevent or detect these.

On Monday, I went back into the dairy and applied the fixes — and explained to the CFO why. At the time, security was not recognized as a separate skill or even a job; it was just something good network admins did.

Without realizing it, I had become a white hat hacker and I moved full time into security about two years later!

Richard N., London

Project manager

Have you seen those sleek racing rowboats, with the person in front shouting, "Stroke! Stroke! Stroke!" to keep the rowers in sync? Similarly, *project managers* keep a project going in the same direction and at the right pace to ensure that it is completed correctly and on time.

My security career started as a developer

I was working as an engineer writing code for operations in a nuclear power plant. One day (in the early '80s), I asked the boss how we secured this stuff and who was responsible for making sure our network and supporting computing systems were secure. Two days later, I got a call from corporate headquarters and talked to our CIO. I explained my concern, and that was the beginning of my security career. I became responsible for securing our corporate network and, from there, went on to become one of the first security engineers for the company.

Bruce Lobree, Seattle

Project managers, or PMs, keep projects running smoothly and ensure that all required resources are available as needed. In many cases, PMs can use their general knowledge of IT security to ensure that security-related activities are included in a project's schedule and carried out by people with the right skills. Some of the things that PMs need to know include the following:

- Laws and regulations applicable to the organization
- Security policies that are relevant to whatever project PMs are working with at the time
- Client or customer security-related expectations
- Security tools used in the organization to verify software security

Business analyst

Depending on the organization, a *business analyst* may be a jack-of-all-trades or focused on one set of activities. In this book, a business analyst is the former. Examples of business analyst activities include

- Running reports
- Analyzing the content of reports to assist other workers in their jobs
- Conducting research tasks and projects on internal business matters
- Organizing information into usable or readable form

A business analyst can also be thought of as a technical assistant.

Like other IT workers, a business analyst must be familiar with the concepts of safe computer usage and prudent handling of sensitive data, so that they don't unwittingly bring harm to the information by compromising sensitive data and systems.

Most people in security start out in another IT job, and move laterally into a security position.

IT manager or IT director

An *IT manager* (in smaller organizations, *the* IT manager) or *IT director* directs the work of others in the IT organization. To get security savvy and do the right thing security-wise for the organization, an IT manager needs to understand many aspects of information security, including the following:

- ✔ **Security policy:** The security policy includes both the policy for general workers as well as IT-specific policies related to the design, implementation, and management of information systems.

- ✔ **Security aspects of applicable business processes:** These aspects include but are not limited to change management, configuration management, incident management, asset management, and employee onboarding and offboarding.

- ✔ **Leadership by example:** An IT manager is watched by almost everyone on the team, so he or she should lead by example to ensure that IT staffers also toe the line on security policy, procedures, and expected behavior.

Human resources employee

Human resources (HR) workers play a big part in information security. They are the linchpin in the procedures followed when hiring and terminating employees. HR has many other important security-related aspects, including the following:

- ✔ **Background checks:** A background check is relatively straightforward in the United States but trickier in countries that restrict or ban them. Still, it's important to fully understand the criminal history and ethics of an employment candidate.

- ✔ **Discipline:** HR often coordinates formal disciplinary action for all kinds of misbehavior, including violations of security policy. HR must understand the serious nature of different information security violations so that appropriate disciplinary actions are taken in the event of a breach or misconduct.

My security career started on a committee

I got a job as an IT director for one of the departments in a large municipality. Shortly after arriving, I began work on their first information security committee. Our task was to create a new InfoSec policy. Eventually, we decided that we needed to hire a CISO for the city.

The person we hired was and is someone many of you would recognize, but I'll leave out his name to protect the innocent (and guilty!). We quickly became good friends and respected colleagues, and when the position of deputy CISO was created, I applied and was hired.

David R. Matthews, Seattle

All IT positions require security skills

Making the transition from a non-security job to a security job is not as difficult as you might think. Many companies require relevant, security-related skills for almost every position in IT.

Security is the responsibility of not just the security manager but also every IT worker in the organization. Every position in IT requires security skills and knowledge related to each particular position.

✔ **Job descriptions:** HR usually creates and manages the job descriptions in an organization. Security is an essential ingredient in virtually all IT positions, and in many others as well.

In many organizations HR manages only full-time employees, not contractors, consultants, or temporary workers. As a result, access management processes suffer greatly. When contractors, consultants, or temps leave an organization, the personnel responsible for locking their user accounts often don't know, creating a big security risk and a significant compliance issue. Organizations can get into a lot of trouble if they have active accounts for contractors and temps who are no longer active.

Getting an Entry-level Security Position

When it comes to security jobs, most companies don't hire people without experience. However, with the shortage of security talent, organizations are becoming creative: If they can't find a security professional to fill an open role, they'll train a person for the position.

An organization hiring one or more entry-level security people will, or should, have security professionals with industry experience already on staff, so you'd be a part of a team that includes people with more experience.

Organizations offer several types of entry-level positions. Although they probably don't add *junior* to the job title, it's included here so you can better understand the role.

Junior security analyst

A *junior security analyst* is an assistant to a senior-level security analyst, engineer, administrator, or manager. In a general sense, a junior security analyst is responsible for completing tasks that involve the creation or analysis of security-related information, such as the following:

- **SOC operations:** Many larger organizations have a security operations center, or SOC, to monitor and manage security-related tools and systems for detecting security incidents, which are relayed to the appropriate personnel. A junior security analyst may be given a variety of chores related to operations in the SOC.

- **IT audits:** An IT auditor often needs an assistant to help with a variety of tasks, such as collecting and managing audit evidence as well as creating audit reports.

- **Policy management:** A junior security analyst might monitor the compliance of security policies. For instance, a junior analyst may conduct clean desk reviews, observe users' security-related behavior, or conduct in-person surveys and interviews.

- **Risk management:** A junior security analyst might manage the contents of the organization's risk register and carry out tasks regarding risk treatment, such as documenting risk mitigation or risk acceptance artifacts.

ANECDOTE

My security career started at a detective agency

In the 1980s, my school library had a Teletype that students could use to run a program that would identify our career aptitudes. The user would answer 250 multiple-choice questions, and the program would produce three suitable occupations. The program always reported my first occupation as fur designer. I was so incensed by the prospect that I spent weeks reading *ComputerWorld* and IBM 360 operator manuals until I could figure out how to dial into the mainframe to obtain system operator (SYSOP) privilege and change the occupation results. The mainframe exposed more than 100 time-sharing accounts serving not only many of the area's school districts but dozens of manufacturing and banking companies.

A few years later, I had a job as a typist and clerk for a detective agency — and a lot of mainframe hacking experience poking around with a personally owned Teletype and modem, One day, I mentioned my first mainframe exploits to the detective agency owner. He jumped on the opportunity to provide remediation services to several of those companies. I provided the bulk of the actual work, before I was even a high school graduate.

Todd Plesco, Mission Viejo, California

✔ **Security reporting:** The tools and systems that protect an organization contain a lot of security-related information. A junior security analyst might create security metrics and reports that management uses to understand the effectiveness of their security systems.

Junior security administrator

A *junior security administrator* is a helper on a team of security administrators. Some of the roles that this entry-level security administrator might perform include the following:

✔ **User account administration:** In this role, you create user accounts, make access permission changes to existing accounts, and lock or remove a user account when someone leaves the organization. You might also create or manage roles, which are used to control access to data and application functions.

✔ **Firewall administration:** Administering firewalls involves the regular upkeep of their *rulesets,* the data that a firewall uses to determine whether traffic should be blocked or permitted to pass. Firewalls are also configured to log certain traffic, so you might also examine logs.

✔ **Intrusion detection system (IDS) and intrusion prevention system (IPS) administration:** An IDS and IPS are similar to a firewall, in that they contain rules to manage and logs to examine.

✔ **Data loss prevention (DLP) administration:** A DLP system is used to detect (and, possibly, block) sensitive data being transmitted out of an organization's network. A DLP system requires a lot of tuning so that routine business operations are not affected. The junior security administrator makes these adjustments, as well as examines logs and takes appropriate action.

✔ **Antimalware administration:** Organizations small and large need antimalware to keep computer viruses, Trojan horses, and worms out of the network. Larger organizations may accomplish these tasks through a centralized management console, which views and manages the health of antimalware software on workstations and servers. A lot of detail work is required, generally in coordination with senior-level security people. For example, a higher-up may determine which patches are to be applied to which assets at what time, and the junior-level person applies those patches correctly.

✔ **Spam administration:** Practically all organizations employ spam filtering, often through a central console that manages filtering rules, exceptions, and a quarantine area for suspected spam messages. The spam-filtering system and its configuration requires regular attention, to make sure that legitimate email keeps flowing uninterrupted while spam is blocked and put aside.

✔ **SIEM (security incident and event management) administration:** A SIEM is a system that collects log data from lots of systems to correlate little events that help us understand bigger ones, such as employee abuse, system malfunction, and security breaches. A SIEM requires a lot of upkeep in two main areas: configuring alarms and alerts, and setting up feeds from new systems and devices.

✔ **Vulnerability management:** This set of activities may involve running security scanning tools such as Nessus, NMAP, or Rapid7 to look for vulnerabilities in workstations, servers, and network devices. Or you could load the raw output from scanning tools into the vulnerability management module of a GRC platform such as RSAM, Lockpath, or Archer. Also included in vulnerability management is the management of systems to push security patches and configuration changes to servers and workstations.

In all these roles, you learn one or more aspects of security administration and security operations. As you gain experience, you can work your way up to more senior roles.

Rolling Up Your Sleeves as a Security Practitioner

Many kinds of security jobs exist in business and government today. This section describes the most common ones.

Security analyst

Security analysts are thinkers, responsible for transforming data and events into usable information for themselves and others. Their industry expertise guides them in reaching meaningful and correct conclusions. Their communication skills enable them to impart their conclusions to others so that the organization can benefit from their work.

This description sounds vague because a security analyst's work can range across the entire spectrum of security management, security operations, and security administration. A security analyst may be spending time conducting research — interpreting current events, new encryption algorithms, or many other things, and then figuring out how these external developments should shape the organization's short-term operations or long-term strategy.

Still stumped? Here are some examples of work that a security analyst may perform:

- ✔ Analysis of events in a SIEM, DLP, IDS/IPS, or FIM system to determine the cause behind "interesting" events found in their logs

- ✔ Analysis of cryptographic algorithms used in industry to help determine whether cryptosystems in the organization are still effective or need to be upgraded to something better

- ✔ Analysis of the organization's control and management framework against industry standards to determine whether changes are needed

- ✔ Analysis of current trends in malware and the organization's current controls to determine whether advanced malware protection (AMP) tools are warranted

Security specialist

A *security specialist* is a security expert across a wide range of security disciplines, techniques, and tools. You might think of a security specialist as a security analyst, security engineer, forensic investigator, IT auditor, and security architect rolled into one.

The role of security specialist is similar to that of a general practitioner in the health care industry.

Security engineer

A *security engineer* installs, configures, and manages various security tools and systems used by the organization. A senior-level security engineer is also involved in the testing and selection of new security tools and systems.

A security engineer will work with many types of security tools and systems, such as the following:

- ✔ Firewalls
- ✔ Next-generation firewalls
- ✔ Intrusion detection systems and intrusion prevention systems
- ✔ Data loss prevention systems
- ✔ Spam filters
- ✔ Anti-malware
- ✔ Advanced malware protection systems

- ✔ Web access filters
- ✔ File integrity monitoring tools
- ✔ Cloud monitoring and control tools
- ✔ Netflow tools
- ✔ System and network forensics tools

Security engineers rarely work in a vacuum. Instead, they partner with many other people in the organization. For example, a security engineer works with network engineers to ensure the smooth and proper operation of all network-based tools, and with the systems administrator or systems engineers to ensure the smooth and proper operation of all system-based tools.

Security architect

A *security architect* is a designer of processes and systems. This role is typically the most senior position in information security for an individual contributor.

Generally, a security architect has responsibilities in one or more of the following disciplines:

- ✔ Security technology
- ✔ Security processes
- ✔ Security framework and controls
- ✔ Security policy

A security architect determines *how* risks will be reduced in an organization. This role is in contrast to determining *what* risks will be reduced, which is often the job of the chief information security officer (CISO), described later in the chapter.

Forensic investigator

A *forensic investigator,* sometimes known as a forensics analyst or forensics specialist, conducts forensic investigations on computers and networks, usually after a security incident or security breach has occurred.

A *forensic investigation* is a detailed analysis of an event. In the context of computers and networks, this investigation involves an examination of computers and other devices, so that an event can be better understood.

My Ben Braddock moment

In *The Graduate,* Ben Braddock (played by Dustin Hoffman) is a recent college graduate with no well-defined plans. I had my own Ben Braddock moment when someone asked me about the next steps I should take to add value and expertise to my career path. My friend leaned over and, instead of saying "plastics" like Dustin Hoffman's adviser, said "forensics."

A great deal of my work since then has been a direct result of that life-changing word. I went back to school and earned several certificates in computer forensics. While I was there, I took a class in the legal issues around e-discovery, and that topic has been a rewarding interest of mine ever since.

David R. Matthews, Seattle

The forensic investigator uses a variety of tools and techniques to answer the basic "what happened?" question. Forensic investigations are usually conducted in two types of situations:

- ✔ **Break-ins:** When an external adversary breaks into a system or network, the investigator must figure out how the break-in occurred and what the person did.
- ✔ **Policy violations:** This situation mainly involves employee misconduct.

Forensic investigators often must employ "chain of custody" procedures because the results of their investigation become part of a lawsuit or criminal trial. The tools, techniques, and even the character of the forensic investigator may be called into question when the results of the forensic investigation are part of the evidence in a trial.

Because they often have access to information of the highest sensitivity, forensic investigators must be highly trustworthy, even by security professional standards.

IT auditor

An *IT auditor* (also known as an IS auditor or a security auditor) determines the effectiveness of security controls, and communicates that level of effectiveness to others through written reports that describe controls, their intended function, and how well they carry out that function.

Large versus small organizations

The day-to-day life of a security professional can vary widely due to many factors, including the size of the organization. For example, in a small organization, you would tend to be a "jack of all trades and master of none." You may be involved in many facets of information security and may often be faced with the difficult decision of focusing on certain activities at the expense of others. Security pros in smaller organizations are rarely bored, however, because each day can be wildly different from any other.

In a larger organization, you'll have an opportunity to specialize in an individual aspect of information security, such as vulnerability management, software development security, or physical security. Because you'll stay in one focus area most of the time, your knowledge will deepen and you'll learn valuable skills.

In general, if you like structure and predictability, a position in a larger company might be right for you. But if you like variety and not knowing what the day will bring, a smaller company might be what you need.

If you're picturing an auditor as someone with a checklist, you're right: Experienced auditors use checklists to make sure they don't forget any aspect of a control they are examining. However, they also have a deep understanding of the technologies and details involved in the controls they examine, and they understand that the true effectiveness of a control requires more than a checklist.

IT auditors must be independent and objective, so it is best if they are not members of the department they are auditing. Otherwise, it might appear that the auditor was being controlled by the department that he or she was auditing.

Getting to the Top in Security Management

Some people are satisfied in an individual contributor role and have no interest in management. Others yearn to develop big visions, lead big teams, and do big things. This section describes pinnacle IT security roles in an organization, and the sensitivity and responsibility each entails.

Security manager

A *security manager* is a line manager who manages one or more individual contributors on a security team, including all the positions discussed previously in this chapter. Expected to have years of experience in one or more of these positions, a security manager assigns tasks, resolves disputes, and mentors his or her employees to further their professional growth. This role is like any other managerial in a technical organization.

For the right person, managing a team of security professionals can be the best job ever. As with most technology management jobs, you need to know how to do many of the tasks and jobs that you expect your staff to do because they'll look to you to understand how to do their job even better. Establishing credibility in a technology management job requires the ability to show others how to do their job and inspiring them to do it well.

Check out *Leadership For Dummies* by John Marrin for more information on leading teams of workers.

Security manager jobs can be gratifying for people who have vision but who lack the time to do all the work themselves.

Compliance officer

Usually found in organizations with industry regulations, a *compliance officer* ensures that the organization is compliant with applicable laws and regulations. Although this role is not a security position per se, I include it here because compliance is so often associated with information security.

Examples of industries and their applicable regulations follow:

- ✔ **Financial services:** GLBA (Gramm Leach Bliley Act), NCUA (National Credit Union Association), FDIC (Federal Deposit Insurance Corporation), SSAE16 (Statement on Standards for Attestation Engagements No. 16, Reporting on Controls at a Service Organization)

- ✔ **Public utilities:** NERC (North American Electric Reliability Corporation) and FERC (Federal Energy Regulatory Commission)

- ✔ **Healthcare organizations:** HIPAA (Health Insurance Portability and Accountability Act)

- ✔ **U.S. government agencies:** FISMA (Federal Information Systems Management Act)

✔ **Merchants and other entities that process credit card data:** PCI-DSS (Payment Card Industry Data Security Standard)

✔ **Organizations that write software for processing credit card data:** PA-DSS (Payment Application Data Security Standard)

In addition, organizations voluntarily comply with other standards, including the following:

✔ **ISO27001** (Information technology – Security techniques – Information security management systems – Requirements)

✔ **SOC2** (Report on Controls at a Service Organization Relevant to Security, Availability, Processing Integrity, Confidentiality or Privacy)

Privacy officer

A *privacy officer* (PO) or *chief privacy officer* (CPO) is typically found in organizations that store or process large amounts of sensitive data about individuals and is responsible for two primary aspects about that data:

✔ **Protection from disclosure:** Protecting sensitive data from disclosure is really just about data security controls in the context of sensitive data about people. Like other sensitive data in the organization, this information must be adequately and effectively protected.

✔ **Assurance of proper handling:** An organization must have proper practices regarding handling and possible onward distribution of a person's sensitive information. For example, an organization that collects contact information from its customers is generally prohibited from selling that information to other companies for marketing.

Sensitive data includes names and contact information, financial information (including social security and other account numbers), and medical information. Each regulation or standard has its own definition of sensitive information and required protection and handling requirements.

Because a chief privacy officer is generally in an organization with a chief information security officer (CISO) or chief security officer (CSO), a CPO's job typically will focus on business use and proper handling of customer sensitive information. The protection of that information is the job of the CISO or CSO.

Chief information security officer and chief security officer

The chief *information security officer* (CISO) and the *chief security officer* (CSO) are the top security jobs in government and industry.

The CISO and CSO typically report to the president or CEO of a corporation or to a cabinet member or department head in government.

The CISO deals primarily with the security of information systems and often with physical security. The CSO is concerned with security related to both technology and non-technology issues.

The CISO and CSO are typically responsible for the following:

- Security policy
- Risk management and risk treatment
- Security architecture
- Security operations
- Security incident response

CISOs and CSOs operate in the rarefied air of corporate (or government) executive management, where the loftiest issues concerning the organization are discussed. Corporate or government politics deeply affect the CISO and CSO, and a lot of their time is spent negotiating with other executives to ensure that the organization is on the right footing for managing security and technology-related risk.

Understanding Success in a Security Job

A basic truth of information security jobs can be frustrating to some people but an exciting challenge to others: Your guidance on improving security and reducing risk will often be ignored.

Many security professionals have a difficult time with the feeling of being ineffective. You can spend considerable time on a project and provides recommendations for improving security, but many of those recommendations might be disregarded. A track record of such events can make most professionals feel like a failure.

Security professionals need to understand that they are a *change agent*. Because information security practices are often not intuitive to others, your job will involve working with others so that they will embrace small or large changes and do their part to improve security in an organization. To be an effective change agent, you need negotiation and persuasion skills so that others will understand and embrace your point of view and realize why it's important to the organization.

However, even if you're a skilled negotiator, you won't always get your way. This is not a failure because it's your job to make sure that decision makers make informed decisions — in other words, it's your job to inform them of the risks associated with their choices. As long as decision makers make informed decisions, considering a variety of factors that include security issues, you've done your job, whether or not you agree with the decisions. This aspect of information security jobs has nothing to do with technology and everything to do with people.

Chapter 3

Exploring Current Issues in Information Security

I'm delighted that you're interested in an information security job. With this book, I hope I can help you go into this field with your eyes wide open. This chapter describes the issues that the information security industry faces today — issues that we talk about with other professionals. You discover the everyday challenges — and opportunities — that we encounter when protecting your companies, customers, computers, information, and users.

Malware and Exploits

Malware, short for *malicious software,* is software that has some harmful purpose, by itself or as part of a bigger system. In this section you look at the types of malware, their internal components, evasion techniques, and the types of attacks that use malware.

Types of malware

In almost every field of information security, you will be engaged in the war against malware. The types of malware are viruses, Trojan horses, and worms.

Viruses

Computer *viruses* are fragments of computer code that attach to program files, disk boot sectors, or document files. When computer viruses are attached, the file (or disk) is said to be infected. The computer code in the virus is activated when its host (the program file, disk boot sector, or document file) is executed, accessed, or opened.

Generally, when activated, a virus will attempt to attach itself to other files, disks, or documents. In this way, computer viruses move from computer to computer.

In addition to code to help propagate itself to other objects, a computer virus often has code to carry out other functions. For instance, a virus can delete or overwrite computer files, display information on the computer's screen, play sounds, or attempt to communicate to other computers through any active network interfaces. Whatever you can imagine that a virus could do, someone has probably written a virus to do just that.

Several types of viruses exist, including the following:

- ✔ **Resident:** Remains in memory, typically from boot-up to shutdown.
- ✔ **Non-resident:** Starts running, performs its tasks, and then exits. It does not remain in memory.
- ✔ **Boot sector:** Attaches itself to a floppy, USB, or hard drive boot sector instead of to an executable program and is executed when the media is logically mounted. Okay, so floppy discs haven't been around for years, but mentioning them gives you some background on how long boot sector viruses have been in existence.
- ✔ **Macro:** Attaches itself to a macro inside a word processing document or a spreadsheet file, and is typically executed when the document or spreadsheet is opened.

Some well-known computer viruses include these:

- ✔ **Elk Cloner:** The first computer virus to affect Apple computers
- ✔ **Brain:** A boot sector virus that was among the first viruses to infect PCs
- ✔ **Concept:** The first macro virus, which attacked Microsoft Word documents
- ✔ **Jerusalem:** A virus that destroyed all executable files on infected machines on every Friday the 13th

A computer virus is so-named because of its similarity to biological viruses that invade the living cells of organisms. Biological viruses are not separate living organisms; they depend on the cells they invade for replication and transportation. By itself, a biological virus is just a strand of information that can do nothing.

Trojan horses

A *Trojan horse*, like a computer virus, is a type of malware that cannot propagate unless activated. (The malware got its name from the Trojan horse in the famous battle between the Greeks and their attack on the city of Troy.) A Trojan horse relies on a human to activate it, typically through a ruse or a trick; the user is generally offered a computer program for some given purpose. When the user executes the program, the Trojan horse carries out the malicious purpose for which it was designed.

Following are two famous Trojan horses:

- **Torpig:** Turns off antivirus programs and permits its creator to remotely access compromised systems

- **Cryptolocker:** Encrypts files on a user's hard drive and on any file shares accessible from the target computer and then offers a ransom to the user for a tool to decrypt their files

Worms

A *worm* is a type of malware that can propagate on its own or with a little help from humans. Famous computer worms include the following:

- **Christmas Tree EXEC:** The first self-replicating computer worm

- **Morris worm:** Written as an experiment by Robert Tappan Morris, a student at Cornell University, and propagated through a series of known vulnerabilities and configurations across the early Internet in 1988

- **ILOVEYOU:** A rapidly spreading mass-mailing worm that caused significant disruption

- **Code Red:** A rapidly spreading worm that exploited vulnerability in the early Microsoft web server system called Internet Information Services (IIS)

- **SQL Slammer:** The fastest spreading worm of all time, crashing the Internet within 15 minutes of its release and attacking vulnerabilities in Microsoft SQL Server and Microsoft SQL Data Engine (MSDE)

- **Stuxnet:** Possibly developed by the United States and Israel and designed to attack centrifuges used to refine weapons-grade uranium in Iran

In 1949, years before the first computer network was built, John von Neumann wrote an article titled "Theory of self-reproducing automata." He was decades ahead of his time when he envisioned computer worms.

Malware components

Malware often consists of several components, each of which has a specific task. These components are

- **Exploit:** This code is written to take advantage of (*exploit*) a vulnerability in a target system. For example, a program running on a system might be vulnerable to a buffer overflow attack. A Trojan horse might lack this component, because a Trojan horse is designed to trick the user into running the program.

- **Dropper:** This code is used to perform an installation of additional programs or malware. The dropper might copy the malware from inside the install package or download it over the Internet.

- **Malware:** This code fulfills the purpose of the attack. The malware could steal passwords as users type them, or eavesdrop on network traffic, or scan a hard drive for sensitive data and send it to the malware's creator.

To better understand these components of malware, here's an analogy in the physical world. A burglar breaks into a business. The weak lock on the back door is the *vulnerability*. The lock-picking set that the burglar uses to open the back door is the *exploit*. The *dropper* is the burglar walking through the unlocked door into the building. The *malware* is the burglar installing a hidden video surveillance camera or stealing valuables from the business.

Trojan horses generally don't have an exploit component. The human who executes or installs the Trojan horse takes the place of the exploit component.

Evading detection

In the earlier days of antivirus history a virus writer would create and release a new virus, and then a few months later antivirus companies would create the capability to neutralize the virus. After many years of this, virus writers developed increasingly advanced techniques for evading detection by antivirus software, such as the following:

- **Hosts file manipulation:** By manipulating the *hosts* file (a flat file containing DNS hostnames and their respective IP addresses), a virus can attempt to prevent the target computer from obtaining security patches and antivirus updates.

✔ **DNS settings manipulation:** This technique is another way of preventing the target system from obtaining security patches and antivirus updates.

✔ **Process hiding:** Malware will try to hide through a few different techniques, such as giving itself a legitimate sounding name (for example, Explorer), attaching itself to a legitimate process, or manipulating the operating system so that its presence is overlooked.

✔ **Polymorphism:** Malware is typically recognized by its *signature,* similar to a criminal's unique fingerprint. Malware employing polymorphism can evade signature-based detection by changing its signature on every computer it infects.

✔ **Hiding in USB firmware:** A newer type of attack called BadUSB involves malware installed in the firmware of a USB device, which — like a boot sector virus — is activated upon insertion of a USB device. This attack is scary, except in organizations that have locked down the use of USB storage devices.

Types of malware attacks

Adversaries use a variety of techniques to try and get malware onto a target system. The more common techniques are described in this section.

Spam

Plain old unwanted emails can contain attachments (ZIP files, EXE files, documents, spreadsheets, images, PDF documents, and so on) that contain malware. This type of attack is more correctly called a spam plus Trojan attack, because the email containing the malicious attachment usually makes a falsified claim regarding the attachment.

Phishing

This attack is similar to spam, except the email message includes a URL to a website containing malware just waiting to exploit a browser vulnerability. If you're working your brain cells, you'll recognize this as a social engineering attack because the attacker is trying to trick users into doing something they ought not do.

"Found" USB device

A favorite technique is to load malware on a USB device, and then leave it where someone is bound to find it. Curious employees spot the little gem and think, "Oh boy, a USB drive. I wonder what's on it!" And then the trouble begins.

Downloaded software

Many of us love to download new programs, wallpaper images, and other fodder for our computer's giant hard drives. However, downloaded software may contain malware that sneaks in during the software install.

Watering hole attack

A cheetah can go and chase its prey all over the place, or it can just hang out at the local watering hole and wait for its prey to show up. Watering hole attacks are like that: If an adversary is targeting a particular organization, it will install malware on a website that it thinks people in the target organization will frequent.

Zero-day attacks and advanced malware prevention

A *zero-day attack* is a malware attack for which few or none of the antimalware vendors have the capability to detect, never mind prevent.

The two popular uses for the term *zero day* follow:

- ✔ **Brand new exploit:** This proper use of the term *zero day* refers to malware (the exploit portion, specifically) that attacks a vulnerability unknown to the target's manufacturer. For example, an adversary discovers a new buffer overflow vulnerability in Microsoft Internet Explorer and creates exploit code that permits the attacker to execute arbitrary code on the target machine, permitting a dropper to install malware on the machine. The term *zero day* refers to the number of days from public disclosure of a vulnerability to its successful exploit; an attack on an unknown vulnerability means that zero days have passed from public disclosure of the vulnerability to its exploitation. In the case of a zero-day exploit, no public disclosure has been made.

- ✔ **Unknown malware:** This popular, though technically incorrect, use of the term *zero day* means that a specific instance of malware has never been seen by antimalware vendors — hence, no signature or defense exists for it. In this form of the term, zero-day malware may be unique and unknown to antimalware vendors but exploiting a previously known vulnerability.

In both cases, zero-day attacks are unknown to antimalware vendors as well as other defenses such as an Intrusion Prevention System (IPS). Only advanced malware prevention tools will be able to detect and block zero-day attacks.

In the information security profession, the malware battle is considered lost. Antimalware defenses can no longer prevent all infections due to the new methods of propagation, exploitation, and hiding created by our adversaries.

Antimalware

Antivirus software, now often called *antimalware,* attempts to detect and block all types of malware. Here is a brief history of the advances in antimalware from its humble beginnings:

- ✔ **Self-contained and scan only:** The earliest antimalware programs came prepackaged to detect and neutralize all known varieties of malware. The only way that early antimalware worked was through a whole-disk (or whole-floppy) scan.

- ✔ **Real-time detection:** Antimalware improved to include detection of an infection in real-time. This process required tight integration with the computer's operating system: Every time a program opened a file, the antimalware program would first examine the contents of the file to see whether it contained malware.

- ✔ **Signature updates:** As the number of viruses and other types of malware grew, it became evident that antimalware needed to be updated periodically so that newly discovered malware could also be detected and blocked.

- ✔ **Heuristic detection**: Antimalware vendors, discouraged by the sheer number of new viruses being created every day, turned to another technique called *heuristics,* in which antimalware observes the behavior of programs and blocks them if they were acting malwarelike.

Advanced malware prevention (AMP) tools detect and block many kinds of advanced malware, including polymorphic malware, zero-day attacks, and advanced persistent threats (APTs). Instead of relying on signatures, AMP tools take other approaches, including the following:

- ✔ **Malicious network traffic detection:** AMP tools that connect to network span ports can observe all network traffic in to and out of an organization. These tools are able to detect command and control traffic, which is a hallmark of bots and botnets (described in the next section). Depending on their configuration, AMP tools can either detect or detect and block such traffic.

- ✔ **OS process analysis:** AMP tools that work on servers and workstations keep a close eye on processes running on the system, recording what they do and blocking malicious ones.

The scourge of malware

In the earliest days of malware, five to ten new computer viruses occurred in a year. Today, Kaspersky Lab claims that it detects over three hundred thousand malware variants *every day*. Even if the actual number was one hundred times less, the traditional model of antimalware and its periodic updates can no longer effectively address the tremendous growth in malware.

In 2014, one of the major antimalware vendors publicly stated that antimalware was no longer effective against the advanced techniques employed by malware. As experienced security professionals, we agree.

Assaults on Organizations

The unrelenting assaults on governments and businesses by cybercriminal organizations is the central theme of information security at every level, from executives to analysts. Indeed, cybersecurity is an important topic at the highest levels of government and private industry. Senior officials and executives are expressing concern over high-profile break-ins and their own organizations' defenses. This section describes the types of attacks we're facing today.

Break-ins

Malware is not the only tool in an attacker's toolbox. Just as lock picking is one way to break into a building, other techniques are frequently used to break into computer systems. Some of these techniques follow:

- ✔ **Password guessing:** Intruders will attempt to guess a user's login credentials so that they can access a system. From there, the intruder may steal data, perform fraudulent transactions, or gather information that will lead to a break-in on another system. Tools are available that rapidly guess likely passwords, but sometimes attackers guess passwords manually.

- ✔ **Eavesdropping:** Intruders will use a number of techniques to eavesdrop on a network connection or even a telephone conversation to pick up valuable information that they can use to break into a target system.

- ✔ **Social engineering:** Intruders will trick other people to perform certain acts or reveal certain information, all of which helps the intruder break into a target system. Intruders can trick users into giving them various bits and pieces of information that, when put together, will give an intruder enough information to slip into an organization's network.

✔ **Theft:** In a time-proven technique, an attacker steals a computer (or smartphone or tablet computer) and hopes to find information on the device to break into that device or break into another system.

In the early days of computer crime, malware didn't yet exist, so attackers relied on the preceding techniques, which they performed manually. These techniques are still used regularly even with some punchy malware.

Social engineering is one of the biggest problems in computer security today. When organizations do a good job of protecting their computers and networks, intruders turn to "hacking the people" instead, with great success.

Bots and botnets

A product of networking and the global Internet, bots and botnets represent a remarkable feat of distributed computing. They would be something to admire if it weren't for the fact that they exist primarily to carry out malicious deeds. Still, bots and botnets require our respect, for they can be powerful and inflict much mischief and damage when so directed.

In the early 2000s, malware creators expanded their vision and created a concept wherein a single operator could create a piece of malware that would give him or her automated remote control of many computers at once. Any one of these compromised computers is called a *bot* (short for robot), and a collection of these bots under central control is known as a *botnet* or *bot army*. The person who operates the bot army is a *bot herder*.

By themselves, bots are capable of a variety of tasks, including the following:

✔ **Hosting phishing sites:** A phishing scam typically involves an imposter website. Rather than going to a cloud service provider such as AWS or Azure, an adversary will use compromised systems, modifying them so that they are web servers that steal login credentials or implant malware on new victim computers (sometimes for the purpose of growing a bot army).

✔ **Relaying intrusions:** While carrying out illicit activities online, adversaries are usually careful to cover their tracks, typically by relaying their traffic through a number of compromised systems.

In addition to the preceding capabilities, a bot army can be used for additional tasks, such as

✔ **Relaying spam:** A spammer always needs to find new compromised machines through which he or she can relay spam messages. This is because of spam services that quickly detect spam relays and block them.

A bot army is an effective tool for relaying spam as the spammer can use bots in quick succession, evading spam-blocking tactics.

✓ **Participating in a distributed denial of service attack (DDoS):** In this attack, hundreds or thousands of computers are directed to flood a target system (or network) with a high volume of network traffic. The objective of a distributed denial of service attack is the prolonged incapacitation of a target system so that it is unusable by its legitimate users.

Two famous botnets are

✓ **Storm:** This botnet started out as the Storm worm, infecting each vulnerable target system with the storm bot software, forming the storm botnet. Little known fact: Though called a worm, Storm was a Trojan because it spread through email and relied on users to open attachments containing malware.

✓ **Conficker:** This worm and its variants infected many versions of the Windows operating system, as old as Windows 2000 and as new as Windows 7.

Advanced persistent threats

An *advanced persistent threat (APT)* is a broad technique of cyberespionage, system compromise, and data exfiltration inflicted on a specific target and with a specific objective. The term *APT* is also frequently used as a label for a person or a group of people using such tools.

Depending on the sophistication of the APT team, the techniques for a specific campaign may be custom developed to target the technologies used by the organization. A result of this customization is a zero-day attack (described earlier, in the "Zero-day attacks and advanced malware prevention" section).

Disruptive Trends

Attacks and cybercrime are not the only things vying for information security professionals' attention. Another issue is the parade of technical innovations that provide businesses with compelling opportunities for improved productivity and service levels. At the same time, these innovations — like many new technologies — are not fully "baked" at first and often don't have all the security features that organizations need.

Some new technologies, such as virtualization, are more mature, but organizations (including their security teams) are still playing catch-up in terms of knowing how to configure and operate them in a way that protects them from internal and external attacks.

Mobility trends

Everything was fine in corporate IT organizations until users started bringing their own personal computers, tablet computers, and smartphones to work and using them to get their jobs done. Security professionals need to address several issues pertaining to *BYOD* (*bring your own device,* or *bring your own disaster,* as many security professionals like to call it):

- ✔ **Endpoint security:** When personally owned devices are used to conduct business, the organization may have a more difficult time employing its antimalware, patch management, and encryption enterprise tools. In addition, many mobile platforms lack mature enterprise management capabilities and antimalware.

- ✔ **Control of sensitive information:** When personally owned endpoints (laptops, tablets, smartphones, or anything else that employees own that they use to conduct official business) are lost or stolen, the organization may have more limited means of remotely wiping data on these devices. And when an employee leaves, determining whether he or she really (and effectively) erased company data will be difficult.

Many mobile device management (MDM) tools are available for enterprises, but these tools are still maturing. Few if any offer truly comprehensive management and data protection capabilities across the variety of devices that employees are likely to use for business.

Virtualization

Virtualization is the practice of installing one or more instances of actively running operating systems on a single hardware server. The primary business driver for virtualization is the preservation of capital. The main technology drivers are more efficient use of server hardware and the capability to quickly move a running system from one hardware platform to another.

The master virtualization program is called a *hypervisor,* and the operating systems running on a hypervisor are called *guests.* In addition to operating systems such as Windows, Linux, and MacOS, network operating systems can run as guests, including routers, firewalls, intrusion detection systems (IDS), and data loss prevention (DLP) systems. Hence, it's now possible to build an entire infrastructure stack, including network infrastructure, on a single hardware server.

This powerful capability is part of what keeps an information security professional up at night. The lack of "air gaps" between infrastructure components in a virtualized environment provides more opportunities for attackers to successfully infiltrate virtual systems.

Another concern of IT managers and security managers alike is *virtualization sprawl*, the uncontrolled implementation of new virtual servers without proper approval. Unlike the former physical world, where management's approval to purchase server hardware served as the means to control the implementation of new servers, with virtualization it's possible to create a new server with just a few clicks.

Cloud computing

The trend in cloud computing can be summed up as follows: Organizations tend to acquire new business applications hosted by other organizations, rather than hosting the applications themselves on purchased computer hardware. In other words, why buy new hardware, operating system, database management system software, and application software, when you can pay some other company to do all that for less money?

The lists of pros and cons for cloud computing are long. The economic drivers swing heavily in favor of cloud computing, but many IT and security organizations are unprepared to manage the security of cloud apps as effectively as on-premise apps.

The most important issues that security professionals face regarding cloud computing include the following:

- ✓ **Cloud sprawl:** Because it is so easy to begin using a cloud-based application, IT and security organizations often have little visibility into just how extensive an organization's use of cloud services has become. The number of unapproved cloud services in use by your organization is probably worse than you think.

- ✓ **Data security:** Knowing which controls a cloud services provider uses and their effectiveness can be difficult. In other words, the protection of information stored in the cloud can be difficult to verify.

- ✓ **Data control:** An organization that isn't aware of all the cloud apps it uses has lost control of its data. If you don't know where your data is, how can you control it?

✔ **Legal issues:** Security and privacy laws crisscross the world, making data jurisdiction and data sovereignty stickier issues than ever. For instance, how do you know if it's even legal to store certain data in certain locations (provided you even know the physical locations of data stored in the cloud).

As scary as this all sounds, hope is on the horizon. Later in this chapter, the "Cloud Security Alliance" section provides information that will help you get better visibility and control over your data in the cloud.

The Internet of Things

The Internet of Things (IoT) is the name given to the coming phenomenon of the wave of Internet-connected smart devices. Soon, nearly everything we purchase that uses electricity will have a CPU and be connected to the Internet, including our home appliances, our vehicles, our gadgets, and even *us*.

In the context of information security as we know it today, this proliferation of Internet-connected devices will intensify the vulnerability management problem. With so many more devices with latent vulnerabilities, adversaries will have a new playground to explore.

Regulatory Compliance and Privacy

Security professionals have a love-hate relationship with laws and regulations. As information security laws began to be passed in the 1980s and 1990s, we danced gleefully in the aisles at work because we now had an additional tool when trying to convince others of the need for security. We were able to also say, "It's the law!"

But the love was short-lived, and soon we were grumbling because we were not able to choose which forms of security to implement. Instead, we were required to implement security controls even when doing so made no sense. Soon we learned to be selective and prudent when stating "it's the law."

FISMA

The Federal Information Systems Management Act, or FISMA, requires that all U.S. federal government systems meet minimum security standards. Many U.S. states, counties, and cities have also adopted the same level of standards.

NIST SP800-53 and FIPS-200

In simplest terms, FISMA requires that U.S. federal government agencies comply with several standards, including NIST (National Institute for Standards and Technologies) Special Publication 800-53, *Security and Privacy Controls for Federal Information Systems and Organizations,* and FIPS (Federal Information Processing Standards) Publication 200, *Minimum Security Requirements for Federal Information and Information Systems.*

Many nongovernment organizations voluntarily comply with the NIST and FIPS standards, because they recognize their value and understand that doing so will increase their security.

Certification and accreditation

Government agencies are required to undergo a process that includes an assessment of an information system and a formal approval process that authorizes the agency to begin (or continue) use of the system. These processes are together known as *certification and accreditation,* or *C&A.* The certification part is the assessment of the system against NIST 800-53, FIPS-200, and possibly other standards and requirements. The accreditation part is the formal authorization to use the system after the assessment has been completed and analyzed.

New systems are required to undergo C&A, and most systems are required to be recertified periodically, typically every one to three years.

FEDRAMP

Organizations that provide services to the U.S. federal government are also required to comply with NIST 800-53 and FIPS-200. Government agencies are required to utilize a process called FEDRAMP (Federal Risk and Authorization Management Program) to assess service providers before they are used. This requirement primarily applies to cloud service providers and other instances of government agencies outsourcing IT infrastructure or applications to service providers.

HIPAA and HITECH

Healthcare providers, insurance companies, and most U.S. based companies offering health insurance benefits are required to comply with HIPAA (Health Insurance Portability and Accountability Act) and HITECH (Health Information Technology for Economic and Clinical Health Act).

HIPAA requires that organizations storing electronic protected health information (EPHI) take certain measures to protect the confidentiality, integrity, and availability of EPHI. Organizations required to comply with HIPAA are known as *covered entities.*

HITECH expanded the reach of HIPAA by requiring business associates that store or process EPHI to comply with HIPAA as well. The term *business associates* means any organization that provides services to a covered entity. HITECH also added new breach notification requirements, ensuring that citizens will be notified if their health information is inappropriately disclosed or compromised.

Sarbanes-Oxley

The Sarbanes-Oxley Act of 2002 is a law that was passed as a result of several corporate scandals involving falsification of financial records of public companies. Often known as SarBox or just SOX, this law has had a significant effect on security policy and security controls in U.S. publicly traded companies.

SOX Controls

The primary consequence of SOX was the enactment of controls in the following IT functions:

- ✔ **Security policy:** Organizations are required to have a security policy that is relevant, periodically reviewed and approved by management, and enforced.

- ✔ **Access management:** Organizations are required to have effective and mature access management processes and tools, so that only authorized personnel have access to appropriate systems, roles, and functions.

- ✔ **Change management:** Organizations are required to be in complete control of the IT systems and infrastructure that supports their financial systems, so they must have a mature change management process that ensures that only approved changes may be made to systems and that unapproved changes will be detected and corrected.

- ✔ **Incident management:** Organizations are required to have tools and processes in place to detect incidents in a timely manner and to respond to incidents properly and effectively, resulting in incident resolution as well as a complete understanding of the extent of any incident.

- ✔ **Vulnerability management:** Organizations are required to have tools and processes in place to periodically examine systems for vulnerabilities and to correct those vulnerabilities timely and effectively.

- ✔ **Event logging:** Organizations are required to have tools and processes in place to ensure that all events are recorded, and that those recordings are archived, for in-scope systems. Periodic review — or automated alerting — of events is also required.

> ✔ **Internal audit:** Organizations are required to take full ownership of the state and effectiveness of their internal controls, including periodic internal audits of those controls and effective responses to issues found during those audits.

The context of these controls is an organization's key financial system, as well as supporting systems and infrastructure. Any additional applications related to revenue or expenses may also be in-scope.

The intent of these IT controls is the prevention or detection of any tampering of financial records that is performed through manipulation of underlying IT systems and infrastructure.

Audits

U.S. public companies are required to undergo an annual financial audit by a U.S. registered public accounting firm. Before SOX, the IT portion of a public audit was brief and superficial. After SOX, IT audits are typically thorough and arduous, with considerably more attention on IT operations for in-scope systems, infrastructure, and personnel.

State data breach laws

Starting with California's well-known SB1386 in 2002, the majority of U.S. states, as well as many other countries, have enacted laws that require the disclosure of security breaches involving certain records of their citizens. The crux of California's breach notification law is that notification is required if the data in question was not encrypted; if data in encrypted form is acquired by an unauthorized party, no notification is required.

The ever-changing patchwork

From 2002 to the present day, U.S. states have been enacting and updating their laws regarding the protection of citizens' data. These U.S. state laws alone present a challenge to many organizations that routinely process personal data on U.S. citizens: Just keeping up with all the changes in these laws is problematic.

Reaching across borders

Many U.S. state privacy laws claim jurisdiction of companies that have private records on its citizens, regardless of the location of those companies. Information security professionals often wonder whether those laws are enforceable across state lines. For instance, suppose that a company in Colorado has a compromise of private information for citizens in California. Will California's breach notification law truly be able to enforce that law on a company located in Colorado — or anywhere else?

EU data privacy laws

In 1995, the European Union passed the European Privacy Directive, sometimes referred to by its number, 95/46/EC. This directive established an operational model for the collection, storage, processing, and distribution of personal information of European citizens.

The directive defines the rights of European citizens with regards to the use of their personal information. European citizens have the right to know what information is being kept about them and how it is used, and the ability to correct that information or request its removal. The directive also imposes requirements on organizations to use reasonable means to protect this information and to facilitate citizens' rights as described.

The European Privacy Directive prohibits European companies from transmitting private citizen data to countries outside Europe that have weaker privacy laws, such as the United States. However, the United States and the European Union bridged this gap through the use of Safe Harbor Principles, where individual U.S. companies can voluntarily agree to protect data on European citizens in accordance with the European Privacy Directive. This agreement can be accomplished through individual legal contracts between European and U.S. companies. U.S. companies can also voluntarily register their businesses on the U.S. Department of Commerce Safe Harbor website, which legally obligates those U.S. companies to protect data on European citizens to the same level as the European Privacy Directive.

Privacy

The term *privacy* has several meanings and interpretations. In several contexts, privacy is a social and political hot button. But this is not a book about politics or philosophy, so the discussion here is focused on how privacy pertains to business and information security. First, a definition: *Privacy* is concerned with the safeguarding and proper use of citizens' personal and sensitive information.

Let's dissect this definition a little more:

- ✔ **Safeguarding personally sensitive information:** In this vein, privacy is information security focused on one type of data — that of citizens' personal information. In practice, protecting personally sensitive information is really not any different from protecting any other information in an organization. For us to do our jobs, we need to understand how this information is collected, stored, processed, and removed. Then we can use the tools in our toolboxes to maximize protection.

✔ **Proper use of personally sensitive information:** Mainly, is the data safeguarded (see the first bullet), and is it used only for purposes explicitly stated, or is it also sold to marketing companies who will bombard us with unwanted emails, telephone calls, and junk mail? This aspect of privacy is of concern to us, but it's somewhat outside our core concern — unless you're the chief privacy officer in an organization, in which case it's your main concern!

Permitted uses of private information

A common practice for organizations that collect personally sensitive information about citizens is the publication of a privacy policy. Often seen on corporate and government websites, a privacy policy typically provides a detailed account of the methods used to collect, store, and process users' personal information. Usually, a privacy policy explains how this information may be forwarded to other organizations for a variety of purposes, methods available for users to verify, correct, and remove their data, and the ability to opt out of certain activities, features, and uses of their data.

In the United States, the Federal Trade Commission has kept a close eye on organizations' published privacy policies and has levied fines or lawsuits on organizations that violate their own published privacy policy.

Cookies, beacons, and other online tracking

In the online world, many people are wary of the methods used by certain organizations to track users' Internet usage for the purpose of delivering targeted advertising. One of the more controversial practices is Google's method of reading the contents of an e-mail message and delivering ads to the user based on keywords in the message. Another less controversial method, but one that still has many persons' blood boiling, is the use of tracking cookies, web beacons, and other tricks to track the Internet site visitation habits of individual users.

Cookies are small data objects sent from a website and stored by a user's browser on the user's local computer. There are three types of cookies used today:

✔ **Session cookie:** This type of cookie is used between web servers and users' web browsers to establish and maintain a user's session with the website. Web servers use session cookies to distinguish one user from another. Also known as authentication cookies, session cookies are usually considered an acceptable use of cookies.

✔ **Tracking cookie:** This cookie is typically used to improve a user's experience when visiting a website. For instance, tracking cookies store a user's language preference, landing page, currency, and so on. A tracking cookie is also called a persistent cookie and originates from the same domain in the browser's address bar.

> ✔ **Third-party cookie:** This tracking cookie is sent from a website not in the browser's address bar. Third-party cookies are often used for advertising tracking and other uses often not associated with the core functionality of the website that a user is visiting.

Web beacons, also known as *web bugs* or *tracking bugs*, are objects that a user's browser or email client downloads when a user is viewing a web page or HTML-encoded email message. When a user's browser or email client downloads a web page or email message containing a web beacon, this downloading is logged in the beacon's web server log, facilitating tracking of the viewing of the web page or email message by the user. Web beacons take the following forms:

> ✔ 1x1 GIF (image) file that is transparent or the same color as the web page, which makes it effectively invisible to the end user
>
> ✔ 1x1 HTML frame that is invisible to the user
>
> ✔ JavaScript file that is invisible to the user

Flash cookies are tracking objects similar to browser cookies and are used by Adobe Flash browser plug-ins. Flash cookies can be used for purposes similar to those for tracking cookies.

Information Security Standards

Standards are statements of how things are done. Individual organizations often develop standards that describe how they do certain things, such as how to

> ✔ Harden (protect from attack) an Internet-facing Windows server
>
> ✔ Build and install IT components in retail locations
>
> ✔ Configure end user workstations

Within an organization, standards help drive consistency, which in turn improves service levels and security.

At the industry level, standards have a similar purpose: They drive consistency in the way that typical things are accomplished. In information security, several excellent standards represent effective methods for security processes and security technologies. In this section, you discover the most popular security standards that have had a positive, lasting effect and serve as guideposts along the road to more secure organizations.

ISO 27001

ISO 27001 is a highly respected international standard for information security management. ISO 27001 uses the term *information security management system (ISMS)* to describe the processes and records required for effective security management in any size organization.

The full name of the standard is *Information technology — Security techniques; Information security management systems — Requirements.* This complicated name is related to the two major sections of the standard as described next.

Requirements

The requirements section of the standard describes the necessary characteristics for an organization to properly manage its ISMS. The requirements section consists of the following:

- **Context of the organization:** The intended scope of the standard in an organization
- **Leadership:** The executive management commitment to maintaining an effective ISMS and security policy, and formally establishing security-related roles and responsibilities
- **Planning:** Activities such as risk assessments and risk treatment
- **Support:** Providing the necessary resources, training, and communications regarding security
- **Documented information:** Consistent practices related to security-related documents and records
- **Operation:** Performing risk assessments and risk treatment
- **Performance evaluation:** Security monitoring, internal auditing, and management review
- **Improvement:** Watching for and seizing opportunities to make security processes and controls better over time.

Controls

The controls section of ISO 27001 contains a set of industry standard controls, organized in the following categories:

- Information security policies
- Organization of information security
- Human resource security
- Asset management

- ✔ Access control

- ✔ Cryptography

- ✔ Physical and environmental security

- ✔ Operations security

- ✔ Communications security

- ✔ Systems acquisition, development, and maintenance

- ✔ Supplier relationships

- ✔ Information security incident management

- ✔ Information security aspects of business continuity management

- ✔ Compliance

Becoming ISO 27001 compliant

An organization that wants to improve its security management system using ISO 27001 as its standard would undergo the following activities:

- ✔ **Gap analysis:** The first step in achieving compliance, a gap analysis is performed either by the organization or by an outside expert. A gap analysis helps the organization understand which requirements and controls it does and doesn't comply with.

- ✔ **Remediation:** For any requirements and controls with which the organization is not compliant, it can make changes to its personnel (such as training), processes, and technologies to become compliant.

- ✔ **External audit:** An organization that needs to demonstrate compliance via an external audit can hire a competent security assessment firm to perform an audit with a detailed audit report and opinion of compliance.

- ✔ **Certification and registration:** An organization can choose to undergo a higher-quality external audit by employing one of the organizations authorized to certify and register an organization as ISO 27001 compliant. The advantage is that the audit firm is held to a high standard on ISO 27001 audits. ISO 27001 certification is generally more costly than an external audit but may be required in some circumstances.

Individuals in an organization can receive training and earn an *ISO 27001 Internal Auditor* certification. Organizations committed to ISO 27001 compliance will often obtain this certification for one or more of their employees, who through this training will better understand the meaning of ISO 27001 requirements and controls, as well as the proper techniques to determine compliance.

A single user copy of the ISO 27001 standard costs nearly $300. This cost is the single barrier preventing wider adoption of this high-quality standard.

COBIT

Control Objectives for Information and Related Technology (COBIT) is an IT process and governance framework created by ISACA (Information Systems Audit and Control Association) in the mid 1990s.

Before 2012, ISACA maintained five IT management libraries:

- ✔ COBIT 4.1 (the process framework)
- ✔ Val IT 2.0
- ✔ Risk IT Framework
- ✔ IT Assurance Framework (ITAF)
- ✔ Business Model for Information Security (BMIS)

In 2012, ISACA released COBIT 5, which is an integration of these five models. COBIT 5 components are

- ✔ IT governance and practices
- ✔ Process descriptions
- ✔ Control objectives
- ✔ Management guidelines
- ✔ Maturity models

ISACA offers the COBIT framework and related documentation to its members for free as a download. Hard copies are available for purchase.

NIST 800-53

Special Publication 800-53, *Security and Privacy Controls for Federal Information Systems and Organizations*, is a highly recognized and respected framework of security controls for both government and private organizations. It's published by the National Institute for Standards and Technology (NIST), a branch of the U.S. Department of Commerce.

All agencies of the U.S. federal government are required to comply with NIST SP 800-53; however, many state and local governments, as well as private organizations, also use NIST SP 800-53 as their security controls framework.

How InfoSec issues affect us

Information security is the fastest-changing discipline in both information technology (IT) and general business. Here are some examples of the things that are changing rapidly:

✔ **Attackers and attack techniques:** Even more quickly than we find ways of stopping them, attackers are improving their attack techniques and attacking in new ways.

✔ **Malware innovation:** Malware is becoming faster, stealthier, and more potent. Today's malware has rendered traditional antivirus and antimalware all but obsolete.

✔ **New, disruptive tools and technologies:** Hardware and software tech firms are inventing and creating lots of cool, new, and disruptive technologies, such as Apple iPhone, Google Glass, Nest, Uber, and smart utility meters.

✔ **Standards and regulations:** Laws on data protection and privacy are ever changing.

✔ **Internet of Things (IoT):** If we thought things were complicated now, an explosion of Internet-connected devices is just around the corner, creating a heyday for attackers, who will then have more types of devices to explore and vulnerabilities to exploit.

A recent industry report claims a world shortage of over one million information security professionals. A lot of work must be done to keep our adversaries at bay and effectively protect our critical information. As a result, we frequently have to determine which of the important issues of the day warrant our attention.

The primary way in which the explosion of information technology affects us is in how we spend our time. Security professionals need to spend several hours each week reading about current events, innovations, and industry changes to be properly informed and, therefore, effective in our jobs. Often we feel battle-weary, and yet the fight goes on every day. InfoSec work is highly rewarding work, but it is not easy work.

NIST SP 800-53 is comprised of several categories:

✔ Access control

✔ Audit and accountability

✔ Security assessment and authorization

✔ Configuration management

✔ Contingency planning

✔ Identification and authentication

✔ Incident response

✔ Maintenance

✔ Media protection

✔ Physical and environmental protection

✔ Planning

✔ Personnel security

✔ Risk assessment

✔ System and services acquisition

✔ System and communications protection

✔ System and information integrity

Cloud Security Alliance (CSA)

Cloud Security Alliance (CSA) is an organization that has developed standards and guidance for cloud service providers as well as organizations utilizing cloud-based services such as software as a service (SaaS), infrastructure as a service (IaaS), and platform as a service (PaaS). Noted CSA publications follow:

✔ *Cloud Controls Matrix:* This matrix of recommended controls for cloud service providers provides relevance tags for SaaS, PaaS, and IaaS, as well as mappings to many other controls frameworks, including AICPA, BITS, COBIT, European Privacy Directive, NIST SP800-53, HIPAA, ISO27001, and PCI-DSS.

✔ *Enterprise Architecture:* This extensive one-sheet infographic portrays cloud security controls in four main categories:

- Business operations support services: compliance, data governance, operational risk management, human resource security, security monitoring services, legal services, and internal investigations

- Information technology operation and support: IT operations, service delivery, and service support

- Services: presentation services, application services, information services, and infrastructure services

- Security and risk management: governance, risk, and compliance; InfoSec management; privilege management infrastructure; threat and vulnerability management; infrastructure protection services; data protection; and policies and standards

You'll want to print this infographic and hang it in your office as a handy reference.

> ✔ *Security Guidance for Critical Areas of Mobile Computing:* This extensive whitepaper describes the current state of mobile computing and provides guidance for policies, controls, and tools for the safe utilization of mobile devices in an organization.
>
> ✔ *Security Guidance for Critical Areas of Focus in Cloud Computing:* This lengthy whitepaper contains detailed narratives on cloud computing lexicons, governance, risk, and implementation guidance.
>
> ✔ *Consensus Assessments Initiative Questionnaire:* A potential consumer of cloud-based services can send this detailed questionnaire to a cloud services provider to better understand the service provider's safeguards and controls.

Although these standards are voluntary, they represent significant improvement in the development of controls and guidance for cloud service providers and consumers of cloud services.

PCI Security Standard Council

Organizations that store, process, or transmit credit card data are subject to one or more standards meant to ensure the protection of credit card data. *PCI (Payment Card Industry) Security Standards Council,* a non-profit organization formed by the major credit card brands (VISA, MasterCard, American Express, Discover, and JCB), manages these standards and certifications.

PCI-DSS

The *Payment Card Industry Data Security Standard (PCI-DSS)* is an industry standard established and maintained by the PCI Security Standards Council. Usually known as PCI-DSS or just PCI, this standard requires organizations that store, process, or transmit credit card data to comply with all applicable requirements in the standard. The following organizations are required to comply:

> ✔ Card issuers such as banks and credit unions
>
> ✔ Payment processors and gateways
>
> ✔ Merchants
>
> ✔ Any service provider that handles cardholder data

PCI is primarily enforced through the major credit card brands. Any organization that is unable or unwilling to comply with PCI can be fined by one or more of the card brands, and even be cut off from being able to issue or process cardholder data.

Organizations that process a smaller number of credit cards per year are permitted to self-certify to the PCI-DSS. Larger organizations are required to undergo an annual on-site audit by an organization certified to conduct these audits.

All organizations that process any number of credit card records are required to undergo a quarterly security scan of its external assets, performed by an organization certified to perform these scans.

PA-DSS

The *Payment Application Data Security Standard (PA-DSS)* is an industry standard for the certification of commercial payment applications that process credit card transactions. The PA-DSS is especially useful for merchants and other organizations seeking software applications; by selecting a PA-DSS–certified application, they can reduce the scope of audits and compliance efforts.

Qualified Security Assessor (QSA)

Qualified Security Assessor (QSA) is a certification affixed to an organization that performs PCI audits. All individual employed in a QSA-certified organization that will be performing PCI audits are also required to undergo annual training and examination for QSA certification.

Internal Security Assessor (ISA)

Internal Security Assessor (ISA) is a certification earned by a security or audit professional as an employee of an ISA sponsor company. An ISA sponsor company is a merchant or service provider that will agree to sponsor one or more of its employees for PCI training. By having an employee ISA certified, the organization can better understand what they must do to maintain PCI compliance.

Individual QSA and ISA certifications are granted to security professionals with their present employers. If the QSA or ISA professionals leave their employer, they lose QSA or ISA certification and must become recertified by their next employer.

Approved Scanning Vendor (ASV)

An *Approved Scanning Vendor (ASV)* is a company that has been certified by the PCI Security Standards Council to perform the quarterly security scans that all merchants and service providers are required to undergo.

PCI Forensic Investigator (PFI)

A *PCI Forensic Investigator (PFI)* is a company that has been certified by the PCI Security Standards Council to perform forensic investigations on organizations that have suffered a security breach of its cardholder data.

Part II
Having the Right Stuff

Image courtesy NovaInfosec

In this part . . .

- ✔ Discover the education required to break into the information security field.

- ✔ Understand the training and certifications you can earn in the InfoSec profession.

- ✔ Study the technology concepts that information security professionals work with on a regular basis.

- ✔ Look at the practices used to build and manage an information security program.

Chapter 4

Education, Training, and Certifications

In This Chapter

▶ Understanding education opportunities in information security

▶ Obtaining training opportunities to advance in the profession

▶ Earning certifications that reflect your skills and knowledge

A successful career in information security requires you to commit to a lifestyle of continuous learning just to keep up with current threats, trends, and techniques.

A wide array of learning opportunities are available for people who want to get into the information security field, as well as continuing education for those already in the field. The choices you make will depend on several factors, including the following:

▸ Work experience

▸ Prior education

▸ Age

▸ Level of management or specialization you want to attain

 A good educational foundation is essential for entry in the information security profession, and a steady intake of continuing education is essential from then on.

Higher Education

Undergraduate and graduate degrees in management information systems, computer science, and similar subjects have been offered for decades. More recently, many colleges and universities are offering degree programs in one or more aspects of information security. Colleges and universities also offer continuing education programs in information technology and security.

Undergraduate programs in information security

Universities around the world offer undergraduate degrees in information security — too many to list in this book, and that's a good thing. You can probably find a university near you that offers a degree in information security. Many universities are also offering online degrees.

Typical degrees being awarded include the following:

- Bachelor of Science in Information Security
- Bachelor of Science in Security and Risk Analysis
- Bachelor of Science in Security Engineering
- Bachelor of Science in Information Technology — Security
- Bachelor of Science in Computer Science and Information Security

The variety of degree programs will help you build the foundation of your career as you begin your formal education.

Your best long-term strategy should include the completion of an undergraduate degree in a technical field. The more college education you have, the more you will enjoy more opportunities for jobs and career growth.

Graduate degrees in information security

Like undergraduate degrees, graduate-level degrees in information security are offered by many universities. A graduate degree is a great path for advanced studies and will help you compete for advanced positions in information security. Many middle- and upper-management jobs in information security require advanced degrees.

Graduate degrees being awarded include the following:

- University of Washington: MS in Cyber Security Engineering
- Western Governors University: MS in Information Security and Assurance

- ✔ Champlain College: MS in Digital Forensic Science

- ✔ Lewis University: MS in Information Security — Technical

- ✔ Capella University: MS in Information Assurance and Security

- ✔ Northcentral University: Ph.D. in Business Administration — Computer and Information Security

Some security organizations also offer graduate degrees, including these two:

- ✔ SANS (SysAdmin, Audit, Networking, and Security) Institute: MS in Information Security Engineering, and MS in Information Security Management

- ✔ International Council of E-Commerce Consultants (also known as EC-Council), Master of Security Science

A good reference for locating graduate-level education can be found at www.gradschools.com.

Continuing education

Continuing education is the practice of continually obtaining training courses to expand one's knowledge and skills. In the information security profession, continuing education is essential to our success for several reasons:

- ✔ **High rate of change:** The information security business is undergoing an extremely high rate of change. New threats, vulnerabilities, techniques, and security breaches happen daily. Unlike many other professions that move much more slowly, InfoSec undergoes constant transformation.

The value of a college degree

The advantage of a formal university education is that you have the opportunity to immerse yourself in information security and really live and breathe it. Additionally, companies and the federal government are actively and heavily recruiting from university programs dealing with information security. Internships are also available, and the major consulting companies are looking for individuals with some skill in the field.

The disadvantages? Getting a college degree is costly and time-consuming and can be especially difficult if you're not in a position to go back to school full time. Thankfully, programs are available that accommodate those with a job and family life, but it's a considerable investment in time and resources regardless.

Glen Sorensen, Seattle

✔ **Certification requirements:** You'll need to earn one or more vendor or nonvendor certifications (which are described later in this chapter). Many of these certifications require that you undergo continuing education to remain in good standing.

Certificates from colleges and universities

Many colleges and universities have continuing education programs designed for working professionals. Often these are evening or weekend programs in which students earn certificates. Many are offered online, which gives you a wider choice of certificate offerings.

Examples of these certificates include the following:

✔ Certificate in Information Security and Risk Management, from the University of Washington

✔ Certificate in Computer and Network Security, from Stanford University

✔ Certificate in Information Systems Cybersecurity, from Penn State University

Courses from professional organizations

Many professional organizations offer training courses in different fields in the information security profession. These courses are offered in a variety of formats and timelines, including:

✔ Training weeks or boot camps

✔ Training day or days immediately before or after a professional conference

✔ Self-paced online training

✔ Classroom training

Examples of these types of education courses include:

✔ **RSA Conference:** SANS and (ISC)^2 certification training offered the two days before the main conference

✔ **SANS Institute:** Training weeks offered in several cities worldwide each year

✔ **ISACA:** Training weeks, plus one and two-day workshops offered immediately before conferences

✔ **BlackHat:** Several days of training offered immediately before the main conference

Other continuing education opportunities

Besides certifications and formal training courses, you can continue your information security education in other ways, including the following:

- ✔ Vendor product training
- ✔ Vendor product demos
- ✔ Security organization chapter lectures
- ✔ Lectures at security conferences

Military education

Today's military organizations still have their traditional weapons: guns, warships, submarines, fighter planes, and bombers. These large organizations require a lot of information technology to support them. So that they can protect their own networks, military organizations train many of their personnel in different facets of information security. The internal networks in military organizations utilize the same technologies as commercial networks, so most of the skills learned while in the military will translate directly into private sector or public sector jobs.

Military organizations also have offensive and defensive cyberwarfare capabilities. Specialists who work in these areas will also learn valuable skills that will translate nicely into information security jobs in private organizations and as security consultants.

Examples of military training in information security include the following:

- ✔ **U.S. Army School Cyber Leader College:** Information Assurance and Computer Network Defense training and certification
- ✔ **U.S. Navy:** training in information warfare, cyberwarfare engineering, and cryptography
- ✔ **U.S. Air Force:** training in cybersurety and cybersystems operations

Vendor Certifications

Vendor certifications play an important role in many information technology career paths, and information security is no different. Formal education and training (discussed earlier in this chapter) provide you with important fundamental knowledge and theories that will endure throughout your career.

Vendor certifications, on the other hand, can serve as an important capstone that provides practical, hands-on knowledge of current security technologies.

Most vendor certification exams are administered at Pearson VUE (`www.pearsonvue.com`) and Prometric (`www.prometric.com`) testing centers. These testing centers have strict identification requirements to verify the candidate's identity before taking any exam. Most exams are computer-based and provide test results immediately after completion of the exam. Visit the testing centers' respective websites to locate a test center near you, schedule an exam, find out about specific identification requirements, and pay your test registration fees.

Vendor certification programs are continuously updated. The information presented here is current as of this writing, but you should always visit the vendor's website before pursuing a certification to ensure that you have the latest information about that certification and its requirements.

Check Point

The Check Point Certified Professional Program (`www.checkpoint.com`) provides product-focused certifications based on one of the most popular firewall products on the market: Check Point Firewall-1. Certifications include the following

- **Check Point Certified Security Administrator (CCSA):** An entry-level certification for security administrators who have 6 to 12 months of work experience with Check Point security solutions. Candidates must pass a single exam that covers the following topics:

  - Understanding Check Point technologies

  - Describing deployment platforms and security policies

  - Monitoring traffic and connections

  - Implementing network address translation (NAT)

  - Configuring user management and authentication

  - Using Check Point's SmartUpdate

  - Implementing identity awareness

  - Configuring virtual private network (VPN) tunnels

  - Resolving security administration issues

✔ **Check Point Certified Security Expert (CCSE):** The next certification level. Candidates must first earn the CCSA certification, and then take an additional exam that covers the same topics as the CCSA exam but at a more advanced level.

✔ **Check Point Certified Managed Security Expert (CCMSE):** For security administrators who manage large or virtualized network environments. The candidate must first earn the CCSE certification, and then pass an additional exam covering the following topics:

- Installing, configuring, and managing the multi-domain management (MDM) environment

- Understanding common deployment scenarios

- Understanding the traffic inspection process

- Configuring domain management server (DMS) high availability

- Configuring and implementing a global policy

- Applying common troubleshooting practices

To help you prepare for your certification exams, Check Point offers three-day courses for both the CCSA and CCSE certifications, and a five-day course to prepare for the CCMSE certification. These courses are available through authorized training partners around the world.

Cisco

Cisco (www.cisco.com) offers five levels of network certifications to support its network, server, and security solutions: entry, associate, professional, expert, and architect. Cisco security certifications are Cisco Certified Network Associate (CCNA), Cisco Certified Network Professional (CCNP), and Cisco Certified Internetwork Expert (CCIE), as well as the Cisco Cybersecurity Specialist certification.

Cisco Certified Network Associate (CCNA)

Cisco's associate-level certification is considered the foundation level of networking certification. The CCNA Security certification validates associate-level knowledge and skills required to secure networks built on Cisco infrastructure and technology. A CCNA Security network professional can demonstrate the skills necessary to

✔ Develop a security infrastructure

✔ Recognize threats to and vulnerabilities in the network

✔ Mitigate security threats and vulnerabilities

CCNA Security certification first requires candidates to earn either the Cisco Certified Entry Networking Technician (CCENT) or CCNA Routing and Switching certification. The candidate must then pass the Implementing Cisco IOS (Internetwork Operating System) Network Security (IINS) exam. This 90-minute exam consists of 55 to 65 questions covering the following topics

- ✓ Common security threats
- ✓ Security and Cisco routers
- ✓ Authentication, authorization, and accounting (AAA) on Cisco devices
- ✓ IOS access control lists (ACLs)
- ✓ Secure network management and reporting
- ✓ Common Layer 2 attacks
- ✓ Cisco firewall technologies
- ✓ Cisco intrusion prevention systems (IPS)
- ✓ VPN technologies

CCENT certification requires the candidate to pass the Interconnecting Cisco Networking Devices Part 1 (ICND1) exam. CCNA Routing and Switching Certification requires the candidate to pass the ICND1 and ICND2 exams, or the CCNA Composite Exam (CCNAX).

Recognition of a different sort

Cisco security certifications can also earn you important recognition by the U.S. National Security Agency (NSA) and U.S. Department of Defense (DoD).

The CCNA Security certification complies with the Committee on National Security Systems (CNSS) 4011 training standard, which applies to certain information security professionals responsible for identifying system vulnerabilities, investigating and documenting system security technologies and policies, and analyzing and evaluating system security technologies. The CCNA Security certification program satisfies the formal NSA and CNSS training requirement for information security professionals who work with federal agencies and private sector organizations to protect their information and defend the nation's vital information assets.

The U.S. Department of Defense has also certified the CCNA Security certification as DoD 8570.01-M compliant. The DoD 8570 Directive provides guidance and procedures for the training, certification, and management of DoD employees who perform Information Assurance (IA) functions. These employees are required to hold an approved certification for their particular job role and classification. The CCNA Security certification has been approved for DoD Information Assurance Technician Levels I and II.

If you're interested in working in the public sector, be sure to check out Chapter 9!

Cisco Certified Network Professional (CCNP)

Cisco's professional-level certification represents a more advanced knowledge of networking technologies for experienced networking professionals. CCNP Security certification requires the candidate to earn the CCNA Routing and Switching certification and to pass the following four exams

- ✓ **Implementing Cisco Secure Access Solutions (SISAS):** A 90-minute exam consisting of 65 to 75 questions on the following topics:
  - Identity management and secure access
  - Threat defense
  - Troubleshooting, monitoring, and reporting tools
  - Threat defense architectures
  - Identity management architectures

- ✓ **Implementing Cisco Edge Network Security Solutions (SENSS):** A 90-minute exam consisting of 65 to 75 questions that cover the following topics:
  - Threat defense
  - Cisco security device graphical user interfaces (GUIs) and secured command-line interface (CLI) management
  - Management services on Cisco devices
  - Troubleshooting, monitoring, and reporting tools
  - Threat defense architectures
  - Security components and considerations

- ✓ **Implementing Cisco Secure Mobility Solutions (SIMOS):** A 90-minute exam consisting of 65 to 75 questions on the following topics:
  - Secure communications
  - Troubleshooting, monitoring, and reporting tools
  - Secure communications architectures

- ✓ **Implementing Cisco Threat Control Solutions (SITCS):** A 90-minute exam consisting of 65 to 75 questions covering the following topics:
  - Content security
  - Threat defense
  - Device GUIs and secured CLI
  - Troubleshooting, monitoring, and reporting tools
  - Threat defense architectures
  - Content security architectures

Cisco Certified Internetworking Expert (CCIE)

Cisco's *créme de la créme,* the Cisco Certified Internetworking Expert (CCIE) offers a security track that requires satisfactory completion of a two-hour exam and an eight-hour hands-on lab! There are no formal prerequisites for the CCIE Security certification, but candidates should have a minimum of three to five years of professional work experience in networking and security.

The CCIE exam consists of 90 to 110 questions covering the following topics:

- ✔ Infrastructure, connectivity, communications, and network security
- ✔ Security protocols
- ✔ Application and infrastructure security
- ✔ Threats, vulnerability analysis, and mitigation
- ✔ Cisco security products, features, and management
- ✔ Cisco security technologies and solutions
- ✔ Security policies and procedures, best practices, and standards

After passing the CCIE Security exam, you must pass the CCIE Security lab. You must attempt the lab within 18 months of passing the exam, and must pass the lab within three years of passing the exam (yes, it's that difficult!).

Cisco Cybersecurity Specialist

Finally, the Cisco Cybersecurity Specialist certification recognizes security professionals who possess specialized and proven knowledge of event monitoring, security event/alarm/traffic analysis, and incident response. Candidates must pass a 60-minute exam consisting of 45 to 55 questions covering the following topics:

- ✔ Information gathering and security foundations
- ✔ Event monitoring
- ✔ Security events and alarms
- ✔ Traffic analysis, collection, and correlation
- ✔ Incident response
- ✔ Operational communications

Dell

The technical certification from Dell (www.dell.com) is for security professionals responsible for designing, implementing, supporting or managing Dell SonicWALL security products. Certifications include the following:

- ✔ **Certified SonicWALL Security Administrator (CSSA):** Candidates must pass one of the CSSA certification exams. These exams are bundled with Dell instructor-led courses. For some courses, test-out exams are available, which allow candidates to take the exam without attending the course. CSSA courses and exams include

  - Network Security Basic Administration

  - Secure Remote Access Basic Administration

  - Global Management Solution Basic Administration

  - Email Security

- ✔ **Master Certified SonicWALL Security Administrator (Master CSSA):** Candidates who hold three or more active CSSA certifications are designated Master CSSAs.

- ✔ **Certified SonicWALL Security Professional (CSSP):** Candidates must hold at least one CSSA certification, attend a two-day, instructor-led Network Security Advanced Administration course, and pass a Dell SonicWALL CSSP certification exam.

EMC

EMC (www.emc.com) offers the RSA Certified Security Professional Program for security professionals with the knowledge and skills to deploy and maintain enterprise security systems. Certification exams are administered at Pearson VUE testing centers and include the following:

- ✔ **RSA Archer Certified Administrator:** An exam consisting of 70 multiple-choice, multiple-response, and true/false questions that must be completed in 90 minutes. Exam topics include

  - System integration and configuration management

  - Security administration

  - Communication and data presentation

- ✔ **RSA Security Analytics Certified Administrator:** An exam consisting of 71 multiple-choice, multiple-response, and true/false questions that must be completed in 90 minutes. Exam topics include

    - General product knowledge (features, functions, and capabilities)

    - System configurations

    - Monitoring and troubleshooting

- ✔ **RSA Authentication Manager Certified Administrator:** An exam consisting of 70 multiple-choice, multiple-response, and true/false questions that must be completed in 90 minutes. Exam topics include

    - RSA SecurID and RSA Authentication Manager product knowledge

    - Database management and configuration

    - Troubleshooting and maintenance

EnCase

The EnCase Certified Examiner (EnCE) certification is for information security professionals who have extensive experience in computer investigation methodology and the use of EnCase computer forensics software from Guidance Software (www.guidancesoftware.com).

EnCE certification requires that the candidate have at least 64 hours of approved computer forensic training or 12 months of computer forensic experience. The candidate must then submit the EnCE application to the EnCase Certification Coordinator and register for the Phase I exam.

The Phase I exam is a two-hour exam administered online by ExamBuilder during a Guidance Software EnCE Prep Course, or at Guidance Software's annual Computer and Enterprise Investigations Conference (CEIC). The test consists of 180 multiple choice and true/false questions (174 for international candidates; legal questions are removed) covering the following topics:

- ✔ Computer forensic best practices
- ✔ Legal issues
- ✔ Computer knowledge
- ✔ EnCase software knowledge
- ✔ Evidence discovery techniques
- ✔ File system artifacts

After successful completion of the Phase I exam, candidates will receive an email from Guidance Software containing instructions for completing the Phase II practical exam. This email message includes directions for accessing the EnCase Forensic software, evidence files, and objectives or issues that the candidate must address. The candidate must work through the case, compile a report, and submit the report to Guidance Software within 60 days.

Fortinet

The Fortinet Network Security Expert (NSE) is an eight-level certification program for security professionals with technical experience using the network security platform from Fortinet (`www.fortinet.com`). Each certification level is a prerequisite for the next level. The certification levels, objectives, and requirements are listed in Table 4-1.

Fortinet is retiring the FCNSA and FCNSP certification programs (referenced in the NSE 2 and NSE 4 requirements in Table 4-1). Individuals who currently hold the FCNSA or FCNSP certification will be required to recertify under the NSE program within one year after Fortinet announces the formal retirement date for these programs.

Table 4-1	**Fortinet Network Security Expert Certification**	
Level	*Objective*	*Requirements*
NSE 1	Develop a foundational understanding of network security concepts	Pass six online exams administered by the Fortinet Learning Center
NSE 2	Develop basic Fortinet configuration and administration skills	Pass the Fortinet Certified Network Security Associate (FCNSA) exam at a Pearson VUE testing center
NSE 3	Develop an advanced understanding of network security design and architecture	Pass an online exam administered by the Fortinet Learning Center
NSE 4	Gain a comprehensive understanding of how to design and implement network security infrastructure	Pass the Fortinet Certified Network Security Professional (FCNSP) exam at a Pearson VUE testing center

(continued)

Table 4-1 *(continued)*

Level	Objective	Requirements
NSE 5	Develop a detailed understanding of how to implement network security management and analytics	Complete the FortiManager and FortiAnalyzer classes and pass both the FortiManager and FortiAnalyzer specialist exams administered by the Fortinet Learning Center
NSE 6	Develop an understanding of security technologies beyond the firewall	Must wait at least 90 days after completion of NSE 4 and then complete at least two Fortinet advanced technology classes. Topics include web application firewall (WAF), mail, web, distributed denial-of-service (DDoS), application delivery controller (ADC), and advanced persistent threats (APT)
NSE 7	Demonstrate ability to troubleshoot internet security issues	Must wait at least 90 days after completion of NSE 4, and complete the FortiGate Troubleshooting class and pass in-class practical exam
NSE 8	Demonstrate ability to install comprehensive network security solution in a live environment	Must wait at least 90 days after completion of NSE 7, and then pass an individual oral examination and a practical experience exam

IBM

IBM (www.ibm.com) offers approximately 20 security certifications on its various security solutions, including Access Manager, AppScan, Identity Manager, Network Intrusion Prevention System, QRadar SIEM (Security Information and Event Management), SiteProtector, and Tivoli.

Certification levels include

- ✔ IBM certified solution advisor
- ✔ IBM certified associate
- ✔ IBM certified deployment professional
- ✔ IBM certified advanced deployment professional

Each IBM certification at the solution advisor, associate, and deployment professional levels require the candidate to pass one exam (except the IBM Certified Deployment Professional — Network Intrusion Prevention System certification, which requires two exams) administered by Pearson VUE testing centers. Certifications are not available for all IBM security products at all certification levels, but there are no prerequisites for any certification level.

Requirements for the IBM certified advanced deployment professional certification level vary between three and four tests, and in some cases require an industry certification (discussed later in this chapter), such as the Certified Information Systems Security Professional (CISSP), Systems Security Certified Practitioner (SSCP), or Security+.

McAfee

McAfee (www.mcafee.com) security products are well known and widely used throughout the world. McAfee's security certification program consists of four tracks and validates the candidate's knowledge and skills with various McAfee security products and security topics. Exams are administered by Prometric testing centers. The four certification tracks and specializations include

- ✔ **Certified McAfee Security Administrator (CMSA)**
    - Risk and compliance
    - Endpoint
    - Network
    - Operations
- ✔ **Certified McAfee Security Specialist (CMSS)**
    - ePO (ePolicy Orchestrator)
    - NSP (Network Security Platform)
    - HIPs (Host Intrusion Prevention System)
    - DLPe (Data Loss Prevention Endpoint)
    - SIEM (Security Information and Event Management)
    - NGFW (Next-Generation Firewall)
- ✔ **Certified McAfee Security Professional (CMSP)**
    - Security Engineer
    - Ethical Security Testing
    - Incident Response and Forensics
    - Malware Analysis
- ✔ **Certified McAfee Security Expert (CMSX)**
    - Security Architect

Microsoft

Certification programs from Microsoft (www.microsoft.com) have undergone many changes over the years. The current program provides a certification path for server and desktop professionals that includes a security fundamentals requirement. Microsoft's entry-level certification is the Microsoft Technology Associate (MTA). The MTA: IT Infrastructure certification requires the candidate to pass one of four exams, administered by Pearson VUE and Prometric testing centers, as well as at many schools through Certiport (www.certiport.com) testing centers. The four MTA: IT Infrastructure exams include the following topics:

- Windows operating system fundamentals
- Windows server administration fundamentals
- Networking fundamentals
- Security fundamentals

The Security Fundamentals exam covers the following topics:

- Security layers
- Operating system security
- Network security
- Security software

There are no prerequisites for MTA certification, but candidates should have a working knowledge of Windows Server, Windows-based networking, Active Directory, antimalware products, firewalls, and network devices.

Oracle

Oracle (www.oracle.com) offers two security certifications covering the Oracle Solaris operating system and Oracle database management system.

To earn the Oracle Certified Expert, Oracle Solaris 10 Security Administrator certification, candidates must be certified as an Oracle Certified Professional, Oracle Solaris 10 System Administrator, and pass the Oracle Solaris 10 Security Administrator Certified Expert Exam. This 90-minute, 59-question exam is administered by Pearson VUE and covers the following topics:

- General security principles and features
- Installing systems securely

✔ Principles of least privilege

✔ Cryptographic features

✔ Application and network security

✔ Auditing and zone security

The Oracle Database 11g Security Certified Implementation Specialist certification requires candidates to pass a 105-minute, 70-question exam administered by Pearson VUE. Exam topics include

✔ Overview of Oracle Database 11g security options

✔ Audit vault

✔ Advanced security option (ASO)

✔ Database vault

✔ Enterprise manager data-masking pack

Palo Alto Networks

Palo Alto Networks offers two certification programs based on its next-generation security products. The Accredited Configuration Engineer (ACE) certification exam tests the candidate's knowledge of the core features and functions of Palo Alto Networks' next-generation firewalls. The exam is web-based and consists of 50 multiple-choice questions.

The Certified Network Security Engineer (CNSE) exam is a formal certification administered by Kryterion Testing Network (KTN) centers. The candidate has two and a half hours to complete a 100-question, multiple-choice, multiple-response exam. Exam questions cover the following areas:

✔ **Administration and management:** Demonstrate an understanding of configuration management, upgrading and downgrading PAN-OS (Palo Alto Networks Operating System), role-based administration, configuring the management interface, customizing response pages, reporting, and using the ACC (Application Command Center) to obtain network information.

✔ **Network architecture:** Demonstrate an understanding of interface configuration and features, SSL (Secure Sockets Layer) and site-to-site VPNs (virtual private networks), source and destination NAT (network address translation), and virtual routers.

✔ **Security architecture:** Demonstrate an understanding of packet flow, zone-based security policy, SSL decryption, certificate management, and logging behaviors.

✔ **Troubleshooting:** Illustrate knowledge of using the Get TechSupport file, interpreting CLI (command-line interface) commands, and evaluating firewall logs as methods for troubleshooting.

✔ **User identification:** Display knowledge of installing and configuring the various User Identification agents, the terminal server agent, and Captive Portal.

✔ **Content identification:** Demonstrate knowledge of how to configure security profiles as they relate to URL (Uniform Resource Locator) filtering, antivirus, data-filtering patterns, and vulnerability detection.

✔ **Application identification:** Display an understanding of the workings of security policy as it relates to Application ID, application groups, application filters, application dependencies, rule shadowing, and application override traffic.

✔ **Panorama:** Demonstrate an understanding of how policy is created and pushed from the Panorama server, how Panorama receives logging and reporting events, how objects are managed, and how device groups are created and used as targets in policy rules.

✔ **GlobalProtect:** Display an understanding of how a GlobalProtect Agent, GlobalProtect Portal, and a GlobalProtect Gateway are configured. Understand how HIP (Host Information Profile) matches are used in security rules and how clients are polled for HIP compliance.

Learn more about Kryterion Testing Network Centers at www.kryterion online.com. Learn more about the Palo Alto Networks certification programs at www.paloaltonetworks.com.

Red Hat

The Red Hat (www.redhat.com) Certificate of Expertise in Server Hardening is for security professionals with skills and experience in

✔ Configuring file systems and volumes for more restrictive security policies

✔ Implementing additional user account security and identity management

✔ Configuring enhanced, secure logging, and audit capabilities

✔ Identifying and performing appropriate package updates in response to Common Vulnerabilities and Exposure (CVE) and Red Hat Security Advisory (RHSA) reports

Sourcefire

Sourcefire (`www.sourcefire.com`), which was recently acquired by Cisco, offers four certification programs that enable candidates to become certified on all their security solutions (SFCE) or on individual products (SFCP, SFCP-AMP, and SnortCP). Exams are administered online and consist of 50 to 100 questions that must be completed in one and a half to three hours. Details of the individual certifications follow:

- **Sourcefire Certified Expert (SFCE):** For candidates with in-depth knowledge of Sourcefire System v5, including Next-Generation IPS (Intrusion Prevention System), Next-Generation Firewall, FireSIGHT, and FIREAMP analysis and rules.

- **Sourcefire Certified Professional (SFCP):** For candidates with in-depth knowledge of Sourcefire System v5, including Next-Generation IPS (Intrusion Prevention System), Next-Generation Firewall, FireSIGHT analysis and rules.

- **Sourcefire Certified Administrator (SFCA):** For candidates with in-depth knowledge of Sourcefire System v5 user interface and initial setup of appliances.

- **Sourcefire Certified Professional (SFCP-AMP):** For candidates with in-depth knowledge of FireAMP, Sourcefire Cloud, and the Sourcefire Connector, including File Device trajectory, administration, analysis, and client management.

- **Snort Certified Professional (SnortCP):** For candidates with in-depth knowledge of open source components and technical skills for successful implementation and rule writing.

Symantec

Like McAfee, Symantec (`www.symantec.com`) security products are well known and widely used throughout the world. To support its security solutions, Symantec offers the Symantec Certified Specialist (SCS) and Symantec Certified Professional (SCP) certification programs.

SCS certifications are based on a specific area of expertise with Symantec products. These certifications measure technical knowledge of common tasks such as installation, configuration, deployment, product management and administration, and day-to-day maintenance. To achieve SCS certification, candidates must pass one exam administered by Pearson VUE testing centers. Currently, more than a dozen SCS exams are offered, covering the following security products:

- Symantec Cluster Server
- Symantec Storage Foundation
- Symantec NetBackup
- Symantec Enterprise Vault
- Symantec Endpoint Protection
- Symantec Backup Exec
- Veritas Storage Foundation and High Availability Solutions
- Symantec Management Platform
- Symantec Client Management Suite
- Symantec Clearwell eDiscovery Platform
- Symantec Control Compliance Suite
- Symantec Data Center Security
- Symantec Data Loss Prevention
- Symantec Network Access Control

The SCP certification program validates the candidate's skills and technical competencies necessary to design, architect, and implement multiple solutions in data protection, high availability, or security environments. Candidates must pass two or more SCS exams and one SCP exam administered by Pearson VUE testing centers. Currently, four SCP certification tracks are available:

- **SCP in Cloud Security:** The candidate must pass the Symantec Cloud Security exam and the Cloud Security Alliance's Certificate in Cloud Security Knowledge (CCSK). Go to `https://ccsk.cloudsecurity alliance.org` to learn more.

- **SCP in Data Protection:** The candidate must pass the Administration of Symantec NetBackup for UNIX (or Windows) and Administration of Symantec Backup Exec exams.

- **SCP in Endpoint Management:** The candidate must pass the Administration of Symantec Management Platform and Administration of Altiris Client Management Suite exams.

- **SCP in Storage Management and High Availability for UNIX:** The candidate must pass the Administration of Veritas Storage Foundation for UNIX and Administration of Veritas Cluster Server for UNIX exams.

Industry Certifications

Industry certifications, also known as vendor-neutral certifications, can play an important role in any information security career. Like formal education and training (discussed earlier in this chapter), vendor-neutral certifications demonstrate your understanding of important fundamental knowledge and theories apart from specific products and tools.

As mentioned, Pearson VUE (www.pearsonvue.com) and Prometric (www.prometric.com) testing centers administer most vendor certification exams. These testing centers verify the candidate's identity prior to taking any exam. Most exams are computer-based and provide test results immediately after you complete the exam. Check out the testing centers' respective websites to locate a test center near you, schedule an exam, find out about specific ID requirements, and pay your test registration fees.

Industry certification programs are continuously updated. The information presented here is current as of this writing, but you should visit the organization's website before pursuing a certification to ensure that you have the latest information about that certification and its requirements.

ASIS International

ASIS International (www.asisonline.org), which was formerly the American Society for Industrial Security, offers several security industry certifications including Certified Protection Professional (CPP), Professional Certified Investigator (PCI), and Physical Security Professional (PSP).

Certified Protection Professional (CPP)

The CPP certification is for security management professionals who have seven years of security experience (including three years in a security management position) and a bachelor's degree, or nine years of security experience (including three years in a security management position) if you don't have a bachelor's degree. The CPP exam consists of 200 multiple-choice questions (an additional 25 pre-test questions are included throughout the exam for future exams but do not count as part of your final score) in the following subject areas:

- ✔ Security principles and practices
- ✔ Business principles and practices
- ✔ Personnel security
- ✔ Physical security

- ✔ Information security
- ✔ Emergency practices
- ✔ Investigations
- ✔ Legal aspects

Professional Certified Investigator (PCI)

The PCI certification is for security professionals with knowledge and experience in case forensics. It requires a high school diploma or General Educational Development (GED) equivalent, and a minimum of five years of investigations experience, with at least two years in case management. The PCI certification is applicable to a broad range of investigations that extend well beyond computer crime to include

- ✔ Arson
- ✔ Child abuse
- ✔ Economic crime
- ✔ Forensics
- ✔ Gaming
- ✔ Healthcare fraud
- ✔ Insurance fraud
- ✔ Loss prevention
- ✔ Narcotics
- ✔ Property and casualty
- ✔ Threat assessment
- ✔ Workplace violence

The ASIS Professional Certified Investigator (PCI) certification and the Payment Card Industry's (PCI) Data Security Standard (and various certification programs) are not associated or affiliated in any way. They are different and don't even cover the same topics! Learn more about the Payment Card Industry in Chapters 3 and 5 and later in this chapter.

The PCI certification exam consists of 140 multiple-choice questions. Only 125 questions are scored; the remaining 15 questions are pre-test questions randomly distributed throughout the exam as potential future certification exam questions. The exam covers three security domains:

- ✔ Case management
- ✔ Investigative techniques and procedures
- ✔ Case presentation

Physical Security Professional (PSP)

The Physical Security Professional (PSPS) certification is for security professionals with knowledge and experience in threat assessment and risk analysis, integrated physical security systems, and identification, implementation, and evaluation of physical security measures. PSP certification requires a high school diploma (or GED equivalent) or an associate degree and six years of physical security experience, or a bachelor's degree (or higher) and four years of physical security experience.

The PSP certification exam consists of 140 multiple-choice questions. Only 125 questions are scored; the remaining 15 questions are pre-test questions randomly distributed throughout the exam as potential future certification exam questions. The exam covers the following three broad topic areas

✔ Physical security assessment

✔ Application, design, and integration of physical security systems

✔ Implementation of physical security measures

DRI International

DRI International (www.drii.org), formerly Disaster Recovery Institute International, is a global nonprofit organization that focuses on professional standards for business continuity and disaster recovery planning. DRII certifies more than 12,000 professionals worldwide in more than 100 countries. DRII certification programs include four certified professional designations, three certified specialties, and two risk management certifications.

DRII certifications require that you take at least one examination; some also require you to describe your professional experience and choose references who will vouch for your experience.

DRI International has organized its certifications within several career tracks:

✔ **Continuity:**

- **Associate Business Continuity Professional (ABCP):** An entry-level certification for individuals with less than two years of industry experience

- **Certified Functional Continuity Professional (CFCP):** Requires more than two years of experience in three of the subject matter areas defined in DRII's list of professional practices

- **Certified Business Continuity Professional (CBCP):** Requires more than two years of experience in five of DRII's subject matter areas

- **Certified Business Continuity Vendor (CBCV):** For individuals and vendors who have some knowledge of business continuity planning but are not practitioners in an organization

✔ **Advanced continuity:**

- **Master Business Continuity Professional (MBCP):** For individuals who have superior knowledge and at least five years of experience in the business continuity profession

✔ **Audit:**

- **Certified Business Continuity Auditor (CBCA):** For specialists with two years of experience auditing business continuity programs

- **Certified Business Continuity Lead Auditor (CBCLA):** For audit team leaders with two years of experience building and managing audit programs

✔ **Public sector continuity:**

- **Associate Public Sector Continuity Professional (APSCP):** An entry-level certification for someone just starting out in business continuity in the public sector

- **Certified Public Sector Continuity Professional (CPSCP):** For business continuity professionals in the public sector with two years of experience

✔ **Healthcare continuity:**

- **Associate Healthcare Provider Continuity Professional (AHPCP):** For someone starting a business continuity career in the healthcare industry

- **Certified Healthcare Provider Continuity Professional (CHPCP):** For business continuity professionals in healthcare with two years of experience

✔ **Risk management:**

- **Associate Risk Management Professional (ARMP):** An entry-level certification for professionals who are new in the risk management field

- **Certified Risk Management Professional (CRMP):** For professionals with two years of experience in two of DRII's four risk management practice areas

EC-Council

The International Council of E-Commerce Consultants (www.eccouncil. org), better known as EC-Council, first made waves with its Certified Ethical Hacker certification — not so much with the content of its examination but with the term *ethical hacker.* The fuss is partly to do with the change in usage for the term *hacker,* which used to describe a hobbyist or enthusiast, but now is a mostly negative term meaning someone who breaks into systems to steal data or alter its contents or function.

EC-Council has many security-related certifications. EC-Council certification exams can be taken in any EC-Council Accredited Training Center, Pearson VUE, or Prometric testing center (in the United States). Certifications available from EC-Council include the following:

- ✔ **Certified Secure Computer User (CSCU):** For end users who are not security professionals. This certification focuses on safe computer and mobile device usage, safe Internet usage, and data protection.

- ✔ **EC-Council Certified Security Specialist (ECSS):** A generalist certification that focuses on information security, network security, and computer forensics.

- ✔ **Certified Ethical Hacker (CEH):** An entry certification for penetration testers. This certification is for professionals who have proficiency in reconnaissance and intrusion tools used by hackers. The purpose of this certification is to help protect an organization from cybercriminals through the knowledge and skills of an in-house professional who understands their techniques.

- ✔ **Certified Network Defense Architect (CNDA):** For government agencies. This certification is functionally equivalent to the Certified Ethical Hacker (CEH) certification in every way but the name. It's the CEH certification without the controversial *h* word.

- ✔ **EC-Council Certified Secure Programmer (ECSP):** For software developers with knowledge and skills in secure software development. This certification comes in .Net and Java variants.

- ✔ **EC-Council Certified VoIP Professional (ECVP):** For professionals with knowledge and experience in Voice over Internet Protocol (VoIP).

- ✔ **EC-Council Certified Encryption Specialist (ECES):** For security professionals with knowledge and experience with encryption, hashing, and key management.

- ✔ **EC-Council Network Security Administrator (ENSA):** For network administrators and others who build and configure security systems such as firewalls, intrusion detection systems (IDS), antimalware systems, and security event and incident management (SIEM) systems.

✔ **EC-Council Disaster Recovery Professional (EDRP):** For disaster recovery professionals with experience building and running a corporate disaster recovery program.

✔ **EC-Council Certified Security Analyst (ECSA):** For penetration testers who demonstrate advanced skills in penetration testing and penetration testing programs.

✔ **Licensed Penetration Tester (LPT):** The topmost certification for penetration testers who work as consultants or in client organizations.

✔ **Computer Hacking Forensic Investigator (CHFI):** For computer forensics professionals who investigate cybercrime and internal corporate investigations.

✔ **EC-Council Certified Incident Handler (ECIH):** For experienced incident handlers and other professionals who are called on to respond to security incidents.

✔ **Certified Chief Information Security Officer (C I CISO):** For security professionals with knowledge and experience building and leading corporate information security management programs.

SANS Institute

Along with the (ISC)^2 Certified Information Systems Security Professional (CISSP) certification, discussed later in this chapter, Global Information Assurance Certification, or GIAC (www.giac.org), certifications are among the most widely known and respected security industry certifications today. The SANS (SysAdmin, Audit, Networking, and Security) Institute Global Information Assurance Certification (GIAC) program validates the skills and knowledge of security professionals, practitioners, and developers through nearly 30 certifications, which are grouped into the following categories:

✔ **Security administration:**

- GIAC Security Essentials (GSEC)

- GIAC Certified Incident Handler (GCIH)

- GIAC Certified Intrusion Analyst (GCIA)

- GIAC Certified Penetration Tester (GPEN)

- GIAC Web Application Penetration Tester (GWAPT)

- GIAC Certified Perimeter Protection Analyst (GPPA)

- GIAC Certified Windows Security Administrator (GCWN)

- GIAC Information Security Fundamentals (GISF)

- GIAC Assessing and Auditing Wireless Networks (GAWN)
- GIAC Certified Enterprise Defender (GCED)
- GIAC Certified UNIX Security Administrator (GCUX)
- GIAC Exploit Researcher and Advanced Penetration Tester (GXPN)
- GIAC Mobile Device Security Analyst (GMOB)
- GIAC Global Industrial Cyber Security Professional (GICSP)
- GIAC Critical Controls Certification (GCCC)

✔ **Forensics:**

- GIAC Certified Forensic Analyst (GCFA)
- GIAC Certified Forensics Examiner (GCFE)
- GIAC Reverse Engineering Malware (GREM)
- GIAC Network Forensic Analyst (GNFA)

✔ **Management:**

- GIAC Security Leadership Certification (GSLC)
- GIAC Information Security Professional (GISP)
- GIAC Certified Project Manager Certification (GCPM)

✔ **Audit:**

- GIAC Systems and Network Auditor (GSNA)

✔ **Software security:**

- GIAC Secure Software Programmer - .NET (GSSP-NET)
- GIAC Secure Software Programmer - Java (GSSP-JAVA)
- GIAC Certified Web Application Defender (GWEB)

✔ **Legal:**

- GIAC Law of Data Security & Investigations (GLEG)

✔ **Security expert:**

- GIAC Security Expert (GSE)

The GSE is the most prestigious certification in the GIAC family. To earn the GSE, you must successfully complete a 75-question, three-hour exam, followed by a two-day lab exam. Prerequisites include the GSEC, GCIH, and GCIA certifications.

Most GIAC certifications correspond to SANS Institute training courses. However, attending a SANS course is not required to earn GIAC certification. Exams are typically offered at Pearson VUE testing centers, and take from two to five hours. You have up to four months after registering for an exam to take the exam. SANS GIAC recommends a minimum of 55 hours of study (in addition to any formal training courses) to prepare for a GIAC certification exam. All GIAC certifications are valid for four years.

GIAC certification candidates who register for a SANS training course cannot take the corresponding certification exam until ten days after completion of the training course.

International Information Systems Security Certification Consortium (ISC)²

Founded in 1988, (ISC)² (pronounced "I-S-C-squared") was formed to create a global information security certification program. In 1994, the CISSP certification was established, and it has since been recognized as one of the top security certifications in the profession. Some of the certifications offered by (ISC)² are described in this section.

Systems Security Certified Practitioner (SSCP)

Systems Security Certified Practitioner (SSCP) is the entry-level certification offered by (ISC)². Requiring as little as one year of professional experience, the SSCP certification is great for professionals who are working to establish their security careers.

Certified Information Systems Security Professional (CISSP)

Universally recognized as the greatest of all information security certifications, Certified Information Systems Security Professional (CISSP) covers a broad swath of subject matter in its Common Body of Knowledge (CBK):

- Access control
- Telecommunications and network security
- Information security governance and risk management
- Software development security
- Cryptography
- Security architecture and design
- Security operations
- Business continuity and disaster recovery planning
- Legal, regulations, investigations, and compliance
- Physical (environmental) security

The CISSP exam contains 250 multiple-choice questions and takes six hours.

Several CISSP concentrations are now available to CISSP holders who want to extend their certification into one of three important specialties:

- ✔ CISSP-ISSAP (Information Systems Security Architecture Professional)
- ✔ CISSP-ISSEP (Information Systems Security Engineering Professional)
- ✔ CISSP-ISSMP (Information Systems Security Management Professional)

You can learn more about the CISSP certification in *CISSP For Dummies,* 4th Edition.

Certified Software Security Lifecycle Professional (CSSLP)

The Certified Software Security Lifecycle Professional (CSSLP) certification recognizes expertise in the *security development life cycle,* which is the set of business processes and techniques that ensures the inclusion of security in every step of the software development process.

The range of subject matter in this certification includes

- ✔ Secure software concepts
- ✔ Security software requirements
- ✔ Secure software design
- ✔ Secure software implementation/coding
- ✔ Secure software testing
- ✔ Software acceptance
- ✔ Software deployment, operations, maintenance, and disposal
- ✔ Supply chain and software acquisition

Certified Cyber Forensics Professional (CCFP)

The Certified Cyber Forensics Professional (CCFP) certification is a recognition of skills and experience in the field of *computer forensics,* the science of conducting sound digital investigations that may be used in legal proceedings.

The range of subject matter in this certification includes

- ✔ Legal and ethical principles
- ✔ Investigations
- ✔ Forensic science

- ✔ Digital forensics
- ✔ Application forensics
- ✔ Hybrid and emerging technologies

Certified Authorization Professional (CAP)

The Certified Authorization Professional (CAP) certification recognizes skills and knowledge in the work of authorizing and maintaining information systems in the Risk Management Framework as defined in NIST SP 800-37, *Guide for Applying the Risk Management Framework to Federal Information Systems*.

The range of subject matter in this certification includes

- ✔ Risk management framework (RMF)
- ✔ Categorization of information systems
- ✔ Selection of security controls
- ✔ Security control implementation
- ✔ Security control assessment
- ✔ Information system authorization
- ✔ Monitoring of security controls

Healthcare Information Security and Privacy Practitioner (HCISPP)

The Healthcare Information Security and Privacy Practitioner (HCISPP) certification recognizes expertise in the protection of personal health information. The range of subject matter in this certification includes

- ✔ Healthcare industry
- ✔ Regulatory environment
- ✔ Privacy and security in healthcare
- ✔ Information governance and risk management
- ✔ Information risk assessment
- ✔ Third-party risk management

(ISC)² also offers an *Associate of (ISC)²* Certification, for those who have passed the CISSP exam but who do not yet have the required years of experience to be awarded the CISSP certificate.

ISACA

ISACA (www.isaca.org), formerly known as the Information Systems Audit and Control Association, is a nonprofit organization dedicated to the development of frameworks, standards, guidance, education, and certifications for professionals in security audit and security management.

ISACA certification exams are issued a limited number of times per year, at hundreds of locations around the world.

Certified Information Systems Auditor (CISA)

Enacted in 1978, the Certified Information Systems Auditor (CISA) certification is one of the most prestigious security certifications available in the industry. This certification covers the following subject matter:

✔ Information systems audit

✔ IT governance

✔ Systems and infrastructure life cycle

✔ IT service delivery and support

✔ Protection of information assets

✔ Business continuity and disaster recovery planning

The CISA certification is frequently required for IT audit professionals in employment positions focused on IT audit or IT audit management.

Certified Information Security Manager (CISM)

The Certified Information Security Manager (CISM) certification is recognition of the skills, knowledge, and experience of security managers. The CISM certification covers the following subject matter:

✔ Information security governance

✔ Information risk management and compliance

✔ Information security program development and management

✔ Information security incident management

Certified in the Governance of Enterprise IT (CGEIT)

Certified in the Governance of Enterprise IT (CGEIT) is a certification aligned more with IT management than IT security. The CGEIT certification covers the following domains:

- ✔ Framework for the governance of enterprise IT
- ✔ Strategic management
- ✔ Benefits realization
- ✔ Risk optimization
- ✔ Resource optimization

Certified in Risk and Information Systems Control (CRISC)

Certified in Risk and Information Systems Control (CRISC) is ISACA's newest security-related certification. With heavy emphasis in risk management and controls, CRISC complements CISA and CISM, and the three together provide comprehensive control over information security management and operations.

The CRISC certification covers the following domains:

- ✔ Risk identification
- ✔ Risk assessment
- ✔ Risk response and mitigation
- ✔ Risk and control monitoring and reporting

PCI Standards Council

PCI Standards Council (www.pcisecuritystandards.org) is a nonprofit organization sponsored by the world's leading credit card brands: VISA, MasterCard, American Express, Discover, and JCB. The Council has developed several security standards for use by banks, card issuers, merchants who accept credit cards as a form of payment, and other service providers who process, store, or transmit credit card numbers. In support of this overall program, security professionals can earn several certifications that provide recognition of their expertise and give them certain privileges. The two prevalent certifications are discussed here.

Internal Security Assessor (ISA)

The Internal Security Assessor (ISA) certification is a recognition of knowledge, skills, experience, and training. An individual with an ISA certification can perform internal audits and provide guidance to IT and security personnel in the organization regarding its compliance to the Payment Card Industry Data Security Standard (PCI-DSS).

The ISA certification is valid for an individual only while he or she is employed in the same company. If those with an ISA certification change companies, they must be recertified.

Qualified Security Assessor (QSA)

The Qualified Security Assessor (QSA) certification is a recognition of knowledge, skills, experience, and training in the Payment Card Industry Data Security Standard (PCI-DSS). An individual with a QSA is authorized to conduct third-party PCI-DSS audits of an organization.

An individual with a QSA must be an employee of an organization that itself is QSA certified at the organizational level. Further, those with a QSA certification automatically surrender their certification if they change employers. If they want to continue performing PCI-DSS audits, they must be recertified.

Cloud Security Alliance

The Cloud Security Alliance (www.cloudsecurityalliance.org), or CSA, is a nonprofit organization that develops security standards for cloud service providers as well as organizations that utilize cloud-based services.

Cloud Computing Security Knowledge (CCSK) is a knowledge-based certification that is a demonstration of your knowledge about cloud computing and the controls that need to be in place, both by a cloud services provider as well as by any organization utilizing cloud services in support of its business. The domains of the CCSK certification are

- Architecture
- Governance and enterprise risk management
- Legal issues: contracts and electronic discovery
- Compliance and audit management
- Information management and data security
- Interoperability and portability
- Traditional security, business continuity, and disaster recovery
- Data center operations
- Incident response

✔ Application security

✔ Encryption and key management

✔ Identity, entitlement, and access management

✔ Virtualization

✔ Security as a service

The CCSK examination consists of 60 multiple-choice questions and takes 90 minutes. An 80% score is required to pass. Candidates are assessed $345 to take the exam, which users take online at `http://ccsk.cloudsecurityalliance.org`.

Chapter 5

Key Technology Concepts

In This Chapter

▶ Becoming familiar with key concepts in IS technologies

▶ Understanding the issues that concern security professionals

▶ Learning the language of the technology side of information security

*Y*ou *can't protect what you don't understand.* To be an effective information security professional, understanding how information technology works is not negotiable. The task of protecting electronically stored information is a technical challenge: The more you know about IT, the more effective you'll be as an information security professional.

This chapter is modeled precisely after five of the ten categories in the *Common Body of Knowledge* (CBK) in the CISSP (Certified Information Systems Security Professional) certification. The five categories in this chapter are more technology-centric. The other five categories of the CISSP CBK are covered in Chapter 6.

For a deeper dive into the CISSP common body of knowledge, pick up the latest revision of the book, *CISSP For Dummies,* 4th Edition.

 It would be unwise to think of the topics in this chapter as being strictly technology based, just as much as it would be to consider the topics in Chapter 6 as being strictly management based. Management and technology have a symbiotic relationship.

Access Control

At its heart, access control is all about who (or what) is allowed to access something. When access control is performed correctly, unauthorized personnel are denied access to sensitive data. Often, access controls — even a single user ID and password — are the only defense between sensitive data and criminals who want it.

Access control terms

access review	password	single-factor authentication
accumulation of privileges	password quality	social engineering
authentication	password recovery	telnet
biometrics	phishing	token
FTP, FTPS, and SFTP	rainbow table	user ID
hashing	replay attack	watering hole attack
key logger	salting	
multifactor authentication	session hijacking	

Basic concepts in access control

The basics of access control are all about the technologies and business processes used to manage authentication. There are a lot of ways to get access
control wrong, and few ways to get it right. The concepts in this section are
the most important in all of information security.

Authentication

Authentication is the process of asserting one's identity — including required
proof such as a password, token, or biometric — to a system to access its
resources. The identity takes the form of a *user ID,* which is a value assigned
to a person or machine.

Single-factor authentication generally involves the presentation of a *user ID*
and *password.* This common form of authentication is vulnerable to attack by
adversaries.

A *password* is a secret word, phrase, or random characters used as a part of
single-factor authentication. The quality of a password is an important factor
that helps resist some forms of attack. Characteristics of password quality
include length (how many characters), complexity (whether the password
must contain lowercase letters, uppercase letters, numerals, and special
characters), expiration (how much time may elapse before a user is required
to select a new password), recovery (the process used when users forget
their password), and reuse (whether previously used passwords may be
used again).

Passwords are typically stored in hashed form. *Hashing* is an irreversible cryptographic function that facilitates the confirmation of a correct password during the login process but prevents the extraction of passwords. Hashing is explained in more detail in the "Cryptography" section, later in the chapter.

Multifactor authentication generally involves the presentation of a user ID, together with a token or biometric. This type of authentication is generally stronger than single-factor authentication. A *token* is a hardware device that is used in multifactor authentication, and represents a far stronger form of authentication than single factor. Some form of a biometric can also be used in multifactor authentication, such as a fingerprint, a palm scan, an iris scan, or a voiceprint.

Access control attacks and countermeasures

Adversaries who are attempting to access resources in a target system frequently attack access controls. Methods of attack include the following:

- ✔ **Replay attack:** An attacker intercepts an authentication, typically over a network, and replays the captured login credentials to try to gain unauthorized access to the target system. A replay attack can be successful even when some forms of token authentication are used, provided the attacker replays the captured login credentials soon after capturing them.

- ✔ **Stealing password hashes:** The attacker obtains the database of hashed passwords from a system. If the hashing method used is weak, the attacker may be able to employ rainbow tables or other techniques to obtain account passwords. A *rainbow table* is a simple (but very large) lookup table containing all possible password hashes and their corresponding passwords. The technique known as *salting* (mixing in random numbers when storing the hash of a new password) prevents the use of rainbow tables.

What you know, have, and are

The concepts in single-factor and multifactor authentication are sometimes difficult to understand. In the information security profession, three phrases often used to simplify these concepts:

- ✔ **What you know:** User ID and password authentication. The user ID and password are something that a user would know.

- ✔ **What you have:** Token or smart card authentication. The user must have the physical object (and use it properly) to log in.

- ✔ **What you are:** Biometric authentication. Some physical aspect of a user, such as a fingerprint, retina scan, or even voiceprint.

✔ **Interception of passwords in transit:** An attacker may be able to intercept login credentials if they are transmitted "in the clear" (unencrypted) over a network. Older but still-used protocols such as Telnet and FTP (File Transfer Protocol) employ the transmission of login credentials without encryption. Discontinuing Telnet and FTP in favor of ssh (Secure SHell), FTPS (File Transfer Protocol Secure), and SFTP (Secure File Transfer Protocol) eliminates this threat.

✔ **Session hijacking:** An attacker attempts to steal session cookies from a user's web session; if successful, the attacker will be able to hijack the user's session. The attacker may then be able to perform all functions that the user could perform. Proper session management, including full session encryption and encryption of session cookies, can prevent session hijacking.

✔ **Key logger:** An adversary may be able to use one of several methods to get key logger malware installed on a user's system. If successful, the key logger will be able to intercept typed login credentials and transmit them to the adversary, who can use them later to access those same systems. Multifactor authentication and advanced malware prevention (AMP) tools can help thwart key loggers.

✔ **Social engineering:** Adversaries have a number of techniques available to trick users into providing their login credentials. Techniques include

   • **Phishing:** The attacker sends an email that attempts to trick the user into clicking a link that takes the user to a *phishing site,* which is an imposter site used to request login credentials. If the user provides those credentials, the attacker can use them to access the real site.

   • **Watering hole attack:** An attacker selects a website that he or she believes is frequented by targeted users. The attacker attacks the website and plants malware on the site that can, if successful, install a key logger or other malware on the victim's workstation.

Access control processes

Getting access control technology right is a challenge, but it's not the biggest concern. The business processes supporting access controls are critical. If not implemented and managed correctly, the best access control technology is of little use — similar to owning a car with the best burglar alarm and then parking the car unlocked with the keys in the ignition switch.

Key processes in access control include the following:

✔ **Access provisioning:** The process of provisioning access for a user should follow a strict, documented process. Every request should be properly approved by one person/group and performed by a different person/group. Records for all steps must be retained.

✔ **Internal transfers:** Access management personnel need to be notified when an employee is transferred to another position, so that the issue of accumulation of privileges can be prevented.

✔ **Employee termination:** Access management personnel need to be notified immediately when an employee leaves the organization, especially if the person is being terminated. All user accounts should be locked or removed and then double-checked.

✔ **Managing access controls for contractors, temps, and others:** All personnel with access to organization systems and applications need to be managed using the same set of processes. Too many organizations do a substandard job of managing temporary workers. The result is the existence of user accounts for personnel who no longer work in the organization.

✔ **Password recovery:** Organizations need a solid process for users who forget their passwords. Otherwise, attackers may be able to use this process to take over employees' user accounts.

✔ **Periodic access reviews:** Every aspect of access management needs to be periodically reviewed to ensure that every instance of access provisioning, termination, and transfers are performed correctly. The consequences of messing up access control processes can result in active user accounts with excessive privileges, and user accounts still associated with terminated personnel.

Emerging issues in access control

Issues that keep information security professionals up at night include these:

✔ Key logging malware

✔ Stolen password hashes

✔ Users who select poor (easily guessed) passwords

✔ Users who reuse personal passwords on business sites

Telecommunications and Network Security

In a large room crowded with information security professionals many years ago, the CISO for a global financial services organization told us that we could be effective in our jobs only to the extent that we understood the business and the technologies it used.

Telecommunications and network security terms

ATM	firewall	router	WEP
CAT-6 cable	frame relay	routing table	MAC address
denial of service	IP address	SONET	WiMAX
DLP	IPS	T-1	MPLS
DMZ	packet header	TCP/IP	WPA
DOCSIS	payload	VoIP	WPA2
DS-1	POTS	VPN	
E-1	PSTN	Watering hole attack	
encapsulation	QoS	ISDN	

Networking at the business level and at the telecommunications level is common among virtually every organization. Hence, it is vital that every information security professional have some degree of working knowledge of networking technologies. Networks are the pipes that run the Internet and facilitate commerce, and the avenues through which our adversaries conduct their attacks. If we don't know enough about network technology, how can we play a meaningful role in protecting our organizations' assets?

Basic concepts in telecommunications and network security

You need to understand the important concept of encapsulation because it is used throughout almost all network technologies. In *encapsulation,* messages of one protocol are placed in messages of another protocol. For example, SMTP (Simple Mail Transport Protocol) messages are placed in TCP (Transmission Control Protocol) messages, which are placed in IP (Internet Protocol) messages, which are placed in DS-1 frames, which are placed in OC-48 frames.

Here's an analogy. You write a message on a sheet of paper (SMTP message), place it in an envelope (TCP message), and place the envelope in a mailbox (IP message), where a mail truck (switch) picks it up and delivers it to a distribution center (router). There, the envelope (TCP message) is placed in a bin (IP message), which is driven to another distribution center (router). There, the bin (IP message) is placed in a larger bin (DS-1 frame) and driven to an airport (DACS), where the larger bin (DS-1 frame) is placed on an air-plane (OC-48 frame) that flies through the air (optical fiber). At the other end of the flight, the process is reversed, and the recipient receives the note on the sheet of paper.

Network technologies

A plethora of network technologies exist; I discuss the important ones in this section.

Wired telecom network technologies

Wired telecom networks connect homes, businesses, schools, and governments through technologies that use copper or fiber optic cabling to carry many types of signals. These signals include the following:

- ✔ **DS-1 (Digital Signal one), T-1, E-1:** *DS-1* is a family of multiplexed telecommunications technologies that have carried voice and data for decades in the United States and Europe. In the United States, *T-1* is the basic protocol, which runs at 1.544Mbps. It's often multiplexed into 24 64Kbps voice channels for use by ordinary phone and fax lines, often known as *POTS (plain old telephone service).* In Europe, *E-1* is the basic protocol, at 2.048bps, or 32 voice channels. Speeds higher than DS-1 are available, such as DS-3 (44.736Mbps), DS-4 (274.176Mbps), and DS-5 (400.352Mbps).

- ✔ **SONET (Synchronous Optical Networking):** This new high-speed tele-communications backbone technology runs over fiber optic cables on land and in submarine cables. SONET runs at dizzying speeds, including OC-1 (48.960Mbps), OC-3 (150.336Mbps), OC-12 (601.344Mbps), OC-96 (4,810.752Mbps), and OC-192 (9,621.504Mbps).

- ✔ **DSL (Digital Subscriber Line):** This family of protocols is delivered to homes and businesses over the same pairs of copper wires as telephone service but at a higher frequency.

- ✔ **DOCSIS (Data Over Cable Service Interface Specification):** This family of technologies transports TCP/IP over cable television service to homes and businesses.

- ✔ **MPLS (MultiProtocol Label Switching):** This packet-switched technology transports a variety of protocols such as TCP/IP, Ethernet, ATM, and VoIP over long distances. MPLS includes Quality of Service (QoS) settings to ensure that protocols such as voice and streaming video are transported without annoying interruption even when networks are congested.

✔ **Dark fiber:** This option is not really a technology but a telecommunications medium available to businesses. Businesses can connect their own telecom equipment to fiber optic cabling to connect their networks between buildings in a city or metropolitan area, using any protocol they want.

Older technologies you don't need to be too concerned with anymore (unless you're a technology history buff) include ISDN, ATM, Frame Relay, X.25, and PSTN.

Wireless telecom network technologies

Wireless telecom networks are used to connect individuals, homes, and businesses through the use of several technologies, including the following:

✔ **GPRS (General Packet Radio Service):** This technology is encapsulated in the GSM (Global System for Mobile communications, originally *Groupe Spécial Mobile*) cellular protocol.

✔ **LTE (Long Term Evolution):** This wireless telecom standard provides voice and data service with speeds up to 300Mbps.

✔ **WiMAX (Worldwide Interoperability for Microwave Access):** A wireless telecom standard that provides data rates up to 40Mbps for mobile stations and 1Gbps for fixed stations, WiMAX was developed to be a wireless alternative to DSL and DOCSIS.

Other notable technologies include CDPD, CDMA, and packet radio.

Wired consumer and business network technologies

Although many standards have been used for wired network technologies, the long-term trend has been a general migration to TCP/IP on Ethernet over copper cabling or fiber optic cabling. The dominant technologies follow:

✔ **CAT-6 (Category 6) cabling:** The darling of homes and businesses running wired networks over distances of up to 100 meters, CAT-6 cabling can run Ethernet speeds up to 10Gbps.

✔ **Fiber optics:** Businesses often run fiber optics in larger buildings to connect networks from floor to floor, as well as from building to building. Fiber-optic cabling is made of glass and transmits signals as visible light, as opposed to CAT-6 and other metallic cabling, which transmits signals as electrical signals.

Has-been cabling used in the past includes Thinnet, Thicknet, Cat-3, and Cat-5.

Wireless consumer and business network technologies

Wireless network technologies are wildly popular in a number of typical settings. The technologies in use are

- ✔ **Wi-Fi:** A technology widely used in residences, small and large businesses, retail stores, restaurants, government buildings, and even outdoors, is the IEEE 802.11 family of wireless protocols. A variety of security protocols are used on Wi-Fi, ranging from none (no encryption at all), *WEP* (Wired Equivalency Protocol, now considered obsolete), *WPA* (Wireless Protected Access, which is just okay), and *WPA2* (preferred by anyone thinking about security). The range of Wi-Fi is about 20 meters indoors and farther outdoors.

- ✔ **Bluetooth:** This popular wireless protocol connects devices in close proximity to one another. Wireless earsets and headsets were the first really popular use of Bluetooth.

- ✔ **NFC (Near Field Communications):** This very short range (6 cm) wireless protocol was developed for use in contactless payment systems.

Runner-ups include *iRDA* (the infrared point-to-point technology that has all but disappeared), *wireless USB* (up and coming, and possibly a force in the future).

TCP/IP

Developed in the 1970s as a robust military communications network that had some self-healing properties and resilience, *TCP/IP* has formed the basis for virtually every home, business, and commercial network, as well as the global Internet itself.

TCP/IP is a packet-based technology in which messages are bundled into *packets* that are *routed* to their destinations. A single packet has a source address, a destination address, a protocol number, and payload (the contents of a message).

TCP/IP addressing

The source address and destination address follow a numbering convention, with a global authority that assigns addresses to organizations. In TCP/IP version 4, the form of an address is

```
xxx.xxx.xxx.xxx
```

where each *xxx (octet)* is commonly portrayed as a decimal value and can range from 1 through 255. In TCP/IP version 6, the form of an address is

```
XXXX : XXXX : XXXX : XXXX : XXXX : XXXX : XXXX : XXXX
```

where each *xxxx (hextet)* is a hexadecimal value that can range from 0000 through FFFF.

TCP/IP routing

In TCP/IP, packets are processed by *routers* as they make their way from their source to their destination. You can think of a router as a traffic cop (in a street intersection) who tells you which way to turn. A router examines a packet's destination address, consults its *routing table,* and then sends the packet in the correct direction to get it closer to its ultimate destination.

Routers exchange routing information, so that each router has a better idea about which direction to send each packet. They exchange this information through several routing protocols, such as RIP, BGP, IGRP, OSPF, or IS-IS. These routing protocols each have best uses: Some are used by Internet backbone routers, and others are better suited for routers inside a company. Some become obsolete, and newer and better ones are developed.

TCP/IP protocols

TCP/IP has two basic protocols, on top of which nearly all the others are used — via encapsulation (the nesting process explained earlier). These two basic protocols are

- ✔ **UDP:** Formally known as *User Datagram Protocol*, UDP is a simple, connectionless protocol typically used to send a message in a single packet.

- ✔ **TCP (Transmission Control Protocol):** This connection-oriented protocol is usually intended for a longer conversation between systems. A TCP session is established by something called a three-way handshake that works something like this:

```
Station A: Hello, I&rsquo;m Station A and I&rsquo;d
           like to talk to you, Station B.
Station B: Hello, I&rsquo;m Station B and yes
           I&rsquo;d like to talk to you, Station A.
Station A: Hello Station B, I&rsquo;m happy we have
           agreed to talk to each other.
```

The TCP and UDP protocols contain hundreds of established protocol standards, a few of which are well known and frequently used, such as

- ✔ **HTTP (HyperText Transport Protocol):** Using port 80, transports user web traffic without encryption.

- ✔ **HTTPS (HyperText Transport Protocol Secure):** Using port 443, transports web traffic with encryption.

- ✔ **SMTP (Simple Mail Transport Protocol):** Using port 25, transports email without encryption.

- ✔ **DNS (Domain Name Service) protocol:** Using port 43 (on both TCP and UDP services), translates domain names such as `www.dummies.com` into IP addresses.

- ✔ **FTP (File Transfer Protocol):** Using ports 20 and 21, enables bulk file transfers without encryption.

- ✔ **SSH (Secure SHell) protocol:** Using port 22, provides administrative access to systems and network devices.

The OSI Network Model is something you should become familiar with to understand concepts such as encapsulation.

Network security

Several network-centric security devices are used to protect systems, networks, and information from intruders. I describe the more common types in this section.

Firewalls

Firewalls are inline devices placed between networks to control the traffic that is allowed to pass between those networks. Typically, an organization will place a firewall at its Internet boundary to prevent intruders from easily accessing the organization's internal networks.

A firewall uses a table of rules to determine whether or not a packet should be permitted. The rules are based on the packet's source address, destination address, and protocol number. Firewalls do not examine the contents of a message.

Firewalls are used to create a demilitarized zone (*DMZ*), which is half-inside and half-outside networks where organizations place Internet-facing systems such as web servers. This strategy helps protect the web server from the Internet and also protects the organization in case an adversary compromises and takes over control of the web server. Figure 5-1 depicts a typical DMZ network.

Intrusion prevention system (IPS)

An *intrusion prevention system (IPS)* is an inline device that examines incoming and outgoing network traffic, looking for signs of intrusions and, when any intrusion is detected, blocking such traffic.

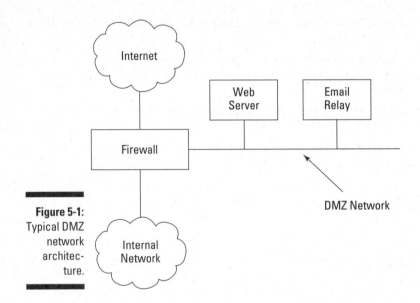

Figure 5-1:
Typical DMZ
network
architec-
ture.

Unlike a firewall, an IPS does examine the contents of network packets, not just their source and destination addresses. This approach is based on the principle that malicious traffic may be characterized by its contents, not merely its origin or destination.

Like a firewall, an IPS is typically placed at or near Internet ingress and egress (entrance and exit) points, so that all Internet incoming and outgoing traffic, respectively, can be examined and any malicious traffic blocked.

Data loss prevention (DLP) system

A *data loss prevention (DLP) system* examines (primarily) outgoing traffic, looking for evidence of sensitive data being sent out of the organization inappropriately. A DLP system is configured to look for specific patterns in outgoing data and send alerts or just block traffic meeting certain criteria.

Web-filtering system

A *web-filtering system* examines the websites that an organization's personnel are visiting. The web-filtering system logs all web access by personnel and can also be configured to block access to various categories of websites (for example, pornography, gambling, weapons, or social media sites) as well as specific sites. The purpose for web-filtering systems is generally twofold: to prevent access to sites that are clearly not work related and to protect the organization from accessing sites that may be hosting malware.

Virtual private network

A *virtual private network (VPN)* is a technique used to encapsulate network traffic flowing between two systems, between a system and a network, or between two networks. Typically, encryption is employed along with encapsulation so that the contents of the traffic cannot be read by anyone who intercepts the traffic.

VPNs are most commonly used for remote access, as well as to protect information flowing over the Internet between specific organizations.

Attacks and countermeasures

Intruders are incredibly efficient at finding ways to break into an organization's networks. They do so to steal valuable data that they can easily monetize. The techniques used and the defensive countermeasures, include the following:

- ✔ **Phishing:** Adversaries compose realistic-looking emails to trick users into clicking links to *phishing sites,* which are malicious sites that will attempt to install malware on victims' workstations or steal login credentials. Countermeasures include spam filters, antimalware, intrusion prevention systems, and security awareness training.

- ✔ **Watering hole attack:** Adversaries find websites that they think an organization they're targeting might visit. They take over those websites and install malicious software that visitors will unknowingly install, leading to an intrusion. Countermeasures include web-filtering systems, antimalware, and intrusion prevention systems.

- ✔ **Denial of service attack:** Adversaries will attack a target system to incapacitate it, either through a high volume flood of data or through malicious traffic designed to incapacitate the target system. Countermeasures include firewalls, intrusion prevention systems, and cloud-based denial-of-service defense services.

Emerging issues in telecommunications and network security

New developments that keep information security professionals on edge include the following:

- ✔ **The Internet of Things (IoT):** Many new devices are being connected to the Internet, and we all know that many of them do not have well-implemented security.

- ✔ **BYOD (bring your own device):** Network interoperability and the proliferation of powerful consumer devices such as iPhone and Android means millions of workers are using their personal devices at work as work tools. Personally owned devices in a business network result in a wide range of issues, including malware control and data control.

- ✔ **IPv6:** The shortage of available IP addresses and other issues are compelling organizations to migrate to IPv6. Although it is more secure by design, few network and security professionals are as familiar with IPv6 as they are with IPv4. Implementing IPv6 can lead to security holes through improper configuration.

Software Development Security

Software programs play a key role in facilitating access to sensitive information. For this reason, software is often attacked, in the hopes that a weakness in a software program will enable the attacker to obtain the entire trove of information to which the software program has access. Organizations must ensure that their software programs have no vulnerabilities that can be exploited by others.

Basic concepts in software development security

As I've said elsewhere in this chapter, a security professional can only protect what he or she understands. Software is a key target of unrelenting attacks, so it's important to understand how software works and how it is built and maintained. Buckle up!

Software development security terms

application whitelisting	cross-site scripting	mobile code
authentication bypass	database management system (DBMS)	software development life cycle (SDLC)
buffer overflow		
compiler	injection attack	source code
cross-site request forgery	logic bomb	

Types of software

Software comes in many shapes and sizes. Some programs work by themselves, and others work as a part of a larger system. Some of the types of software include the following:

- **Agents:** These small programs run on a local system with some type of connection to a master program or console someplace else. For example, an agent on a workstation can facilitate the installation of security patches as directed by an administrator on a central console.

- **Applets:** These programs operate within the context of another program. For example, Flash Player operates within a web browser.

- **Client-server:** In this application architecture, some of the application resides on a workstation (usually having to do with data display and data input), and some resides on a central server (usually having to do with data storage and retrieval).

- **Distributed:** This application architecture consists of several components residing on different systems.

- **Web:** This application consists of a web browser on a user's workstation (or mobile device), a web server, and often an application server and a database management system.

- **Utilities:** Usually standalone programs, utilities are used by system administrators to maintain a system. Think of utilities as the brooms, dustpans, and Crescent wrenches of information systems.

- **Operating systems:** These programs facilitate the use of computer hardware, including storage, memory, and peripheral devices. Examples of operating systems include Microsoft Windows, Ubuntu Linux, Apple OS X, and Android.

Application models and languages

The building blocks of applications are their *source code*, written in a specific *language* such as C, Java, and Assembler. A program is run on a computer in two ways:

- **Compiled:** The program is processed once, in advance, by a compiler, which transforms it into machine-readable form called an *executable*. A program needs to be compiled just once, and the executable can be run over and over.

- **Interpreted:** The program is interpreted in real-time. The process is similar to compiling, except that it must be done each time the program is to be run.

A number of alternative application models are in use today, including the following:

- **Object-oriented (OO) system:** This hierarchical system consists of classes (software libraries), objects, methods, and logical construction that includes concepts such as encapsulation, inheritance, and polymorphism. OO is a world all its own.

- **Neural network:** Designed to mimic the operation of the human brain, a neural network is given a large collections of relevant situations and outcomes. With enough of these, the neural network can make meaningful predictions regarding a particular problem. An example of a neural network is forecasting the time and location of a hurricane's landfall.

- **Expert system:** This system accumulates knowledge on a particular subject regarding past events. An inference engine analyzes this information to arrive at a decision or a solution to a problem.

Threats to software programs

Plenty of threats are carried out against software programs every day; they are the "low-hanging fruit" targets in the cybercrime world. The most well-known threats, plus countermeasures, follow:

- **Buffer overflow:** In a *buffer overflow* attack, the attacker is providing data in an input field in which the software program requesting data is doing little or no input validation or boundary checking. In a successful buffer overflow, the input data literally overflows the memory storage area intended for the input data. The overflow data consists of machine-readable instructions that the attacker hopes will be executed, leading to control of the application program and perhaps the entire machine. The main countermeasure against buffer overflow is boundary definition and checking.

- **Authentication bypass:** Often, only a user ID and password are protecting sensitive data. For this reason, attackers will use every trick in the book to bypass authentication to get straight at sensitive data.

  All attack types listed here represent some method for bypassing authentication.

- **Injection attack:** Similar to a buffer overflow, an *injection attack* inserts some sort of scripting language into an input field, in a way that tricks the target system into executing the script. Types of injection attacks include SQL injection (instructions to the back-end DBMS) and script injection. The countermeasure to injection attacks is careful parsing and filtering of all input data, so that no commands are allowed or accepted.

- **Malicious software:** Often used with buffer overflow and injection attacks, *malicious software* (often known as malware) is designed to steal or alter data, steal login credentials, or permit a takeover of the target system for most any malicious purpose. Countermeasures to malware include antimalware (formerly known as antivirus) and intrusion systems (IPS).

✔ **Mobile code:** Similar to malware, mobile code is downloaded and executed in real time. The most common type of mobile code is code downloaded by a web browser, such as JavaScript. Countermeasures against mobile code include tighter controls to browsers and other software to limit or prohibit mobile code from being downloaded and executed. Application *whitelisting* (the use of a tool or technique to permit only known programs to run) can also be an effective countermeasure.

✔ **Logic bomb:** A *logic bomb* is code that performs some malicious action, such as deleting or altering data. A programmer or an outsider might place a logic bomb in an application. Countermeasures against logic bombs include code reviews and tight access control to source code.

✔ **Back door:** A *back door* is a feature that a developer places in an application that enables some type of undocumented feature or access to the system or database. Back doors are often used during development and should be removed. Countermeasures against back doors include code reviews and tight access control to source code.

✔ **Object reuse:** *Object reuse* is a flaw in an application or its underlying operating system that permits another process to access residual data no longer used by the application. Examples include released memory space that wasn't cleaned up and temporary files. Countermeasures include proper OS selection and configuration to prevent other processes from accessing residual memory, and better access controls for (or erasure of) temporary files.

✔ **Social engineering:** *Social engineering* is any act in which attackers are attempting to trick a user into performing some action. Social engineering can take place in person (an attacker pretending to be a package delivery person), by telephone (a person pretending to be IT or a user who needs help), and online (by phishing). Unlike a lot of online attacks for which many effective countermeasures are available, social engineering attacks can often be successful.

Security in the development life cycle

Many attacks against applications can be defeated if the application itself is designed and constructed properly. Security can be introduced into the software development life cycle (SDLC) with minimum disruption, as follows:

✔ **Conceptual stage:** The program or major changes to it are being considered. Security professionals who get involved at this stage bring regulations, standards, and common attacks to the surface, so that the conceptual design can be free of fatal design flaws.

✔ **Requirements definition stage:** A suite of security requirements is introduced, in addition to other types of requirements.

✔ **Design stage:** Here, when the detailed design is coming together, key security components and features will be a part of the program.

✔ **Coding stage:** Developers develop the actual source code using safe libraries, and their development tools are configured to perform rudimentary security checks to uncover security flaws at the code level.

✔ **Testing stage:** All security requirements identified in the requirements definition stage are tested and verified.

✔ **Maintenance stage:** After the program is in production, any changes to it go through the stages just listed, so that the changes will have the required security features and characteristics.

Database management system

A *database management system (DBMS)* is a software program that manages structured collections of information (*databases*) and facilitates the storage and retrieval of information to and from these databases.

A DBMS employs sets of rules that preserve the integrity and structure of the databases, as well as access controls that determine whether specific people (or programs) are permitted to access or update specific data items in a database.

The most common type of DBMS is a relational DBMS, which is used by Oracle, Microsoft SQL Server, and MySQL. Other types are object, network, hierarchical, and distributed.

Emerging issues in software development security

As is the case in all areas of IT, security in software development will always be evolving, with no end to new concerns:

✔ **Outsourced software development that introduces flaws:** An organization that uses outside developers or entire development firms may create a situation in which security flaws (such as buffer overflows, injection attacks, back doors, logic bombs) may be introduced into the system.

✔ **Open source software that is less secure than we believed:** Open source software enjoyed a reputation as being secure, because so many people were able to examine and test the source code for security flaws.

However, flaws in commonly used open source software have burst that bubble, casting doubt into the security of all open source software.

✔ **High cost of security tools:** Good tools are available to identify many security flaws that give attackers the welcome mat. Some tools examine running programs; others examine source code. These tools can be expensive, and the engineers using them often command high salaries (which may be one reason why you're reading this book).

✔ **Increase in supply chain attacks:** In the context of software development, supply chain attacks include compromises of compilers, software libraries, and utilities that introduce security flaws into programs.

Cryptography

Cryptography is the art and science of hiding data in plain sight, and plays a key role in protecting data from onlookers and adversaries. In this section, you examine this mysterious craft and discover how it's used to protect sensitive data.

Although cryptography is often used as part of a complex system, it's often easier to think of cryptography in isolation, in the simple-use case of a message sent in plain sight from a sender to a receiver.

Cryptography terms

block cipher	encryption	plaintext
certificate authority (CA)	encryption algorithm	pseudorandom number generator
ciphertext	encryption key	public key cryptography
cryptanalysis	hashing	steganography
cryptosystem	key management	stream cipher
decryption key	key length	watermarking
digital certificate	message digest	
digital signature	nonrepudiation	

Basic concepts in cryptography

Encryption is the process of transforming plaintext into ciphertext, via an encryption algorithm and an encryption key. *Decryption* is the process of transforming ciphertext back into plaintext, again with an encryption algorithm and the encryption key. In part, the strength of encryption is based on the *key length* (the number of characters that make up the encryption key) and the complexity of the encryption key.

An implementation of encryption and encryption keys is known as a *cryptosystem*. An attack on a cryptosystem is called *cryptanalysis*.

Most encryption algorithms employ a pseudorandom-number generator (PRNG), which is a technique for deriving a random number for use during encryption and decryption.

Types of encryption

The two basic ways to encrypt data are by block cipher and by stream cipher. Details follow:

- **Block cipher:** A *block cipher* encrypts and decrypts data in batches, or blocks. Block ciphers are prevalent on computers and on the Internet, where they encrypt hard drives and thumb drives, and protect data in transit with SSL and TLS. Notable block ciphers are

  - **Advanced Encryption Standard (AES):** Selected in 2001 by NIST (National Institute of Standards and Technology) to replace DES, AES is based on the Rijndael cipher and is in wide use today.

  - **Data Encryption Standard (DES):** The leading official encryption standard in use from 1977 through the early 2000s. DES was considered obsolete mostly because of its short key lengths.

  - **Triple DES (3DES):** Derived from DES, 3DES was essentially DES with a longer key length and, hence, more resistant to compromise than DES.

  - **Blowfish:** Developed in 1993, Blowfish was developed as an alternative to DES, which was nearly twenty years old. Blowfish is unpatented and in the public domain.

  - **Serpent:** Another public domain algorithm, Serpent was a finalist in the AES selection process.

- **Stream cipher:** A *stream cipher* encrypts a continuous stream of information such as a video feed or an audio conversation. The most common stream cipher is RC4.

Block ciphers are most often used to encrypt Internet based "streaming" services. On the Internet, everything is transmitted in packets, which are individually encrypted using block ciphers.

Hashing, digital signatures, and digital certificates

Hashing is used to create a short, fixed-length *message digest* from a file or block of data; this is something like a fingerprint. Hashing is often used to verify the integrity and/or originator of a file. Common hashing algorithms include:

- **MD-5** is a formerly popular hashing algorithm developed in 1992. It is now considered too weak for reliable use and obsolete.

- **SHA-1** is another popular hashing algorithm that was determined in 2005 to be too weak for continued use. By 2010, U.S. government agencies were required to replace SHA-1 with SHA-2.

- **SHA-2** is a family of hashing algorithms including SHA-224, SHA-256, SHA-384, SHA-512, SHA-512/224, and SHA-512/256. These are all considered reliable for ongoing use.

A *digital signature* is a hashing operation carried out on a file. Depending on the implementation, the digital signature may be embedded in the file or separate from it. A digital signature is used to verify the originator of a file.

A *digital certificate* is an electronic document that consists of a personal or corporate identifier, a public encryption key, and is signed by a certificate authority (CA). The most common format for a digital certificate is known as *X.509*. The use of digital certificates and other tools such as strong authentication can lead to the failure for an individual to be able to plausibly deny involvement with a specific transaction or event. This is known as *non-repudiation*.

Encryption keys

The two main types of encryption keys in use today are

- **Symmetric key:** Both the sender and the receiver have the same encryption key.

- **Asymmetric key:** Also known as *public key cryptography,* utilizes a pair of encryption keys — a public key and a private key. A user who creates a keypair would make the public key available widely and protect the private key as vigorously as one would protect a symmetric key.

Private keys and symmetric keys must be jealously guarded from adversaries. Anyone who obtains a private or symmetric encryption key can decrypt any incoming encrypted message. The management and protection of encryption keys is known as *key management*.

Often, software programs employ passwords to protect encryption keys. Hence, the strength of the cryptosystem is only as strong as the password protecting its keys.

Attacks on cryptosystems

There are several types of attacks of a cryptosystem — mainly having to do with various opportunities that an attacker may be able to discover. They are

- ✔ **Frequency analysis:** An attacker analyzes ciphertext to see what patterns regarding the frequency of occurrence of each character may lead to the discovery of the plaintext or the encryption key.

- ✔ **Birthday attacks:** An attack on a hashing algorithm, this is an attempt to develop messages that have the same hash value. The name "birthday attack" comes from the birthday paradox that states that out of a group of 23 or more randomly chosen people, a 50 percent chance exists that two of them share the same birthday.

- ✔ **Known plaintext attack:** The attacker possesses both plaintext and ciphertext and uses them in an attempt to discover the encryption key.

- ✔ **Chosen ciphertext attack:** The attacker can choose ciphertext, have it decrypted by the cryptosystem, and obtain the resulting plaintext.

- ✔ **Ciphertext only attack:** The attacker has only ciphertext and uses frequency analysis and possibly other techniques in an attempt to discover the plaintext or the encryption key.

- ✔ **Man-in-the-middle attack:** An attacker is able to observe and potentially interfere with a session (or its initiation, where encryption keys may be exchanged).

- ✔ **Replay attack:** An attacker intercepts communications for playback later.

- ✔ **Rubber hose attack:** An attacker has access to someone in possession of encryption keys or other vital secrets about a targeted cryptosystem, and may use means of coercing those secrets.

- ✔ **Social engineering:** Face it: every system is vulnerable to attack if its owners or administrators can be tricked into providing vital information such as a password.

Encryption alternatives

Two techniques are available that provide some of the same features as a cryptosystem:

- ✔ **Steganography (stego):** A message is hidden in a larger file, such as an image file, a video, or sound file. Done properly, this technique can be as effective as encryption.

✔ **Watermarking:** A visible (or audible) imprint is added to a document, an image, a sound recording, or a video recording. Watermarking is a potentially powerful deterrent control because someone may not want to utilize an object with watermarking, which indicates that some other party owns the object.

Emerging issues in cryptography

Encryption is not a magic sleeping pill. Instead, there are numerous worries ranging from new types of attacks to official government misbehavior. Let's take a look at what's keeping security managers awake at night:

✔ **Man-in-the-middle attacks:** Many attacks on cryptosystems involve a man-in-the-middle attack at the onset of a quote-unquote secure communications session. Flaws in session initiation and key exchange can result in the attacker being able to easily read all encrypted communications between two endpoints.

✔ **Improper uses of cryptography:** Cryptography, like any tool, is useful when used properly. Used improperly, cryptography gives us a false sense of security. Two examples are failing to *salt* (mixing in random numbers when calculating the hash of a plaintext message) when hashing passwords, or failing to adequately protect an encryption key.

✔ **Brute-force attacks:** Advances in distributed computing are making it easier for adversaries to build massive parallel computing machines that can be used to attack cryptosystems. A *brute-force attack* employs fast computers to guess every possible combination until the correct one is found. To stave off these attacks, key lengths are getting longer and longer. However, these longer key lengths require more computing power when performing legitimate encryption and decryption. It's a never-ending game of cat and mouse (in this case we are the mouse).

✔ **Precompromised encryption algorithms:** Revelations in 2012-2013 have revealed the plausibility that various government-spying organizations have been able to subvert the development and/or implementation of certain encryption algorithms and cryptosystems. The result is a serious crisis of trust in the cryptosystems used to protect sensitive information from adversaries.

✔ **Persistent use of compromised cryptosystems:** It's a given that encryption algorithms have a limited "shelf life" before some technique for compromising them is revealed.

Physical and Environmental Security

Physical security is concerned with the protection of personnel at work locations, as well as information systems and related media and equipment. Supporting environmental controls and power protection are also a concern.

Basic concepts in physical and environmental security

This section discusses the most common concepts in security measures that are employed to protect personnel and equipment.

Site access security

Organizations should implement a level of site access security commensurate with the value of information and assets in the facility. The following types of controls contribute to the security of a work location, whether a facility is a data center or primarily used by employees:

- **Key cards:** Plastic cards with a magnetic strip, an RFID circuit, or an embedded processor and memory. Key cards are assigned to individual workers and are used to activate door locks to permit entry. With a key card system, a building can be divided into zones that restrict entry to specific areas or rooms as needed. Key card systems record successful and unsuccessful access attempts. Lost or stolen key cards can be deactivated in the system so that they will no longer function.

- **PIN pads:** Keypads with numbers or letters usually used with key cards. PIN pads reduce the risk associated with a lost or stolen key card: On a door controlled by a key card reader and a PIN pad, both the key card and knowledge of the PIN are required to unlock the door.

- **Biometric access controls:** Devices such as fingerprint readers, palm scanners, and iris scanners. These biometric access controls can be used as a more effective site access control than key cards and PIN pads alone because an intruder could steal a key card and obtain a PIN code.

- **Metal keys:** Still used for individual offices, but no longer recommended for rooms where several personnel need to routinely enter because there is no way to know which person entered a room.

- **Mantraps:** A set of two interlocked doors with a short passage between, to control movement of personnel through a door. A mantrap permits only one person at a time to pass, thereby preventing "tailgating," where one or more people can follow an authorized person into a room or building.

- ✔ **Guards:** Personnel with duties to protect facilities and personnel.

- ✔ **Guard dogs:** An effective deterrent that can assist in searches for persons and in apprehending intruders.

- ✔ **Visitor logs:** Written or electronic records of visitors to a building. Visitors can also be requested to present a government-issued identification to confirm their identity.

- ✔ **Fences and walls:** Deterrent and preventive measures to protect the perimeter of a facility or areas of particular interest. A fence or wall at least 8 feet high with strands of barbed wire or razor wire will keep out all but the most determined intruders.

- ✔ **Video surveillance:** Systems of cameras, monitors, and possibly recording equipment such as digital video recorders (DVRs) used to monitor key locations inside and outside a facility. A video system may include personnel who are observing in real-time, or it may be recording for later viewing when needed.

- ✔ **Exterior lighting:** Protects a facility by illuminating areas where an intruder would otherwise be able to work in darkness in an attempt to enter a facility.

- ✔ **Visible notices:** Posted signs and placards informing personnel of the presence of video surveillance, guards, guard dogs, and other controls. Visible notices can also inform visitors of the consequences of entering a facility.

Physical and environmental security terms

barbed wire	guard dog	smoke detector
biometrics	heating, ventilation, and air conditioning (HVAC)	sprinkler system
digital video recorder (DVR)	inert gas fire suppression	tailgating
electric generator	key card	uninterruptible power supply (UPS)
exterior lighting	line conditioner	video surveillance
fence	mantrap	visitor log
fire extinguisher	PIN pad	wall
guard	razor wire	

Secure siting

Secure siting, also known as a *site survey,* is a process of searching for and analyzing a work site for nearby hazards and threats that could pose a risk to the security or safety of a work site and the personnel and equipment within.

Typical hazards that a site survey would identify include the following:

- **Transportation:** nearby airports, railroads, and highways

- **Hazardous substances:** nearby chemical facilities and petroleum pipelines

- **Behavioral:** nearby sites where mass gatherings, riots, and demonstrations could take place

- **Natural:** risk of flooding, landslide, avalanche, volcano, or lahar

Equipment protection

Measures need to be taken to protect equipment and personnel in work locations, including the following:

- **Theft protection:** locking doors, video surveillance, and cable locks

- **Damage protection:** earthquake bracing, and tip-over prevention

- **Fire protection:** smoke detectors, heat detectors, sprinklers, inert gas suppression, and fire extinguishers

- **Cabling security:** conduit or better siting to avoid exposure of communications or power cabling

- **Photography:** notices and intervention to prevent photography in sensitive areas

Electric power

Information-processing equipment (computers, network devices, and so on) is highly sensitive to even slight fluctuations in electric power. The following specialized equipment ensures a continuous supply of clean electric power:

- **Line conditioner:** Absorbs noise present in utility power, such as spikes and surges.

- **Uninterruptible power system (UPS):** Equipped with backup batteries that can supply power to computing equipment from several minutes to an hour or more.

- **Electric generator:** Powered by gasoline, diesel fuel, natural gas, or propane and can generate electric power for hours, days, or more.

An electric generator and a UPS are typically used together to ensure continuous power. Because electric generators take several seconds to a minute or longer to activate, a UPS supplies power while the generator is starting up.

Many UPSs have built-in line conditioners, so standalone line conditioners are uncommon, except in environments where electric power is reliable but noisy.

Heating, ventilation, and air conditioning (HVAC)

People and information-processing equipment operate best within a narrow temperature and humidity range. (Humans are more tolerant of a wider range in temperature.)

Heating, ventilation, and air conditioning (HVAC) systems regulate temperature and humidity in buildings containing personnel, computers, or both. HVAC systems are especially important in data centers, which generate a considerable amount of waste heat that must be continuously moved away from computers to prevent overheating and premature failure.

Many newer data centers rely on circulation of outside ambient air (with particulate filtering) as opposed to refrigeration to provide cooling at a significantly lower cost.

Redundant controls

Many facilities incorporate redundant controls to ensure continuous availability of environmental needs. Redundancy allows for continuous protection in the event of equipment failure as well as routine maintenance. Examples of redundant controls follow:

- Utility power feeds
- UPSs
- Generators
- HVAC systems

Emerging issues in physical and environmental security

Issues in the physical and environmental security realm that keep security professionals awake at night include the following:

- **Use of cloud services:** Organizations that adopt cloud services give up a large measure of control and visibility into the physical controls protecting equipment that stores and processes their data. Some cloud service providers do not readily provide detailed information that some organizations may need for compliance purposes.

- ✔ **Increased equipment density and available environmental controls:** Newer servers and storage systems are constructed in smaller sizes, allowing for more servers and storage to be installed in a given area. Sometimes, however, data centers are unable to supply adequate power and cooling for this higher density equipment.

Chapter 6

Key Management Concepts

In This Chapter

▶ Courting key concepts in information security management

▶ Understanding the issues that concern security professionals

▶ Learning the language of information security management

A *fool with a tool is still a fool.* The owner of a technology business once told this to his employees. Information technology and information security cannot succeed on tools alone but require business processes that manage their use.

This chapter is modeled after five of the ten categories in the *Common Body of Knowledge* (CBK) in the CISSP (Certified Information Systems Security Professional) certification. The five categories in this chapter are security management centric. The other five categories of the CISSP CBK are covered in Chapter 5.

For a deeper dive into the CISSP common body of knowledge, pick up a copy of *CISSP For Dummies,* 4th Edition.

It would be unwise to think of the topics in this chapter as strictly management based, just as much as it would be to consider the topics in Chapter 5 as strictly technology based. Management and technology are inseparable.

Information Security Governance and Risk Management

Management needs to be in control of its security systems, processes, and personnel. Governance is the approach that facilitates this control.

Risk management is the activity that reveals risks in the organization that must be dealt with. This section covers both topics. Common terms in security governance and risk management

Basic concepts in security governance and risk management

In this section, you see how security managers and CISOs ensure that their security programs are successful.

Alignment to organization

For security management to be effective and relevant, an organization's security program and its mission, objectives, and goals must be aligned. The key reason for this is that *security should be a business enabler*, facilitating the organization's efforts to fulfill its mission and achieve its objectives and goals.

Risk management

Risk management is the set of life-cycle activities that identify risks and take appropriate action with each. These activities follow:

- **Risk assessment:** A *risk assessment* is an up-close look at specific systems, processes, suppliers, or perhaps the entire organization. All plausible risks are identified, and the following key characteristics for each risk estimated:

  - *Probability:* the likelihood that a given threat will be realized

  - *Impact:* the degree of influence on the organization when the threat is realized

  - *Recovery effort:* the effort required for the organization to recover from threat realization

Common terms in security governance and risk management

CIA triad	internal audit	risk treatment
control	nondisclosure agreement	security awareness training
data classification	policy	single point of failure
fail open/fail closed	procedure	standard
governance	process	threat
guideline	risk assessment	

- *Asset value:* The value of the asset, if the nature of threat realization requires its replacement

- *Mitigating controls:* Changes that can be made to reduce the probability, impact, or recovery effort

Often, other characteristics about each risk will be identified, such as the person or group that would perform a recovery effort and implement mitigating controls.

All risks identified in a risk assessment are collected in a *risk ledger*, which could be a simple spreadsheet or records in an information system designed to facilitate risk management processes. Such systems are called governance, risk, and compliance (GRC) systems.

✔ **Risk treatment:** When a risk assessment has been completed, management has an important task ahead: to make formal decisions on what to do about each identified risk. Their choices are

- *Acceptance:* Management (not just security management but business management) decides that the level of risk is acceptable, and that nothing needs to be done to reduce the probability or impact of the identified risk.

- *Mitigation:* Management chooses to implement something that will reduce the probability, impact, or recovery effort (or some combination) associated with a risk.

- *Avoidance:* Management chooses to discontinue the activity associated with the risk.

- *Transfer:* Management decides to transfer the risk to another party, usually by purchasing an appropriate insurance policy, such as cyber risk insurance.

Organizations often perform risk treatment in a formal manner, even collecting ink signatures from executives on the formal acceptance, mitigation, avoidance, or transfer of risk. Security management often does this to formally document executives saying "yes this risk is okay," which may be particularly useful later on if a security breach occurs.

Rarely is all risk removed from an item in a risk ledger. Any leftover risk after applying risk treatment is known as *residual risk*. Residual risk is itself a risk item that requires treatment — usually it is accepted.

Many instances of risk treatment involve a blend of acceptance, mitigation, avoidance, and transfer.

Security governance

Governance is the set of activities performed by management to exert control over the organization. In the context of information security, governance means enacting policies, standards, guidelines, procedures, and controls to ensure that desired outcomes are met.

✔ **Policies:** Formal statements that describe what actions and behaviors are required, and which are forbidden, in an organization. Following are some example policy statements:

- Employees shall not share login credentials with any other persons inside or outside the organization.

- Employees shall not use personally owned devices for storing, processing, or managing company information without management approval.

✔ **Standards:** Formal statements that describe how security policy will be carried out. For example, an organization may develop documents that state which brands of hardware or software will be used, and how systems, devices, and programs will be configured.

✔ **Guidelines:** Statements that provide ideas on how policies and standards may be implemented.

✔ **Processes and procedures:** Step-by-step descriptions of work activities carried out by various personnel in the organization.

✔ **Controls:** Specific instances of policies, standards, and key steps in processes and procedures that management has determined are essential for the proper operation and security of business processes and information systems.

Internal and external audit

Organizations in many industries are subject to external audits, as well as required to perform internal audits. The purpose of an *audit* is to assess the effectiveness of an organization's policies, standards, and controls.

An audit may or may not include an examination of information systems, including their configurations, programs, and access permissions.

Data classification

Data classification is a set of standards, procedures, and controls to ensure the proper handling of sensitive information. Data classification is usually implemented by defining levels of sensitivity, along with detailed explanations on permitted and required handling of data at each level.

For instance, an organization might implement four levels of data classifications: public, confidential, secret, and top secret. For each level, specific procedures will exist for handling of data for various common activities such as email, storage on a workstation, transmission over the Internet, and transmission by FAX.

The intention of data classification is the protection of information at a level corresponding to its sensitivity. It would be a waste of resources to protect all internal information as though it were top secret. On the other hand, protecting all information as confidential would not adequately protect the most sensitive information.

Personnel security

Personnel security represents the set of security-related activities that take place throughout the employee life cycle. These activities include

- **Screening:** A background check to ensure that the candidate's employment history, education, and professional licenses are verified, and that the candidate is free of unwanted criminal convictions.

- **Onboarding:** The employee signs documents, including nondisclosure, intellectual property, noncompete, and security policy acknowledgement, documents. Other essential activities include security awareness training and instruction on other policies.

- **Periodic assessment:** Annual re-affirmation of compliance to security policy and other key policies.

- **Transfer and promotion:** Completion of onboarding activities required for new positions (for example, a more thorough background check for someone in senior management).

- **Termination:** Return of all hardware and information assets, reaffirmation of nondisclosure, intellectual property, and other agreements.

Employment laws, as well as security and privacy laws and standards, require that the preceding activities be enacted through formal written processes and procedures and include detailed recordkeeping.

Security awareness training

Training personnel on security policies, procedures, and safe computing is an essential part of every organization's overall defense against harmful security incidents. Known as *security awareness training*, employees are educated on the organization's security policies and practices.

Many laws and regulations require security awareness training, so organizations usually need to keep accurate records on who has received this training.

Many security awareness training programs include quizzes, to ensure that employees understand what is expected and to provide a record that each employee fully understood the organization's policies.

Other concepts

Several security-related concepts are part of every security professional's vocabulary. These concepts guide you on the proper management security issues you'll encounter:

- ✔ **CIA Triad:** *Confidentiality*, *integrity*, and *availability* — the three pillars of security. Everything the InfoSec profession does to protect an organization's assets and information comes down to these.

- ✔ **Defense in depth:** A strategy for protecting important assets by surrounding them with layered defenses. For example, sensitive written records can be stored in a locking cabinet, which is located in a locked office, which is in a locked building. An intruder would need to defeat several defenses to successfully reach the protected asset.

- ✔ **Single point of failure:** Systems or teams in which a key component has no backup or alternative path. For example, a public-facing website may have redundant routers, servers, databases, and storage systems, but only a single firewall. The firewall is a single point of failure because the entire system would fail if the firewall failed.

- ✔ **Fail open/fail closed:** The result of a control if it fails. For example, a security door might become locked (fail closed) or unlocked (fail open) during a power failure.

Emerging issues in security governance and risk management

A lot of things keep security managers awake at night, besides too much coffee during the day. Noteworthy issues are discussed here.

Managing contractors and other temporary workers

Many organizations do a pretty good job of managing the onboarding and offboarding of employees but come up short when handling the same activities for their external consultants, contractors, and temporary workers. As a result, for example, computer user accounts or building access cards might not be locked when temporary workers leave the organization.

Managing suppliers and business partners

Organizations are discovering that a chain is only as strong as its weakest link. Often this weak link is an external organization that has access to information systems or work facilities, particularly where an external entity's security is not as good as the organization itself. Several notable security breaches have occurred through the exploitation of weaknesses in a supplier's organization.

Security Architecture and Design

Security architecture and design is a catchall category in information security that includes several topics, including computer architecture and security models, computer operating systems, and the process of accrediting and certifying systems for use.

Basic concepts in security architecture and design

The concepts in security architecture and design range from abstract security protection models to the design of modern computers and operating systems. This mix of topics is eclectic but essential for security professionals.

Common terms in security architecture and design

access matrix	Clark-Wilson	operating system (OS)
accreditation	discretionary access control	process
Bell LaPadula	guest	secondary storage
Biba	hypervisor	take-grant
bus	main storage	trusted platform module (TPM)
central processing unit (CPU)	mandatory access control	virtualization
certification	multilevel	

Security protection models

Security models are simple representations of security controls that help us understand methods for implementing security controls, and to better understand controls in an existing system. The models that are cited most often are listed here, with a very brief explanation on how it works:

- **Bell LaPadula:** People can read documents at or below their level of security, and write documents at or above their level of security.

- **Biba:** People can read documents only at their level of security, and write documents at or above their level of security.

- **Clark-Wilson:** A rebuttal to Bell LaPadula and Biba, Clark-Wilson is a somewhat elaborate scheme for creating and protecting sensitive information.

- **Access matrix:** A two-dimensional matrix that defines the persons or groups permitted to access specific data or systems.

- **Multilevel:** A system will contain information at more than one security level. People can read information at or below their security level.

- **Mandatory access control (MAC):** An access manager manages access to information.

- **Discretionary access control (DAC):** The owners of individual documents or folders manage access to information.

- **Role-based access control (RBAC):** Access is assigned to groups of users instead of individual users.

- **Noninterference:** Activities performed by persons at a higher level of security will not interfere with activities performed at lower levels of security.

- **Information flow:** Information at specific levels of security are permitted to flow to specific systems or locations.

The preceding models are not exclusive. Instead, a system's method of access control may involve more than one of the models described here.

Information security professionals often use the terms *subject* and *object* when discussing security protection models and access controls. A *subject* is a person or system that may attempt to access an *object*, which could be a system, file, or record in a database.

System evaluation models

Many information systems manage sensitive information or perform sensitive functions. It can be difficult to know what security characteristics should be part of the design of such systems. Thus, several frameworks for the inclusion of security in systems have been developed, including the following:

- ✔ **Common criteria:** A framework for the specification, implementation, and evaluation of a system against a set of security requirements

- ✔ **SEI-CMMI (Software Engineering Institute — Capability Maturity Model Integration):** A model for assessing the maturity of an organization's security practices

- ✔ **SSE-CMM (Systems Security Engineering Capability Maturity Model):** A model for evaluating an organization's capability to implement security in a system

Certification and accreditation

Because information systems are constructed to perform important functions, several methodologies are used to evaluate systems for their suitability to perform those functions. These methodologies include the practices of *certification* (performing the actual evaluation of a system) and *accreditation* (the administrative approval to begin or continue use of a system). These models include the following:

- ✔ **DIACAP (Department of Defense Information Assurance Certification and Accreditation):** Used to certify and accredit military systems

- ✔ **NIACAP (National Information Assurance Certification and Accreditation Process):** Used to certify and accredit U.S. national security systems

- ✔ **DCID 6/3 (Director of Central Intelligence Directive 6/3):** Used to certify and accredit systems in use by the Central Intelligence Agency (CIA)

- ✔ **FEDRAMP (Federal Risk and Authorization Management Program):** A framework for security assessments, authorization, and continuous monitoring for cloud-based security providers

The Federal Information Security Management Act of 2002 (FISMA) is the federal law that requires all U.S. federal government systems to comply with security standards and evaluation practices.

Computer hardware architecture

Security professionals need to understand how computer hardware functions, so that they can ensure that they are properly protected. Modern computers are made up of the following components:

- ✔ **CPU (central processing unit):** The component where computer instructions are executed and calculations performed

- ✔ **Main storage:** The component where information is stored temporarily. Often known as RAM (random access memory), main storage is usually volatile and its contents are lost if power is removed or the computer is turned off.

✔ **Secondary storage:** The component — typically a hard drive or a solid-state drive (SSD) — where information is stored permanently. Information stored here is persistent even when the computer is switched off. Secondary storage is often organized into one or more *file systems*, which are schemes for the storage and retrieval of individual files.

✔ **Bus:** The component where data and instructions flow internally among the CPU, main storage, secondary storage, and externally through peripheral devices and communications adaptors. Popular bus architectures include SCSI (small computer systems interface) SATA (serial ATA), IEEE1394 (also known as FireWire), and USB (universal serial bus).

✔ **Firmware:** Software stored in persistent memory. Firmware is generally used to store initial instructions that are executed when the computer is switched on.

✔ **Communications:** Components for external communications, including network adaptors (for Ethernet, Wi-Fi, or Bluetooth) and display adaptors (for computers with human interfaces). Most computers include one or more communication components — otherwise, how would you get problems into it and results out of it?

✔ **Security hardware:** Components for various security functions, such as a Trusted Platform Module (TPM), which is used to store and generate cryptographic keys, smart card readers, and fingerprint scanners. Some computers include specialized security hardware.

Computer operating system

A computer operating system (OS) consists of the set of programs that facilitate the operation of application programs and tools on computer hardware. The components of an OS include the kernel (the core software that communicates with the CPU, memory, and peripheral devices), device drivers (which facilitate the use of bus devices and peripheral devices), and tools (used by administrators to manage resources such as available disk space).

The main functions performed by an operating system are

✔ **Process management:** Processes are the individual programs that run on a computer. The OS starts and stops processes and makes sure they do not interfere with each other.

✔ **Resource management:** The OS allocates and manages the use of main storage, secondary storage, communications, and attached devices.

✔ **Access management:** The OS manages authentication as well as access to resources such as files and directories in secondary storage.

✔ **Event management:** The OS responds to events such as the insertion or removal of media and devices, keystrokes, or mouse movements.

✔ **Communications management:** The OS manages communications to ensure that incoming and outgoing communications are handled and routed properly.

An operating system can run directly on computer hardware or through a scheme called *virtualization,* in which many separate copies of operating systems can run simultaneously on a computer. In virtualization, the main controlling program is called the *hypervisor*, and each running OS is called a *guest.* The hypervisor's jobs are to allocate computer hardware resources to each guest and to prevent guests from interfering with each other.

Software threats and countermeasures

Intruders attack software systems to interfere with or take over those systems in many ways. Some of the attack methods, along with their countermeasures, follow:

✔ **Covert channel attack:** A hidden communications channel exists in an existing communications channel, in an attempt to make the hidden communications undetectable. Countermeasures include the use of sniffers, packet analyzers, and intrusion detection systems (IDS) to detect anomalies in communications.

✔ **State attack:** Exploiting a timing flaw in a system. Also known as a *race condition,* a state attack can be used to gain access to a resource used by another process. Countermeasures include source code scans and reviews to detect such flaws in programs.

✔ **Side channel attack:** Observing a system's running states to make inferences about activities in the system. An attacker can use this information-gathering method to compromise a system. Countermeasures include logical or physical shielding to thwart observations.

✔ **Emanation:** Electromagnetic radiation (EMR) emitted from a computer system provides valuable information about the system. At times, emanations can include sensitive data that is being processed by a system. Countermeasures include shielding to prevent the emission of EMR.

✔ **Back door:** A feature in a program that gives someone covert access to the program. Typically, a programmer will put back doors into programs during testing but may forget to remove them all when the program is ready for production use. Back doors can be discovered and exploited by intruders. Programmers with malicious intent can create back doors as a means of illicitly accessing the program. Countermeasures include code reviews to detect back doors and packet analyzers to detect their use.

Emerging issues in security architecture and design

Issues that tend to keep security professionals from getting a good night's sleep include the following:

- ✔ **Internet of Things (IoT):** We worry that insufficient work is put into developing sound security models and designs to prevent attacks in new Internet-connected products that.

- ✔ **Speed to market:** Many organizations, in attempts to get newly developed products to market more quickly, skip security designs, reviews, and controls, thereby leaving products open to attack.

- ✔ **Flawed access control:** Many organizations lack the skills to implement sound, effective access controls in their systems, resulting in unnecessary exposure of sensitive data.

Security Operations

Security operations — also known as SecOps — is another category of information security that contains many separate concepts and topics, all having to do with security's support of the operations of information systems.

Basic concepts in security operations

Security operations encompass a wide variety of concepts and activities related to the security aspect of technology operations. Although these

---

Common terms in security operations

antimalware	data loss prevention	need to know
backup	data retention	remote access
change management	incident management	separation of duties
data classification	job rotation	vulnerability management
data destruction	least privilege	

activities are operational, security professionals at all levels need to be familiar with these concepts.

Operations terminology

Several key terms fit best in the security operations category, including the following:

✔ **Separation of duties:** High-value operations need to be split into tasks performed by different individuals or departments. The classic example is privileged access requests: One person requests it, another approves it, and yet another provides it. No one person should be able to do any two or all three.

✔ **Least privilege:** The concept of least privilege states that people (and machines) should have the lowest possible level of privilege required to perform required tasks. Although it's easier to give everyone higher privilege levels, doing so diminishes the need to keep things well protected and gives intruders greater advantages.

✔ **Need to know:** The concept of need-to-know states that people should have access to only the information (and systems) they need to do their job. For example, just because someone has administrator privileges on one system doesn't mean the person should have it on all systems.

✔ **Job rotation:** Organizations periodically move people from role to role for many reasons, including staving off boredom, cross-training, and deterring individuals from abusing their privileges (because it might be discovered by someone rotating into their job).

✔ **Special privileges monitoring:** Because administrative privileges provide powerful capabilities for system, network, and database administrators are so much greater than other people, many organizations choose to monitor their activities on computers more closely, even to the point of monitoring and logging every command they issue to systems.

Continuous monitoring

The velocity of harmful events has accelerated to a point where data review of incident logs is no longer an effective means of detecting unwanted behavior. Besides, the volume of available log data (gigabytes in the smallest organizations and terabytes in larger ones) is too great for humans to review.

Organizations must centralize their logging. All devices and systems should send their log data to a purpose-built central repository, called a security incident and event management (SIEM) system. But more than that, organizations need tools that not only detect serious security events but also alert key personnel and even remediate the incident in seconds instead of weeks or months as is often the case.

Records management

Records management refers to a family of business processes used to manage and protect business records in an organization. Several security-related disciplines in records are of particular interest to information security professionals:

- ✓ **Data classification:** Organizations define sensitive levels for information, with handling procedures at each level. Enforcement is difficult because compliance is voluntary.

- ✓ **Access management:** The broad topic in which organizations establish access management processes to control who has access to what data, functions, and systems.

- ✓ **Data retention:** Based on business need and regulations, organizations establish minimum and maximum retention times for various types of data. In the absence of specific guidance, the best rule is to keep it long enough but not too long: Data is both an asset as well as a liability.

- ✓ **Data loss prevention:** Organizations need to ensure that sensitive data is adequately protected. Static and dynamic tools can find sensitive data living where it shouldn't and observe (and perhaps block) the data when leaving the environment when that departure is not a part of routine business operations.

- ✓ **Backup:** Hardware problems, software problems, and disasters of many kinds make organizations wish they had a backup copy of critical information. Most organizations routinely copy important data to backup media or servers in some remote location.

- ✓ **Data destruction:** After data is no longer needed, it needs to be destroyed so that unauthorized parties cannot recover it.

Antimalware

Antimalware, antivirus, and advanced malware protection (AMP) refer to tools designed to detect and block malware infections and malware activities.

Organizations often combat malware by having several layers of control in place (known as a *defense in depth*), including the following:

- ✓ **Workstation antimalware:** The front lines of the malware wars, every workstation (and even mobile devices) should have antimalware to block malware.

- ✓ **Server antimalware:** File servers and other systems used to store programs and files should have antimalware, just in case malware sneaks through a workstation.

> ✔ **Email server antimalware:** Email is a favored transportation route for malware, so blocking it at email servers is a good way to keep it from reaching workstations.
>
> ✔ **Spam filtering:** Because many attacks come in the form of phishing, spam filters can be effective at blocking most or all phishing messages.
>
> ✔ **Website filtering:** These appliances block access to websites based on category (generally not having to do with business operations) and block websites known to be compromised with malware.

The recent potency of malware is leading many organizations to enact more controls in the form of intrusion prevention systems, which block the command-and-control traffic associated with malware.

Remote access

Remote access is both the business process as well as the technology that facilitates an employee's ability to remotely access information systems that are not accessible from the Internet.

In the business process sense, many organizations permit only a subset of their workers to remotely access the internal environment. In the technical sense, remote access usually includes encryption of all communications, as well as two-factor authentication to make it harder for an attacker to gain access to internal systems.

The fact that many systems are opting to use cloud-based systems instead of internal systems makes some aspects of remote access obsolete. Or, to put it another way, cloud-based systems turn everyone into remote workers because their information systems are no longer located in their internal networks.

Incident management

Incident management is an IT operations process used to properly respond to operational and security incidents. Organizations should have written incident response plans along with training and testing to ensure that these plans are accurate and that personnel understand how to follow them. Written playbooks for common incidents should be developed.

Security incidents are just a special type of incident management, requiring a few additional considerations such as regulatory requirements and privacy laws.

The steps in a mature incident management process are

- Declaration
- Triage
- Investigation
- Analysis
- Containment
- Recovery or mitigation or both
- Debriefing

Not all security incidents require all these steps, but this framework ensures an orderly and coordinated response to reduce the scope and effect of an incident, and a debriefing and follow-up activities to reduce the likelihood or effect of a similar incident in the future.

Vulnerability management

Vulnerability management is an IT operations process concerned with the identification and mitigation of vulnerabilities in IT systems. An effective vulnerability management process includes procedures for identifying vulnerabilities, prioritizing them, and making changes (through change management) to eliminate vulnerabilities that could be used by an intruder to successfully attack the environment.

Change management

Change management is a basic IT operations process concerned with the management and control of changes made in IT systems. A proper change management process has formal steps of request, review, approval, execution, verification, and recordkeeping. The purpose of change control is the discussion of proposed changes before they take place, so that risks and other issues can surface.

All process and procedures, including those in incident management, vulnerability management, and change management, should be formally documented.

Emerging issues in security operations

Yes, many issues in the world of security operations keep security managers awake at night.

Advanced malware

Innovations in malware packaging have rendered antivirus and antimalware software virtually ineffective against advanced malware. Additional layers of detection and prevention tools are needed to combat the threat. These tools have significant costs in terms of capital as well as manpower to maintain them.

The greatest fear is that malware creators will soon develop new ways of circumventing even advanced malware prevention (AMP) tools, thereby requiring even greater investment in effective defenses.

Rapid incident response

Organizations typically become aware of security incidents weeks or months after their occurrence. However, these incidents are often orchestrated at such great speed that effective incident response is now measured in minutes or even seconds. The increase in attack velocity requires a paradigm shift in the way that organizations monitor their environments and the tools they use to detect and respond to incidents.

Bring your own device (BYOD)

With employees in so many organizations bringing personally owned devices to work for use in their daily job duties, organizations are finding it more difficult than ever to keep track of sensitive data and know when that data is leaving its control.

Use of cloud services

The mass migration to cloud-based services challenges organizations to adapt their security operations to maintain sufficient visibility and control over their technology operations. Cloud service providers perform some security operations functions, which are not necessarily visible to customers. Therefore, understanding the complete coverage of protective controls can be difficult.

Business Continuity and Disaster Recovery Planning

Disasters, natural and man-made, occur with alarming unpredictability, throwing organizations in their paths into chaos. Sometimes, the organization doesn't survive or retains only a shadow of its former self. Much can be done to reduce the potency of disasters, giving organizations a far better chance of survival.

Disaster recovery planning (DRP) and business continuity planning (BCP) may not seem as though they should be part of information security. However, the core information security concept of confidentiality, integrity, and availability (CIA) does include DRP and BCP as a vital activity to ensure the *availability* of key systems in an organization.

Common terms in business continuity and disaster recovery planning

business impact assessment (BIA)	maximum tolerable downtime (MTD)	recovery consistency objective (RCO)
cutover test	parallel test	recovery point objective (RPO)
disaster recovery time objective (RTO)	recovery capacity objective (RCapO)	simulation
		walkthrough

Basic concepts in business continuity and disaster recovery planning

BCP and DRP have their own array of concepts that are essential to information security professionals. Even if you don't anticipate working in the BCP or DRP space, familiarity with these concepts may lead you or your organization to opportunities to improve disaster preparedness.

Types of disasters

Several types of man-made and natural disasters have a direct or an indirect effect on organizations. The types of disasters include the following:

✔ **Natural:**

- *Weather:* hurricane, tornado, ice storm, blizzard, or heavy rain

- *Geological:* earthquake, tsunami, volcano, landslide, avalanche, or sinkhole

- *Other:* pandemic, forest or range fire, flood, or solar storm

✔ **Man-made:**

- *Social or political:* war, riot, demonstration, or strike

- *Utilities:* utility outage or fuel shortage

- *Material:* hazardous material spill or radioactive materials leak

These and other types of disasters can have a direct or an indirect effect on organizations, including the following:

- ✔ Interruptions in transportation
- ✔ Communications outages
- ✔ Workforce shortage

Business continuity planning and disaster recovery planning

Two primary activities take place after a disaster strikes:

- ✔ Continuation of business processes using alternate facilities, equipment, or personnel, which is the purview of Business Continuity Planning (BCP)
- ✔ Salvage of buildings and equipment, and restoration of primary work facilities, which is the purview of Disaster Recovery Planning (DRP)

These two activities are both concerned with getting the organization back on its feet after a disaster. Both are needed for the long-term survival of the organization.

Business impact assessment (BIA)

A business impact assessment (BIA) is a special type of risk assessment that is performed periodically to determine two key things: the most critical business processes in the organization, and the resources and dependencies on other business processes that the key processes rely on for continuous operation.

Upon completion, a BIA generally portrays the most important business processes in order of criticality (the most critical processes are listed first).

For each critical process, the maximum tolerable downtime (MTD) value is identified. MTD is the greatest amount of time that a business process can be incapacitated before the organization's survival is at risk. The value of an MTD is difficult to determine and therefore highly judgmental.

Security professionals can derive value from the BIA by understanding which processes and underlying systems are the most important in an organization. Those systems will be the ones requiring the best protection.

Recovery targets

After identifying the most important business processes and systems in the BIA, the organization needs to establish recovery targets. These are the time intervals required to get processes and IT systems running again. The recovery targets are as follows:

- **Recovery time objective (RTO):** Expressed as minutes, hours, or days, the period of time from disaster onset until the process or system is operational. The value of MTD should drive the RTO value.

- **Recovery point objective (RPO):** Expressed as minutes, hours, or days, the period of maximum data loss after a disaster strikes. For instance, if an organization wants to lose no more than one hour's worth of transactions, the RPO would be one hour.

- **Recovery consistency objective (RCO):** Expressed as the measure of integrity and consistency in data in the emergency operations system compared to the original production system. RCO is a percent value that is expressed as 1 minus (number of inconsistent entries) divided by (number of entries).

- **Recovery capacity objective (RCapO):** Expressed as a percentage, the capacity of temporary processing systems compared to production systems.

Often, an organization will determine that a given system does not have sufficient resilience to successfully meet the recovery objectives after a disaster. In this case, the organization must change its recovery objectives to less ambitious figures or invest in equipment and processes that will facilitate recovery within targets.

Contingency planning

Organizations need to develop written contingency plans that personnel can follow when a disaster occurs. These contingency plans should include the following considerations:

- Primary operations personnel may be unwilling or unable to assist in the continuation and recovery of critical systems.
- Personnel who will be following contingency plans may have less familiarity with these processes and systems.

Testing contingency plans

To determine the quality of contingency plans, organizations should periodically test them. These tests, which should include primary and backup personnel, may also serve as training, which helps these personnel better understand the procedures that should be followed during a disaster.

There are five types of tests:

- **Document review:** Personnel read through contingency planning documents, and note any errors or omissions they find.

- **Walkthrough:** Personnel review contingency planning documents in group sessions, noting errors and omissions they find.

- **Simulation:** A scripted disaster is recited to personnel, who respond as though a real disaster is taking place.

- **Parallel test:** Recovery systems are activated and process live data but in isolation so as not to disturb production systems that are still running. A parallel test helps test workload and whether recovery systems work properly.

- **Cutover test:** Production systems are shut down or disconnected, and recovery systems are activated to manage live workload. This test is a complete end-to-end test of the capacity and integrity of the recovery system. If a cutover test fails, it can mean that the systems being tested stop working, resulting in key business processes grinding to a halt.

Emerging issues in business continuity and disaster recovery planning

Two of the most important issues keeping security professionals awake at night follow:

- **Complex distributed systems:** Organizations are relying more on distributed systems (including cloud-based services) that have a higher degree of interconnectivity. It can be more difficult to develop contingency plans that involve resilience improvements when one or more critical components of a system are owned and operated by another organization.

- **Cloud services:** Organizations that employ cloud services have far less direct physical control over their cloud-based processing systems, making the development of contingency plans, as well as testing, more complicated. Cloud service providers may or may not have their own disaster recovery and business continuity plans.

Legal, Regulations, Investigations, and Compliance

Because of their integral role in supporting business processes, information systems are in the crosshairs of laws and regulations. Computers are frequently involved in civil and criminal investigations, requiring forensic procedures when collecting evidence from computers and other electronic devices.

Basic concepts in legal, regulations, investigations, and compliance

Even though security professionals are not attorneys, they must understand the laws, regulations, and other legal requirements that drive compliance efforts in organizations. Likewise, security professionals need to know how security investigations should be conducted. This is fun stuff!

Computer crime laws

Many countries have enacted computer crime laws that define trespass, theft, and privacy in the context of information systems. In the history of law, computers are still new, and the development of laws is ongoing and changing frequently.

This high frequency in changes of laws, regulations, and legal standards presents a challenge to information security and legal professionals as they strive to be compliant with these laws and also to recognize cybercrimes when they occur.

Common terms in legal, regulations, investigations, and compliance

chain of custody

COBIT

COSO

forensics

ISO27002:2013

Managing compliance

Compliance is a matter of adhering to laws, regulations, contractual obligations, and policies. It takes a determined effort to know all compliance obligations in an organization, and more effort to achieve compliance. Many organizations develop or adopt a framework of controls to track compliance on an ongoing basis. Suitable frameworks include

- ✔ **COBIT (Control Objectives for Information and Related Technology):** Developed by ISACA, COBIT is a highly regarded framework for IT operations.

- ✔ **COSO (Committee of Sponsoring Organizations of the Treadway Commission):** Developed as a result of financial accounting scandals in the 1990s, COSO provides guidance for IT control frameworks for U.S. publicly traded companies.

- ✔ **ISO27002:2013:** The international standard for information security management, which establishes a process of controls development and management

Security investigations and forensics

Security investigations are an organization's response to isolated security incidents that have little direct effect on business operations. Still, the events requiring investigation can be important in other ways because they can have significant legal implications.

Any event that takes place in an organization in the context of computers where possible future legal action is involved may require an investigation with forensic rules of evidence in play. These rules include

- ✔ Evidence collection and preservation

- ✔ Evidence chain of custody

- ✔ Evidence collection recordkeeping

- ✔ Evidence examination recordkeeping

For an organization to prevail in any related legal proceedings, it is important that these forensic procedures be carried out by a trained individual with dedicated tools and hardware.

Emerging issues in legal, regulations, investigations, and compliance

The issues keeping security professionals awake at night include these:

- ✓ **Rapid onset of new laws and regulations:** New laws on computer operations, security and privacy are enacted and updated at a rate that makes it hard to keep up on their details, never mind figure out how to be compliant with them.

- ✓ **Jurisdictional issues:** Many new laws have greater jurisdictional reach than in the past. For example, privacy laws in many U.S. states have jurisdiction across state lines, and international privacy laws affect many organizations not located in countries that passed the laws. These jurisdictional issues are all about cross-border privacy, where each country passes laws requiring the protection of private data associated with its citizens, applicable regardless of the location of the organization that has the data. This issue has many corporate counsels on a steady diet of coffee and Rolaids.

Part III
Finding a Job with the Right Organization

Image courtesy FEMA Photo Library

In this part . . .

- ✔ Look at the sometimes-glamorous life of an employee in a consulting company.

- ✔ See what it's like to work in a company that sells security products or services.

- ✔ Read about full-time work in private industry, where InfoSec professionals help protect their employer's assets.

- ✔ Understand the day-to-day life of working in a government agency or educational institution.

Chapter 7

Life as a Security Consultant

In This Chapter

▶ Deciding whether the consulting lifestyle is right for you

▶ Looking at life in a consulting organization

▶ Considering the potentially lonely life of an independent consultant

▶ Comparing consulting with other types of work

Security consultants have an opportunity to help not just a single employer but many organizations during their professional career. Working as a consultant is different from working in an organization, where you have responsibilities only to your employer and its internal operations. As a consultant, you won't be putting down roots in a single organization (other than the consulting firm itself); instead, you'll be moving from place to place.

Consulting is fast-paced and highly rewarding but also unpredictable and stressful. If you are considering a position as a consultant, check out this chapter for the pros and cons.

Is Consulting Right for You?

In the 1960s, the original *Mission Impossible* TV series always started with a taped message to Mr. Phelps, who was given a life-and-death, world-peace-at-stake assignment in some remote corner of the world. Against all odds, Phelps and his team would overcome seemingly insurmountable obstacles and prevail.

Consulting is a lot like the *Mission Impossible* missions. From one consulting gig to the next, you never know what kind of work, people, or company you'll encounter. Some assignments will be boring, others highly challenging, and others rewarding — for a variety of reasons.

Consulting is fundamentally different from many other jobs. Take a look at the following questions. Are you okay with a job where you

✔ May travel from 25 to 75 percent of the time, away from home for days or even weeks at a time?

✔ Work with different people from day to day or week to week?

✔ Won't know what city you'll be in a week or a month from now?

✔ Are expected to be a seasoned expert but won't know what expertise you'll have to call on a day, week, or month from now?

✔ Help build something but will not be around to see how successful it could become?

✔ Sometimes work for people whom you'll meet only by phone?

✔ Aren't around long enough to form deep relationships with the people you work alongside?

If you answered "Yes" to most or all of these questions, consulting may be right for you. In the rest of this chapter, you find out more about working in a consulting organization or as an independent consultant.

Consulting workload

Consulting is hard work — very hard work — for a variety of reasons. Let's take a closer look at the four major factors that will always try to take you down in a consulting job:

✔ **Intellectual fatigue:** As a consultant, you're expected to be professionally superior to the client organization with which you'll be working.

✔ **Performance fatigue:** Because you're in front of clients, you have to be on your A-game all the time. Your clients expect a professional polish from a high-priced consultant; whenever you speak, all eyes and ears will be focused on you. You might feel as though you're on stage all day, every day.

✔ **Physical fatigue:** You'll probably travel a lot, living out of your suitcase, eating in restaurants, and working evenings. You might not take the time for physical exercise while on business travel or working long hours.

✔ **Multitasking fatigue:** Often, you won't be able to concentrate only on the project right in front of you. You may be drafting security reports for clients you met recently, and reading documents from a client you'll be working with next week or next month.

Consulting requires social skills

One of the things that you always come up against when working as a security consultant is the desire for absolutes. "If I buy this firewall/antivirus/new device, I'll be 100 percent secure, right?" Or worse, "I thought that if I bought that firewall/antivirus/new device, I'd be 100 percent secure, right?" Of course, there's no such thing as 100 percent in security.

Being any kind of IT consultant is only 20 percent tech and 80 percent social skills. If you're not prepared (or just don't want) to respond to questions like these, take a different job path.

Marc Gordon, Seattle

Appearance and approach

As a consultant, you are often the face of the consulting firm (or your own company, if you're an independent consultant). The client is paying big bucks for your expertise. You should *always* behave, dress, and communicate in a bit more professional manner than the client employees (without seeming arrogant).

Even when working for a consulting firm, you have some responsibility for sales — your day-to-day actions, customer service, and exhibited expertise

Confidence as a consultant

You have to come into a room confident that you know what you are talking about and always ready to listen to the customers and their concerns. You have to be able roll with the material you have to work with and understand that everyone's level of risk tolerance — what they are willing or not willing to do — is different.

Since you are not a member of the staff or the team you are working with, the trust level is different and you have to spend a lot of time justifying why you need to see what you need to see. Then you have to build security models, perform risk assessments, or troubleshoot security in a way that aligns with a business you may not know a lot about. You also have to understand that you will be spending a lot of time educating people about security, security controls, and other information related to the industry.

Bruce Lobree, Seattle

all help your consulting firm maintain their reputation with the client, and your success and professionalism will be shared with other companies and clients. You must always be mindful of keeping your eyes and ears open for possibilities of add-on work or new business avenues with a client.

Working for a Consulting Firm

Working in a consulting firm can be a lot like working in a traveling circus. You'll have your circus colleagues but the scenery changes as you move from town to town (or client to client).

A job in a consulting firm will probably allow you to spend most of your time assisting other organizations with various aspects of their security management or operations. Chances are, marketing people and sales people are selling the services that you and your consulting colleagues fulfill with your company's clients.

In many ways, work in a consulting firm can be similar to working in a client organization. You'll be working with colleagues in the organization, which will give you a sense of normalcy (although you'll rarely see your colleagues if you work for a regional or national company). Plus, you'll have company benefits such as a retirement plan (a 401K in the United States), medical insurance, and paid holidays and vacation.

In any job, you have to do what you're told. But in a lot of consulting jobs, you also have to go where you're sent. As a consultant, you'll be haunted by the drive to work on billable projects to bring in the money that ultimately ends up in your paycheck (a portion of it, anyway). You want to avoid being on the bench (being paid while between projects) as much as possible.

Consulting firm processes

Many consulting firms have established processes and procedures for a lot of operational activities. These processes and procedures drive consistency and can help the consulting firm increase its business without falling into chaos. Here are some examples:

- **Time accounting:** An established method for tracking billable hours by client and by project, so that each client can be invoiced accurately for all services rendered.
- **Expense accounting:** An established method for capturing billable and nonbillable expenses, such as travel costs, meals, and supplies.

✔ **Engagement management:** Standard procedures for starting, executing, and completing projects. For example:

- *Pre-sales:* In some consulting firms, consultants participate in pre-sales activities with new clients, so that clients can meet the consultant and ask questions about the proposed engagement.

- *Project kickoff:* A conference call or an in-person meeting, as well as an exchange of documents and client contact information.

- *Project status reports:* The consultant writes these, although he or she may need to follow a company template and format.

- *Written deliverables:* Most consulting engagements include one or more written deliverables. You will probably have a template and examples to follow so that new written reports are consistent with previous ones.

- *Project wrap-up:* Includes delivery of written reports, as well as a closing meeting.

- *Post project:* Includes a final accounting of all billable hours and expenses. Some consulting firms may do a project debrief to discuss what went well, what needed improvement, and how future projects can be performed better.

The consultant or other people or departments may perform many of these tasks. There is no correct method, but you may find some of the differences important. For instance, if you want to focus only on security, look for a consulting firm that doesn't requires you to do a lot of your own overhead.

Subject matter variety

In a smaller consulting firm, you'll be a security generalist and may have a variety of consulting engagements. Depending on your areas of expertise, you could be chosen for many different consulting gigs, such as

✔ **Policy development:** You interview key stakeholders in a client organization and develop the organization's security policy.

✔ **Vulnerability assessment:** You use a variety of tools to identify vulnerabilities in a client's network, web application, mobile application, or internal server or workstation environment.

✔ **Security awareness training:** You create training content for general employees in an organization, and perhaps even conduct that training.

✔ **Risk assessment:** You interview ten to twenty people in an organization, discuss their processes and technologies, and produce a risk assessment that details where things could go terribly wrong.

✔ **Physical security social engineering:** You might pose as a delivery driver, an IT worker, or the like while trying to break into an organization's building.

✔ **Security incident response**: As a solo consultant or part of a team, you investigate a security breach to determine what happened, what weakness permitted the intruder to break in, and what measures can be taken to prevent future incidents.

In a larger consulting firm (and in some smaller ones), you may be specializing in one functional area, and most or all of your consulting engagements will be focused on a particular subject matter or activity. For example, if you were in a security assessments group, you would be performing penetration testing and vulnerability scanning; in an incident response group, you would be one of the paratroopers sent in to investigate security incidents.

Working in pre-sales

In many organizations, consultants will support the sales organization in an activity known as pre-sales, in which you take part in sales calls to prospective clients. You're along for the ride so that you, the security expert, can describe your approach to their particular problems. Seeing (or hearing) you in person also gives the client more confidence in the consulting firm, and in you.

Pre-sales is essential to winning future business, but as a consultant, you will face pressure to maximize billable hours (and complete tasks and projects on time for your clients). Often you end up making up the hours spent on pre-sales by working in the early morning or evening, to keep client projects on schedule.

Consulting is itinerant work

Unless you get a long-term consulting gig, you won't be in one workplace for more than a few days or weeks. Forging long-term relationships with people in your client organizations is difficult because you move on just when you're getting to know and enjoy working with them.

Because you're working as a consultant, you won't be putting down roots, in terms of hanging your hat in one organization. Instead, you're an expert, working on a particular task or project, and then you're gone. You won't be around to see the fruits of your labor — at least not the long-term positive effects of your contributions. However, you'll be able to help a lot of organizations, something you'd have little opportunity to do if working for a typical employer.

Going It Alone as an Independent Consultant

In the movie *Star Wars,* the character Han Solo is the semi-romantic portrayal of an independent consultant. He is his own boss, he chooses what jobs to take, and he's in control of his destiny. You also get the impression that it's a lonely job, with only his sidekick Chewbacca as company.

As an independent security consultant, you decide which companies you'll work with. It's the ultimate in independence and the ultimate in risk, like climbing a mountain with no one to belay you if you fall.

Independent consulting is a lifestyle. It's difficult to master, and few are up to it. However, if you're independent consulting material, the rewards can be great. As an independent consultant, it's just you and your clients: You have no coworkers and none of the encumbrances of working in a company with others.

Independent consultants have to do a lot of things on their own:

- ✔ **Marketing and sales:** Independent consultants have to do their own marketing and sales. This task requires a different set of skills and can take considerable time. Sales is a difficult job.

- ✔ **Legal:** As an independent consultant, you'll need to manage your contracts or have outside legal counsel from time to time. You'll want to develop template documents for nondisclosure agreements, statements of work, and a master services agreement.

- ✔ **Accounting:** Unless you're an expert with small business accounting and taxes, you'll probably want to find an accountant to keep your books or complete your tax filings or both.

- ✔ **Earned time and benefits:** I'm sure you appreciate the concept of paid vacations, holidays, and sick days. As an independent consultant, you still need time off, but you're not billing hours while you're not working for a client. You also have to pay for all other benefits, including medical insurance, life insurance, and health club discounts.

- ✔ **No colleagues:** Without colleagues to talk with, independent consultants must look to the professional community for like-minded security professionals with whom they are willing to share ideas, struggles, and joys. Put another way: If you need help on a project, you have to find that help on your own.

The prospect of independent consulting is an intense, rewarding challenge to some, and terrifying to others. It's definitely not for everyone.

The Good, The Bad, and The Ugly of Consulting

Table 7-1 provides a comparison of working in a consulting firm, as an independent consultant, and in a regular organization (which could be a public company, a private company, an institute of higher learning, or the government).

Table 7-1	Consulting Work versus Internal Work		
	Consulting Firm	*Independent Consultant*	*Internal Company*
Marketing and sales	Provided by consulting firm	Provided by independent consultant	N/A
Legal support	Provided by consulting firm	Paid by independent consultant	Provided by employer
Benefits	Paid by consulting firm	Paid by independent consultant	Paid by employer
Support	Coworkers at consulting firm	Must find trusted associates	Coworkers at employer
Job variety	You can work with several companies	You can work with several companies	You can work with only one company
Billing rate	You receive a small fraction	You receive all but must pay for overhead	N/A
Long-term relationships	Only within the consulting firm	Hard to come by	Definitely

Chapter 8

Working for a Security Vendor

As an employee in a security company, you'll have a role in the sales, support, implementation, or management of the company's products or services. Most of these positions are "customer facing," meaning you'll be working with customers in person or by phone. You'll need above-average people skills because you'll be representing your company in front of customers and prospective customers, often with a sales executive but sometimes alone.

In this chapter, you find out about a variety of security-related roles in security vendor organizations.

Working in Sales as a Pre-Sales Engineer

As a pre-sales engineer, you accompany sales executives on sales calls to clients and prospective clients, explaining the wondrous features of the hardware products, software products, or managed services that your company provides. You'll be looked upon as the expert in the room who can take your salesperson's comments deeper with real-life examples about how your company made other clients successful.

This job, however, entails a lot more than just smiling, nodding, and tossing in an occasional tale or two:

> ✔ **Conducting product demos:** You might conduct a demonstration of your company's product or provide a depiction of its operation. You describe in technical terms what your product is doing and explain what the customers are viewing. In some cases, you set up a demo, also

called a POC (proof of concept), in the customer's environment. When this is the case, you'll have limited time and possibly operational limitations. However, a POC will give an organization a good understanding on whether your product will actually work for them.

✔ **Designing solutions:** You design solutions that will work in your customers' environments.

✔ **Creating price quotes:** You may also be responsible for creating price quotes that your customer will use to make a purchasing decision.

✔ **Developing architectures:** You may work alongside experts in the customer's organization to develop an architecture (a drawing, a technical specification, or both) that depicts your company's product in their environment. The plan to use your product in the customer's environment may necessitate changes to the customer's environment and additional equipment from other vendors.

As a part of the sales organization, you'll probably have a sales quota, a commission, or other incentives to help your sales executive sell as much product or service as possible.

If you work with more than one sales executive, you'll have to decide when two sales executives want you to attend a sales meeting at the same time in different locations. Even when everyone in a company can view their coworkers appointment calendars, sometimes conflicts are unavoidable.

You'll also need to attend training sessions about your company's products (including new features and information on size, scope, and price). These sessions will add to your expertise and give your customers confidence that you really do know what you're talking about when you help them imagine success with your products.

If you work for a reseller, you'll need to gain expertise in each of the products that your company sells. In larger companies, you might have to be familiar with products from dozens of manufacturers.

Rolling Up Your Sleeves as an Implementation Engineer

As an implementation engineer, you install and configure your company's product in the customer's environment. Often, you visit the company's headquarters or other locations where the product will be installed or used. For a cloud-based product, you may still be on-site to work with the customer's employees to get the product up and running correctly and perhaps provide informal training.

A job as an implementation engineer is great when things go well, but sometimes you will have unanticipated challenges, such as the following:

- ✔ **Functionality gap:** Sometimes salespeople are overzealous when pitching the product. When customers discover that the product does not in fact take out the garbage or create lattes, they may display their dissatisfaction.

- ✔ **Product DOA (dead on arrival):** It can be embarrassing when a product simply doesn't work!

- ✔ **Product undersized:** The product may be too small (not enough storage, or network throughput, for instance) and not work well in the customer's environment.

- ✔ **Missing components:** The pre-sales engineer might not have included all necessary components for the product to work properly.

- ✔ **Licensing issues:** Sometimes there are difficulties activating a license that's required to get a product running.

- ✔ **Underqualified customer personnel:** Sometimes the customer's organization doesn't have a person with the necessary skills and knowledge to successfully operate the product after you've set it up.

These situations will draw on your relationship and negotiation skills. You'll need to stay cool, help your customer separate emotion from fact, and keep your customer at ease and give him or her confidence in your ability to solve the problem. You are, after all, the expert in all things about your product and your organization — but be sure that you know who in your organization can help you in a crisis.

Helping Customers in Technical Support

As an expert in one or more of your company's products, you receive calls for assistance from a customer who is having some kind of difficulty.

Like an automobile mechanic whose customer complains vaguely about a rattle, your customer's call for help may include imprecise or ambiguous descriptions of a problem. Your skills as a kind, empathetic, expert listener and troubleshooter will guide you as you ask key questions to get to the root cause of the problem.

Customers are not often in a good mood when they're having difficulty with a system. What's more, they may be under pressure to get systems up and running again, and your product's problem may be standing in the way. You'll need to stay cool and collected, keeping the customer confident in your company's ability to stand behind them and solve their problem.

If you're in luck, your company will have good information to help you troubleshoot your customers' problems, with a knowledge base (KB) or other references to guide you. As you gain expertise, you may be contributing to the knowledge base, helping your colleagues and those who follow you.

Watching the Fort for a Managed Security Service Provider

A managed security services provider (MSSP) is an organization that provides services to customers who do not have the resources to perform these services on their own. An MSSP will provide one or more of the following services to its customers:

- **Monitoring:** You use systems or network monitoring tools to observe the general health of a customer's critical systems or support the network infrastructure or both. When alarms (visual alerts indicating a malfunction or security issue) are displayed, you'll follow procedures that could vary from customer to customer.

- **Systems management:** You manage network devices, servers, and storage infrastructure for multiple customers. You make configuration changes, upgrade device software, and watch the health of the infrastructure.

- **Incident response:** You monitor systems and networks for security incidents. When an incident is detected, you use tools to drill into affected systems to begin isolation, containment, and recovery operations. You participate in conference calls with affected clients to listen to their needs and inform them of your company's efforts.

A position in an MSSP is a great place to start a security career because you are exposed to enterprise tools and mature processes, and are surrounded by security experts with a lot more experience than you.

"When it rains, it pours." This saying by a table salt manufacturer applies to the MSSP business. Boredom can give way to frantic intensity when two or more customers have serious issues simultaneously. This type of job can be a bit like that of an airline pilot: interesting and challenging at takeoff and landing but boring in between. But in an MSSP, as when flying an airplane, constant diligence is key.

Chapter 9

Working as an In-House Security Professional

. . . .

In This Chapter

▶ Understanding work in the private sector

▶ Comparing smaller and larger organizations

▶ Looking at security jobs in various industry sectors

. . . .

*M*ost information security professionals work as in-house experts, directly or indirectly contributing to the protection of their employer's information assets and personnel.

Information security jobs in private sector and nonprofit companies vary widely by industry, company size, and other factors. Some people prefer to be a one-man-band in a small company, responsible for all aspects of information security. Others prefer larger companies and to work as part of an information security team or department. There's no right or wrong here — only deciding what you'll like best and where you can be successful.

Living Your Destiny

Probably the most impactful characteristic of being an in-house versus a consulting security professional is that you're in the organization for the long haul. Consultants or contractors come in for a specific task or project and then leave, usually long before anyone realizes the consequences (good or bad) of their work. But as an in-house security professional, you'll reap the fruits of your labor for years.

When you make good decisions, you'll enjoy the outcome and at times even bask in it. But when you make poor decisions, you'll be around to see the consequences and any discomfort that may result. However, you can also improve both bad and good situations to make them even better.

Working in the Private Sector

Private individuals (or a group or people) own and run *private sector organizations.* A private sector company may also be publicly owned, meaning that all or a part of its ownership is through publicly traded shares.

The majority of jobs in the United States are in the private sector. In late 2014, there were 119 million non-farm jobs in private industry and 22 million jobs in government.

Industry regulations

People in many professions tend to work in one industry for much of their career, although they may change employers within an industry. Employers tend to select candidates for employment based on their past experience in the industry, which also tends to keep people in a particular industry sector.

Each sector in the information security field has its own regulations regarding the protection of information and information systems. Familiarity with these regulations also tends to keep an information security professional tied to a specific industry sector. Table 9-1 provides a sample of industries and the regulations related to information security.

Table 9-1   Industry Sectors and Information Security Regulation

Industry	Information Security Regulation
Any public company	Sarbanes-Oxley
Financial sector	Gramm-Leach-Bliley Act (GLBA)
Public utility	North American Electric Reliability Corp (NERC); Federal Energy Regulatory Commission (FERC)
Healthcare	Health Insurance Portability and Accountability Act (HIPAA)
Pharmaceuticals	Food and Drug Administration (FDA)
Any company doing business with the public	Federal Trade Commission (FTC)
Any company accepting credit card payments	Payment Card Industry Data Security Standard (PCI-DSS)*
Any company using personally identifiable information (PII)	U.S. state laws requiring public disclosure of breaches of PII

*PCI-DSS is not a regulation but an industry standard with enforcement mechanisms that arguably make it as effective as government regulation

Many organizations are subject to multiple sets of regulations. For instance, a publicly traded healthcare organization that accepts payments by credit card would be subject to the Sarbanes-Oxley Act, Health Insurance Portability and Accountability Act (HIPAA), Payment Card Industry Data Security Standard (PCI-DSS), and U.S. state laws requiring public disclosure of breaches of personally identifiable information. As a result, the organization may have to enact a complex set of IT controls and endure multiple external audits per year. These requirements, in part, drive demand for information security professionals: Companies need people who are familiar with these different security control frameworks and can implement them effectively and efficiently.

Comparing private versus public companies

A *public company* is one where all or part of its ownership is through publicly traded shares that are traded in an open market such as the New York Stock Exchange. Table 9-2 highlights key differences between private and public companies.

For a security professional, the only practical difference between working in a private company versus a public company (U.S. based) is that a public company must comply with the Sarbanes-Oxley Act, which requires a public company to enact a framework of IT controls and business controls to protect the integrity of the company's financial accounting system and its financial reports.

Table 9-2	Private versus Public Companies	
	Private Company	*Public Company*
Ownership	One or more private individuals	Public shareholders
Major decisions	Private; made by company management	Public; must be approved by shareholders
Financial disclosure	No public disclosure required	Public disclosure required
Reporting of material events	Not required	Required
Selection of board of directors	Private matter	Publicly disclosed; selected by shareholders

Supporting company goals and objectives

Information security professionals in the private sector (particularly those in management positions) must understand the mission, goals, and objectives of their company and then develop and enact security strategies to support the mission, goals, and objectives. Otherwise, the security team will be out of step with the rest of the organization.

To put it simply, an information security team must support and facilitate whatever business activities the organization wants to undertake. Information security needs to be involved all along the way, to understand new initiatives and to influence small and large outcomes so that those initiatives will be successful and carried out with an appropriate level of risk.

One Size Doesn't Fit All: Small and Large Businesses

For many professionals, including those in information security, considerable differences exist when working in small versus large organizations. Without considering any individual's preferences, the issue is not *good versus bad* — only differences in the job based on company size.

Table 9-3 provides some general differences between small and large organizations. Remember that these are generalizations; every company is different.

Table 9-3	Small versus Large Organizations	
	Small organization	*Large organization*
Size of security team	Can be as small as one	Dozens or more
Variety of work	Higher	Lower
Process maturity	Lower	Higher
Human interaction	More face-to-face	Less face-to-face
Visibility to upper management	Higher	Lower

Chaos versus Calm: Growth, Mergers, and Acquisitions

They say that companies are either growing or dying. Although rewarding professional challenges exist in both types of companies, some characteristics of a company are worth a look.

On the surface, working for a company enjoying a high rate of growth looks like a lot of fun — and it can be. However, a rapidly expanding company experiences growing pains that you won't see in more stable, mature organizations:

✔ **Continuous process transformation:** In a growing organization, business processes are changed to accommodate new business features, offerings, teams, locations, clients — everything!

✔ **Outgrowing business systems:** An organization growing slowly will occasionally outgrow a system here and there, but a rapidly growing company will make more frequent changes, many of which are disruptive.

✔ **Lots of additional staff:** A rapidly growing company can have many new people who are not yet familiar with the company's practices, making work chaotic. Processes are changing, systems are changing, people's roles are changing, and inconsistencies, mistakes, and chaos can result.

Besides organic growth, some companies grow by gobbling up other companies. The result is nearly the same: People come together, with different ways of doing things, and try to figure out how to do things in the new combined organization. Lots of decisions get made in the sloppy effort of joining companies in mergers and acquisitions.

In many companies that grow through acquisition, their internal IT systems are often a patchwork of systems and networks from each acquired company. Often these systems remain for years, with integration and consolidation proceeding slowly, if at all. This adds considerable complexity, which is another aspect of the excitement (or angst) that we get to look forward to each day.

Rapidly growing and changing companies are, by their nature, unstable and chaotic. You'll have to decide whether this kind of work environment is something you can live with.

Working in Global Enterprises

Global organizations have a unique set of challenges that companies in a single country aren't faced with. Sure, there are language, cultural, and geographic challenges that make company operations more interesting. But from the perspective of information security, the issues that we need to be aware of and manage include the following:

- **Data protection laws:** Many industrialized countries have enacted data protection laws that prescribe measures that must be taken to protect certain types of data.

- **Data privacy laws:** Many countries have passed privacy laws that place various requirements on organizations doing business there. Some countries place stiff requirements on companies that transfer data about their citizens out of the country, and other countries do not permit companies to transfer private data out of their home country at all.

- **Employment laws:** Differences in employment law keep information security professionals up at night. For example, some countries do not permit companies to perform criminal background checks on employment candidates. In other countries, background checks are allowed but not effective. And in some countries, common security tools such as logging the websites that employees visit are not allowed.

A multinational company must deal with these different national and local laws, and often conduct its business operations differently in each country.

Another important aspect of work in a multinational organization is the likelihood that some of your team members (including your boss, and people who work for you) work and live in other countries. For some, this enriches the experience through the introduction of language and cultural differences. For others, who prefer to work with people mainly face to face, this arrangement may not be a satisfying one.

Living on the Edge with a Startup

If you look at any of the websites dedicated to startup companies that list open positions, such as angel.co (not angel.com), you'll rarely find a security position — unless the company is security-centric, in which case the design of its products or services are all about security.

Working as a security professional in a startup can be a life-changing experience. If you can tolerate the long hours, chaos, and uncertainty, working in a startup can be rewarding for a number of reasons. First, being part of something new carries a level of excitement (which is sometimes hard to distinguish from a feeling of terror). Also, you'll learn a lot in a startup that you won't learn elsewhere, primarily having to do with operating a small business.

Most startup businesses don't have a lot of money, so information security professionals in these businesses have to find creative ways to protect key assets without spending a lot of cash. Exactly how this is done will vary greatly based on the startup business's purpose and product, and many other factors too numerous to mention here.

The bottom line is that working in a start-up is risky and demanding and can be frustrating. However, if things go right, working in a start-up can also be extremely rewarding.

Working for a Nonprofit Organization

In the legal sense, a *nonprofit* uses surplus revenues to further its goals rather than distributing them as profit or dividends to owners. When most people hear "nonprofit," they think of a charity or a foundation.

One typical characteristic of a nonprofit is its culture of frugality, because every dollar spent on anything other than its mission reduces the fulfillment of its mission. With a few exceptions, IT and information security professionals find work in nonprofits frustrating because they have fewer opportunities to gain experience with new technologies. They may also feel that their tenure in a nonprofit will hurt their long-term career outlook. Further, some nonprofits do not have the means to pay market-level salaries to their professionals, which can make it difficult for nonprofit organizations to find qualified talent.

Every cloud has its silver lining. Working in a nonprofit can be intensely rewarding and fulfilling because you are part of something important that is improving the world. For an information security professional, a nonprofit has another reward: Because the organization may not have the funds to buy the latest security technologies, you'll learn how to do more with less, which is a skill valued not only in nonprofits but also throughout the private sector.

Chapter 10

Serving in the Public Sector or Academia

Government agencies and educational institutions need experienced information security professionals as much as private industry does. Governments and educational institutions rely as much on information systems as the private industry, and they face the same challenges — primarily, protecting sensitive information and keeping unauthorized persons away from applications, systems, networks, and data.

Although the principles of information protection are similar in any kind of organization, working in government and education is different from other types of work. Is it right for you? Only you can decide. In this chapter, you find information to help you make that decision.

Working for a Federal, State, or Local Agency

Agencies at all levels are in need of qualified information security professionals who have many of the same skills sought by the private sector. No matter where you work, your skills and knowledge on the protection of information and information systems can be used to safeguard information that is vital to the ongoing operation of government agencies at all levels.

Public service

Working in any level of government is frequently referred to as *public service.* In a public sector job, you serve the public in a professional capacity, providing assistance to your agency in the quest to facilitate more efficient access to information while protecting that information from and responding to inappropriate access.

Public service is an honorable career pursuit, but it is often considered a career that includes tradeoffs in the following four ways:

- **Compensation:** Generally, public service jobs pay 10 percent to 40 percent less than the private sector. However, you're less likely to work the long hours required in many private sector jobs. You might be home for dinner more often, but your dinner is more likely to be ground beef instead of filet mignon.

- **Skills and knowledge deficit:** In public service, you typically have less exposure to the latest in high-tech innovation. Over the long run, this deficit could put you at a slight disadvantage in the jobs market, where your skills would compare unfavorably against private sector candidates who have more experience with the latest tools and techniques.

- **Lower risk:** In a public sector job, you usually take smaller risks, and your job will be less likely to be affected by mergers, downsizing, and lay-offs. Put another way, you may have greater job security.

- **Benefits:** Public sector jobs often come with excellent benefits, more holidays and time off, good health benefits, and often a pension.

In the public sector, you're somewhat further away from the cutting edge, you will have a somewhat lower salary, but your level of risk and time commitment are lower as well. Is the public sector right for you? Only you can answer that. Let's look at more facts of public service in the rest of this section.

Transparency

Everything that goes on in all levels of the public sector is subject to public examination and scrutiny. The memos you write, the emails you send, and the contracts between your agency and outside companies are available to the public on request, with a few exceptions. (The privacy of citizens and public service employees is protected, and in some cases, sensitive information such as system security configurations are unavailable for reasons that I hope are obvious.)

Some professionals bristle at this level of transparency and consider it an invasion of their professional privacy. However, the rationale behind transparent government is a long-standing one in the United States: It is a protection against tyrannical rule. Transparency is just another aspect of public service that comes with the territory.

The glacial pace of change

Government has a long-standing reputation of making progress slowly. Sure, for the most part, government agencies may not have the latest high-tech gadgetry, but often our government agencies at least have the basics to get the job done. But the sometimes slow pace of progress is not just about technology.

Government should be thought of as an institution with well-defined and deeply entrenched business practices, which are sometimes out of step with the practices in private industry.

Leadership

Another big difference between public sector organizations and the private sector is that leadership changes are based on elections, rather than on a professional hiring process. Thus, executive leadership changes on a regular basis, and leaders are chosen more for their political prowess or governing abilities than for their understanding or even comprehension of the world of information technology.

This same dynamic can raise challenges for nontechnical private sector organizations, but at least the leaders are selected and maintained for their expertise in the business of the enterprise. And in those cases, with the correct information from you and your peers, the private sector executive is likely to be at least trainable in the risks presented by technology.

In the public sector, leaders concentrate on their political priorities, so they often have no time or inclination to consider cyber risk. Fortunately, department heads, at least in larger public sector organizations, often survive several terms of office. Therein lies the hope and possibility of creating and maintaining an information security capability of lasting value and resilience.

Local versus federal

At state and local levels, you'll likely have less exposure to high tech innovations and experience. But as you go up to the federal government and defense work, you're likely to have more exposure to cutting edge technology.

With larger government institutions (especially those that protect information), you can get the benefits of scale. For example, monitoring and reporting of every system on a network may not be cost effective at smaller agencies but is routine at the Department of Defense level.

Tenure

In part, the pace of change in the public sector is a result of people remaining in their government jobs for decades, sometimes in the same job. People resist change, and if the same people are in charge for years or decades, their way of doing things tends to stay the same. These practices are out of step with the way things are accomplished in private industry. This practice drives some people a little crazy, but public service is not for everyone.

One reason why people to stay in public service jobs is the pension, a long-term benefit that has all but disappeared from the private sector. Whereas public sector pay is lower than the private sector, a public sector pension may be quite generous for those who spent their entire career in public service.

Regulations

Aside from the general theme of transparency described previously, government agencies are also subject to regulations requiring them to enact controls to protect information and information systems. The most noteworthy of these is the Federal Information Systems Management Act (FISMA) of 2002, which requires every U.S. federal agency to establish effective information security programs.

At a minimum, federal agencies are required to enact security programs based on two key documents:

- **FIPS 200:** Minimum Security Requirements for Federal Information and Information Systems
- **NIST 800-53:** Security and Privacy Controls for Federal Information Systems and Organizations

Agencies are required to develop a System Security Plan (SSP) for each information system, and undergo periodic certification and accreditation processes for each system to ensure that it meets applicable security requirements and standards. Security professionals in government agencies are typically involved in these processes.

Agencies at all levels that accept payments by credit card are required to comply with the Payment Card Industry Data Security Standard (PCI-DSS), which is not a regulation per se but instead enforced through a card brand's power to withhold an agency's ability to process payments by credit card.

Working for a Military or Defense Contractor

U.S. federal agencies, including the Department of Defense, enlist the help of many outside organizations for the development of military and defense capabilities, including weaponry and other support of active military forces. Conversely, they are also often used to provide staff augmentation to fill in understaffed roles; cyber-related roles are often filled with contractors due to the need for experienced and certified individuals. Although these organizations are considered to be in the private sector, they warrant a separate discussion because there are differences in how they operate.

Depending on the particular firm and its purpose, jobs in military and defense contracting companies can resemble government itself in terms of the rate of change, the longevity of the employees, and the potentially glacial pace of operation. On the other hand, many companies and their positions can be much more like the private sector, with a higher pace of work, more exposure to high-tech innovation, and profit sharing!

Employees in military and defense contractor firms usually undergo onerous background checks at the time of hire. For many people in positions of higher sensitivity, background checks may be periodically conducted throughout their employment.

Defense contractors are a public-private hybrid

By working for a defense contractor, you can get access to some of the benefits of working with large government organizations (and exposure to what they do) without having to work through government bureaucracy, and you get the benefits of working for the private sector (technically). At the same time, although you often get a comparably higher salary, you don't have the job security or necessarily the same hours.

I think government contracting is really in between private and public from a career and benefits perspective. A word of caution: Many of the larger government contracting firms work on a contract-by-contract basis, so while you're an employee of the contractor, after the contract with the government is over, you may not be guaranteed a job.

Brian Haller, Seattle

Going Back to School

Whether you consider working in K through 12 or in higher education, employment in education is public service work (unless you work for a private school).

For the most part, information security work in education is a lot like information security in public service: things move slowly, and there may not be a lot of money in the budget to get the tools you think you need to protect the organization. Chances are, you'll be dealing with people deeply entrenched in their careers; many may be resistant to making the kinds of changes you think are warranted to ensure better protection of sensitive information.

Higher education suffers from a paradox in our profession: Universities are generally thought of as open environments with little or no controls to restrict what students and faculty are permitted to do on campus networks. This practice sometimes contradicts our mission of protecting an environment through controls such as a firewall, an intrusion prevention system (IPS), and a data loss prevention (DLP) system. Often, however, this dichotomy plays out through the creation of a highly protected portion of a university's environment housing servers containing sensitive information. This practice of *network segmentation,* or the creation of various security zones, protects certain systems while relaxing security in other places.

Part IV
Getting Hired!

Find out how to interview the interviewer by visiting www.dummies.com/extras/
gettinganinformationsecurityjob.

In this part . . .

- Build your online persona.
- Study different kinds of resumes and find out which style is best for you.
- Craft a cover letter with the right message for each organization you target.
- Create a strategy for a winning interview that helps you and your prospective employer determine whether you're right for each other.

Chapter 11

Branding Yourself for Your Dream Career

. . . .

In This Chapter

▶ Creating an online public persona with LinkedIn

▶ Networking on Facebook

▶ Building your brand with Twitter

▶ Expressing yourself in a blog and online articles

▶ Keeping your personal and professional lives separate

▶ Helping a recruiter help you find your next job

. . . .

*T*he Internet is your marketing machine, and the world is your audience. It's no longer enough to build a resume and upload it to job search sites such as Monster.com. In today's job search marketplace, you also need to tap into business social networking sites that give you the opportunity to market yourself, to create the *brand of you*.

People are the key to advancing your career — you can't do it on your own. Meeting your peers at industry events will help you understand how other information security professionals overcome obstacles and discover their recipes for career success. Reaching a broader audience through online professional networking on sites such as LinkedIn and Twitter will help you establish more professional connections. Expressing your opinion through your blog, as well as through articles and e-books, will help you establish yourself as an information security professional worthy of a serious look from recruiters and your next employer.

In this chapter, you discover how to build your brand through one-on-one networking and by building a personal brand that will set you apart from others. The topic of branding requires a book unto itself, so check out *Branding For Dummies*, 2nd Edition by Bill Chiaravalle and Barbara Findlay Schenck, which includes a chapter devoted to personal and one-person business brands. Plus, follow the advice in this chapter as you build your professional reputation in information security.

Many great resources are available for establishing and building a network of security professionals. The most important resource is *you*. Building your network involves connecting one-on-one with people, not in using tools to create cool online personas (although those are important as well). Your number one objective is to establish yourself as an interesting professional with unique talents who understands the value in working with other information security professionals.

Meeting People

Building your network begins with meeting other professionals and getting to know them. You can meet people in many ways, such as the following:

- ✔ **Inside your company:** If you work in a larger organization with an established information security team, reach out to them and explain that you want to learn more about their careers. If you tell them that you're interested in an information security career, chances are good that someone will be happy to discuss their career with you.

- ✔ **Security industry associations:** There are a lot of industry associations, and many of them organize local events in midsize and larger cities around the world. Some of these associations are

  - **Association for Computing Machinery (ACM):** Has a special interest group on security, audit, and control. Located at www.sigsac.org.

  - **ASIS International:** Professional association that includes certifications. Located at www.asisonline.org.

  - **Association of Certified Fraud Examiners (ACFA):** Antifraud organization. Located at www.acfe.com.

  - **Business Continuity Institute (BCI):** Focused on business continuity and offers professional certifications. Located at www.thebci.org.

  - **DRI International (DRII):** Organization focused on disaster recovery planning. Located at www.drii.org.

  - **International Council of Electronic Commerce Consultants (EC Council):** Founder of CEH and other certifications. Located at www.eccouncil.org.

  - **Institute of Electrical and Electronic Engineers (IEEE):** Has a special interest group on security. Located at www.ieee-security.org.

- **ISACA:** Formerly the Information Systems Audit and Control Association, founder of CISA, CISM, and CRISC certifications as well as the COBIT standard. Located at `www.isaca.org`.

- **International Information Systems Security Certification Consortium [(ISC)^2]:** Founder of CISSP and other certifications. Located at `www.isc2.org`.

- **Information Systems Security Association (ISSA):** Professional organization with local chapters. Located at `www.issa.org`.

- **SANS (SysAdmin, Audit, Networking, and Security) Institute:** Founder of the GIAC family of certifications. Located at `www.sans.org`.

- **USENIX:** Unix-centric organization. Located at `www.usenix.org`.

✔ **Security conferences:** Conferences are a great way to meet people, including other attendees as well as exhibitors and speakers. Many industry associations just listed host security conferences. A few others follow:

- **Black Hat:** Annual conference in Las Vegas. Information at `www.blackhat.com`.

- **BSides:** Community conferences held in several countries. Information at `www.securitybsides.com`.

- **Gartner Security & Risk Management Summit:** Held annually in the United States, Europe, and Asia. Information at `www.gartner.com/events`.

- **RSA:** Large annual security conference held in San Francisco, as well as in Europe and Asia. Information at `www.rsaconference.com`.

- **SecureWorld Expo:** Over a dozen security conferences throughout the U.S. Information at `www.secureworldexpo.com`.

✔ **Sponsored vendor events:** In medium sized and larger cities, companies that produce security products and services hold vendor events, where they discuss related topics and demonstrate their products. These events are often held in hotel meeting spaces and community centers. To learn about these events, get your name on some mailing lists for vendors.

✔ **Service clubs:** Organizations such as Rotary, Kiwanis, Lions, and Optimists focus on service to communities and are a good place to meet other professionals.

Even if you don't know anyone else who will be attending, you'll have an opportunity to meet other people. If you're not the outgoing type, you'll need to pretend to be. Besides, no one else will know whether you're introverted if you pretend for a while that you're an extrovert.

In most cases, it's not good form to introduce yourself and then immediately start talking about yourself, particularly if you tell them you're looking for a job. Instead, it's better to ask people to tell you something about themselves; people will remember you in a much better light if you ask and listen rather than talk their ears off.

If the subject comes back around and someone asks you, "So, what do you do?", you can describe current and past positions, and that you are looking to get into information security. You might explain a little about what you're doing to get into the profession, and then ask the other person's opinion on your approach. You might get some good pointers and maybe even offers to introduce you to others at the event.

Develop an *elevator pitch* — what you would say about yourself to someone while riding an elevator between floors. You have about 1 to 2 minutes to quickly give an overview of what you do as well as your interest in becoming (or your experience as) an information security professional.

If you're currently employed, bring plenty of business cards. If you're between jobs, or if your employer doesn't provide business cards, get some quality ones printed. (Many sites offer free business cards, but you might consider upgrading to a better cardstock or appearance.) In this day of electronic everything, business cards may seem a little old-fashioned, but a lot of people still use them. Business cards are a great way to capture names and contact information easily, so that you can follow-up with relevant and interesting professionals in the future.

The two most important reasons for meeting people? Companies prefer to hire people they know, and security professionals are usually willing to discuss challenges with others they know.

Networking with others

Networking is critical. If you're an introvert and don't always feel social, which is a category I fit into, networking is a good opportunity to overcome those feelings. Knowing people in security will help alleviate that "unknown quantity" risk that potential employers face and will provide land you interviews for which you'd otherwise be overlooked. For me and many others I know, networking was the key to landing our first job in the field or a subsequent one. Beyond that, I've found that the community freely gives advice and help with security problems.

Glen Sorensen, Seattle

Business Networking with LinkedIn

Launched in 2003, LinkedIn touts itself as the "world's largest professional network." With over 200 million users, LinkedIn is a great resource for establishing one's own brand as well as finding other like-minded people. LinkedIn is located at www.linkedin.com.

LinkedIn is your most important tool to establish your brand and a professional network, to be recognized as a thought leader in your area of expertise, and to seek opportunities or advance your career. If you want to learn a lot more about LinkedIn, pick up a copy of *LinkedIn For Dummies*, 3rd Edition by Joel Elad.

To use LinkedIn, sign up for a free account and build a profile that resembles a resume. You establish connections with people you know (or want to know) for business networking. You can join special interest groups where private discussions take place, and you can search for jobs in any industry and location. You can search for people you might know in the "people you may know" feature. You can also search for people by name, location, or company in the freeform search, where you you can also conduct keyword searches to find people in specific interest areas such as network security.

LinkedIn is quite feature-rich: You can express and describe your professional background in many ways. Many consider a LinkedIn profile to be a living resume, which you can update and improve at any time.

In the remainder of this section, various features of LinkedIn are described.

Photo

You can upload a photo of yourself if you want, and most users do. I recommend that you use a recent, high-quality photo. Using a much older photo may capture the beauty of youth, but people who meet you in person may wonder if you are disingenuous. Also, it's best to have a head shot taken by a professional. Wear professional clothing and keep the colors conservative.

Avoid the following mistakes, which can make your first impression less than professional:

- ✔ **Cropped group photo:** A photo that's obviously cropped makes people wonder if you have any good photos of yourself.
- ✔ **Party photo:** Is that the first visual impression you want to make?

✔ **Look at my cool vacation photo:** Yes, the Eiffel Tower and the Statue of Liberty are cool, but leave those for your *personal* Facebook page.

✔ **Selfie:** Almost without exception, selfies are not kind to one's looks, especially if the camera is too close. Your nose looks huge!

✔ **Company logo:** I'm happy that you are enthused about your company, but others want to know what you look like.

You can change your photo any time. If you have a good photo now, use it. Upload a better one later.

LinkedIn also has a background image feature that enables you to upload a landscape-oriented background. It's appropriate to select something business oriented, or just about anything else that is tasteful and reflects well on you personally.

Headline

The LinkedIn headline is the phrase that appears directly below your name on your profile page. Ideas for your headline include title and company (such as *Systems Engineer at Newco*), mission (for instance, *Systems engineer in oil and gas industry*), and multiple activities (for example, *Systems engineer, ISSA board member, and instructor*).

The headline is short, just one or two lines. To those viewing your LinkedIn page, the headline serves as your personal brand statement. Most career coaches advise you to use your headline to define the unique talent and value you deliver.

Below the headline in a smaller type size is the area where you live. Next is a categorization, which you can select to tie into you or your company. For instance, if you're a security professional in the retail industry, you could select Security and Investigations or Retail.

When writing your LinkedIn profile, be sure to use keywords that others are likely to use when seeking someone like you so you'll show up in their searches. Many recruiters and headhunters use premium LinkedIn accounts to search for candidates.

Background

The section of your profile directly below your photo is where you present your background and experience by completing each of the following sections:

- ✔ **Summary:** Write a few paragraphs about yourself. It's best to think about this like a summary near the top of a resume. Don't make it too long, or people might not read it all the way through.

- ✔ **Experience:** List each job you've had, and you can provide several details about your position, primarily in the freeform text field. For each position, you can specify a title, company, location, and description of your responsibilities and accomplishments.

- ✔ **Projects:** Describe any projects you have undertaken at each job. You can specify which other persons (they must be LinkedIn users) participated in the project.

- ✔ **Organizations:** List any organizations that you currently belong to or did in the past. If you've been out of college for less than five years, you can list campus organizations here if you want.

- ✔ **Volunteer Experience & Causes:** List the organizations where you volunteer your time, money, or other resources. You're seen as a better person if you put others' needs ahead of your own.

- ✔ **Skills:** List individual business and technical skills, separate from your individual jobs.

- ✔ **Certifications:** List each industry certification, including the year earned, when it expires (if it does), when you last held it (if it's not current), and a description of the certification if it's not a common one.

- ✔ **Education:** List your education, including courses, degrees, and significant training courses. My own rule of thumb is that you don't need to list your high school education if you're older than 25 years of age.

- ✔ **Additional Info:** List any outside interests, personal details, and how you can be contacted.

- ✔ **Honors and Awards:** List any honors and awards here.

 Like a functional resume, you can change the order of appearance of the various sections in your LinkedIn profile by simply dragging them up or down.

Connections

Any connections you have will appear in your profile. These are other people you know and have agreed to connect with. When you're connected with someone, you can see more details in their profile, their contact information, and any connections you may have in common. If the connection permits, you can view all of the other person's connections (and they yours). LinkedIn does permit you to conceal your connections from others.

The connection feature is intended to be used with *people you know*. Before requesting a connection from someone you don't know, understand that the person can refuse to connect with you and state that he or she doesn't know you. If you decide to pursue a connection with someone you don't know, be sure to include a personal note in the connection request that includes the reason you want to connect. If you get several such rejections, LinkedIn will temporarily suspend your ability to request connections from other users.

Recommendations

LinkedIn provides a means for users to write a recommendation for one of their connections. A recommendation is just that — a description of how you know the person and why the person is a good professional. For example: "Over the past 7 years, I have had the pleasure of working with Emily on the university certification program. I have found her to be hard working, punctual, and a lot of fun to work with."

When you write a recommendation for another person, that person has the choice of whether to include the recommendation in his or her profile. If you didn't have nice things to say about the person, chances are he or she will not approve it. Also, if you got any facts wrong or just said anything that the recipient doesn't care for, he or she can reject it and request that you change it.

Recommendations can function like prewritten references and improve your professional image.

Updates

LinkedIn has a feature where you can write a message, upload an image, or put in a link to an article. You can do a lot of things with updates:

- ✔ Cite an industry article and include your opinion.
- ✔ Post a significant update about yourself.
- ✔ Cite a blog entry you've recently written.

The updates feature of LinkedIn helps you inform your connections about important professional events and issues. However, the feature is also misused — or at least some would say so. For instance, uploading an image of some clever saying ("Managers tell you what to do, Leaders show you how to do it.") borders on being noise, and uploading a photo of your cat would be considered inappropriate by most. Fortunately, LinkedIn gives you the ability to suppress updates from people who are too chatty about unimportant things. In other words, keep your updates professional and business related!

Groups

LinkedIn provides for the creation of *groups*, which are communities of LinkedIn members, where they can discuss matters on almost any topic. Groups can be moderated, which means that a group owner or coordinator (one or more of its members) can selectively approve or reject individual postings. Membership can be set to automatically approve or be subject to manual approval.

Groups are a great way to find people that are in your field or work for companies that you're interested in. When you join a group, you have a legitimate opening to connect directly with other group members. Also, many recruiters utilize groups to find qualified candidates. Recruiters will also make career-related posts that might help you identify employment trends in your field.

The contents of LinkedIn groups can be kept private, so that only its members can view its proceedings. A LinkedIn group can be made public, which means that non-LinkedIn members can join the group, and the contents of the group's discussions will be searchable by Internet search engines such as Google and Yahoo.

Jobs

Many professional recruiters and headhunters use LinkedIn to search for employment candidates. One sign of an effective LinkedIn profile is a periodic contact from a recruiter who asks you if you have any interest in positions he or she is trying to fill. Recruiters find you through keywords in your profile.

Recruiters can purchase a premium subscription to LinkedIn that affords them additional privileges, such as the ability to send messages to LinkedIn users with whom they are not connected.

LinkedIn is my living resume

I've been using LinkedIn for ten years. I realized its value as a public, living resume. My efforts have paid off through numerous opportunities that otherwise would not have materialized.

My LinkedIn profile is bigger than my resume, and includes projects, publications, and over 60 recommendations from coworkers I have worked with over the past thirty years. The richness of my LinkedIn profile has resulted in a steady stream of contacts from recruiters over several years.

Peter H. Gregory, Seattle

Using LinkedIn successfully

LinkedIn can be a powerful tool to expand your professional network. You'll be seen as a good LinkedIn citizen if you follow these pointers:

- ✔ Keep your summary fairly short and include keywords that describe what you do and are likely to be used by others searching for people with your talents.
- ✔ Describe each employment position with the same level of detail as a resume.
- ✔ Use a high-quality professional photo.
- ✔ Request connections only from people you know, or you might lose the ability to request new connections.
- ✔ Accept connection requests only from people you know (fraudsters use LinkedIn to trick users into providing information to them).
- ✔ List your education and professional certifications.

Because your LinkedIn profile is so much like a resume, you'll want to read Chapter 12. Many of the tips in that chapter will apply to your usage of LinkedIn.

Networking through Facebook

Facebook is one of the world's great social networking wonders. From a professional sense, some aspects of Facebook should be left to nonprofessional uses only, while other features can work to your advantage as you develop your personal brand. Facebook can be found at www.facebook.com.

Facebook profile and timeline

A Facebook *profile* is used to describe yourself in many ways: where you live, where you work, where you went to school, and much more. A Facebook *timeline* (once called the Facebook wall) is the place where you type updates of various kinds and where you can see your posts, friends posts to you, and any posts or photos in which you're *tagged,* or mentioned with a link to your Facebook profile.

You are strongly recommended to keep your Facebook profile private, so that only your friends can see any of your content. Prospective employers search for candidates' Facebook pages to get an idea of their character. Because of the way that some Facebook features work, it's best to keep your Facebook profile concealed from all but those to whom you've accepted as Facebook friends.

Although Facebook is more of a *social* networking site, recruiters or companies often use it to learn about prospective or current employees. It's okay to have personal and fun info on Facebook, but treat it as if you know that a potential employer will look at it — err on the side of being conservative. Do not put anything on an online networking source that you wouldn't be comfortable having your employer see or read.

Facebook groups

Although there are many other more suitable places than Facebook for like-minded professionals to gather and discuss issues, millions of Facebook users connect with colleagues and professionals in their category through Facebook and Facebook groups.

Avoid mixing your personal and professional posts by taking a few key steps. First, from your Facebook page, click Friends in the left column. From the page that appears, click Create List to create a group of people with whom you can share information and stay in touch in one place.

Next, search for or create a group by clicking Create a Group or Find New Groups under the Groups listing in the left column of Facebook. From there, it's a matter of participating by checking updates and sharing posts with others in the group.

If the topic of a Facebook group includes confidential information, or if the members of a group should not be publicly known, you should set up the Facebook group as a secret group.

Facebook company pages

Facebook profiles are generally for personal use, and Facebook pages are for businesses and brands. You must have a Facebook profile before you can create a Facebook page for your business. Pages are public (unlike profiles) and discoverable through Facebook and browser searches. In addition, Facebook page posts are free but only a minor percentage of them will show up in the news feeds of your page followers. The rest get filtered as a result of Facebook's algorithms unless you develop high levels of interaction with your posts or pay to post the information as a promoted post.

Facebook business pages and fan pages are one and the same.

Tweeting with Twitter

The microblogging sensation Twitter is another great way to build your brand. Twitter's function is simple: You build a profile, you follow other Twitter users, and others follow you, if they find what you have to say interesting and valuable. When a user you follow posts something (called a *tweet*), it appears in your timeline, along with posts from everyone else they follow. In your timeline, you view the posts made by everyone you follow, and your followers view your posts as well.

You can also send and receive direct messages with people you follow who also follow you.

Posts and direct messages are limited to 140 characters. You'd be wise to keep your posts even shorter because you want to encourage others to retweet or repost your tweets, and they'll need up to 20 characters to add their own message to yours.

To date, over 250 million users are on Twitter.

Setting up your Twitter profile

To set up a Twitter profile, you select a username and password, upload a photo, and provide a brief description of yourself, which is limited to 160 characters, slightly longer than the 140-character tweet limit. You can also have a background photo that will be visible when someone views your profile.

Tweeting

When you have something to say, you *tweet* it: you post an update, maximum of 140 characters including spaces. Everyone following you will see it in his or her timeline. You can include URLs, which Twitter automatically shortens to take less of your 140-character count, and you can include photos and video (a big draw on Twitter) as well. For all you need to know, check out Getting Started with Twitter in Twitter's help center.

Presenting yourself in 140 characters is difficult, but Twitter users do just that. However, for professional purposes, many tweets also include a URL to an article, which could be your blog post or an article of general interest to other security professionals.

Using Twitter successfully

Twitter can be a great way to expand your professional network. You'll be successful with Twitter if you follow these pointers:

✔ Don't become the town crier by retweeting lots of stories put out by news media outlets such as CNN or AP.

✔ Add value to information rather than just rebroadcasting (retweeting) it.

✔ Maintain separate professional and personal Twitter accounts if you want to use Twitter for nonprofessional networking. Followers are visible to everyone, so consider not following your personal Twitter account from your professional one, and vice versa.

✔ Consider using TweetDeck to schedule Tweets at key times of the day or week. Information is available at `www.tweetdeck.twitter.com`.

Starting a Blog

Everyone has an opinion. A blog is a great way to express yours, particularly when something you have to say takes more than 140 characters. All kidding aside, writing a blog can be a great way to publicly express your opinion and solicit feedback. Blogging about information security can be a way of distinguishing yourself from other employment candidates. However, thousands of information security professionals have blog sites, so you may want to consider a blog as table stakes in our profession.

In case you're the last person living under a rock, a *blog* is a simple website that functions like a journal, with journal entries (short articles) that focus on a single point of view or interest area, with the most recent articles appearing first. A blog can also have pages for static content, such as a page for the blog site owner's biography.

Setting up a blog

Setting up a blog is easy. Go to one of several popular (and free) blogging sites, click the Start a New Blog link, and answer a few questions. First, though, consider the following:

- ✔ **Name and URL:** You can name your blog after your name or choose a keyword (or combination of keywords). You can also register your own domain name and associate it with your blog for a more professional feel. For example, on the WordPress service, you could be jimsmith. wordpress.com, or with your own domain name you could be `www. jimsmith.com`, which would redirect to your WordPress site.

- ✔ **Internet searchable:** You'll probably want your blog articles to be searchable so that people can find your blog's articles. Be sure to use keywords in your headlines, section titles, post content, and summary snippet — or in the first 160 characters of your post, because that's what search engines display if you don't provide a snippet. Again, keywords are critical! Find opportunities to insert your keywords into your blogs.

- ✔ **Statistics:** If you want to know how many visitors read your blog and what keyword searches lead them to you, use a blog that provides these types of statistics.

It's best if you keep your blog simple, so that you can maintain it easily. A few weeks or months after that "new blog smell" wears off, you may not be inclined to do much with it. If you keep the blog simple, it won't require much work to maintain it.

A couple of good books on the topic of blogging are *Blogging For Dummies,* 5th Edition by Amy Lupold Bair and Susannah Gardner and *WordPress For Dummies,* 6th Edition by Lisa Sabin-Wilson.

Blog services

Several excellent free blog sites are available. Check out the following:

- ✔ Blogger, `www.blogger.com`
- ✔ SquareSpace, `www.squarespace.com`

✔ TypePad, www.typepad.com

✔ WordPress, www.wordpress.com

All these sites make it easy to set up a blog. Many blog services offer free and paid versions.

Several high-quality (and often free) blog software packages are available that you can acquire and install on a server. However, information security issues today make keeping your site secure a time-consuming proposition. Why not let a free service take care of all this for you?

Information security blogs

If you're not sure how you want to set up your blog, you might want to check out the following blogs for information security professionals:

✔ Assuming the Breach, assumebreach.blogspot.com

✔ Brian Krebs, www.krebsonsecurity.com

✔ Infosecurity Pro, www.infosecurity.pro

✔ Security on Wheels, www.securityonwheels.com/blog

Besides seeing good examples, you may find them interesting and informative.

Using and maintaining your blog

After you've set up your blog, all you really need to do is write short or long articles with some regularity. You don't need to pen something as long as *War and Peace* every week, but you do need to write a blog entry at least once a month, preferably more frequently. Otherwise, your blog will take on a stale, abandoned look, which may be worse than not having one.

As you get accustomed to your blog, consider adding some other features, such as the following:

✔ **Subscribe:** This feature is a way for readers to subscribe to your blog, so that your blog site automatically emails new blog entries to them.

✔ **About:** The About page is a static page about you, which may include something about your education, work history, professional interests, and so on.

- ✔ **Tag cloud:** If you tag your blog entries, you get a tag cloud, which provides a nice visual depiction of the topics you write about the most. Figure 11-1 shows a tag cloud.

- ✔ **Publications:** If you've written articles, books, or e-books, you might create a static page to list them or perhaps create a static page for each individual publication.

- ✔ **Guest posts:** Invite others to submit posts to your blog, and offer to guest blog on their blogs as well. Reciprocal links can develop traffic and readership for all blogs involved.

It's best to keep your blog fairly simple, so that it doesn't have a cluttered, chaotic look and is easier and less time consuming to maintain.

Anti-Virus application security audit Blog breach **career** CISA CISO CISSP cloud data loss **DRP** Encryption Environment Humor **identity theft** incidents Interviews Law Enforcement my books **News** Off-Topic On writing **Opinion** pandemic passwords phishing **Privacy** professional ethics **Quotes and Excerpts** responsibility **Risks** spam threats **Tips** TJX **tools** Vista Wireless XP

Figure 11-1:
A tag cloud from a blog site.

Writing Articles and E-Books

A great way to establish and expand your brand is to write articles for magazines (print or online) and e-books. Articles and e-books help to promote you as an expert in some facet of information security. They also provide you with valuable content you can feature in your Facebook, Twitter, and blog posts while establishing you as a thought leader in your field.

Writing for the reader

You don't need to invent something to write an article or an e-book; all you need is an opinion, a tip, or a story about something in business, information technology, or information security. Here are some ideas for an article or e-book:

- ✔ Your success story and how others can benefit
- ✔ A description of a problem or challenge
- ✔ An epiphany or some kind of new insight into a classic problem or situation
- ✔ A story of an information security failure
- ✔ Your idea on a new way to solve a classic problem in information security
- ✔ Your recipe for successfully completing something

When pondering the idea of an article or e-book, think about what benefit your readers will gain. These articles are not about you and how smart you are but about how your message can help others. When you're writing something for your readers, it's about them, not you.

Finding an outlet

If you've written a good article, consider submitting it to print or online magazines or websites for publication. Be sure that the content fits well with the established style and target audience. You might consider asking someone who writes an information security blog if you can submit an article as a guest author.

Or perhaps a publishing outlet will find you. The best way to get your article published is to publish it yourself on your blog. As long as the article uses good keywords so that it can be found in an Internet search, a few people might take notice and either post a link to refer readers to it or ask you if they can put a copy of your article on their website.

Chances are you will not be paid, and it's probably best not to even ask. Getting your article on someone else's website is free advertising for your brand, so don't bite the hand that feeds you.

Similarly, there are several outlets for publishing an e-book that are free or modestly priced. Two such outlets are

- ✔ Amazon Kindle, `kdp.amazon.com`
- ✔ Book Baby, `www.bookbaby.com`

If you pursue an e-publication, you can use it as a for-sale item on your website or blog, a gift to encourage blog subscriptions or event attendance, or a means for generating interest from potential clients or media outlets. You can also repurpose the content for use on your blog, on Facebook, or in tweets, always including a link where readers can obtain the complete e-book.

Publishing E-Books For Dummies is a great resource for publishing your own e-books.

You should refrain from writing tales about your workplace or your clients if you're in consulting, even if you change the names of companies and people. You need to avoid the perception that you're disclosing information about your employer or client that should be kept confidential.

Segregating Your Personal and Professional Lives

As you begin developing your professional reputation, you'll want to help others gain a clear and positive idea about who you are, your unique talents and value, and your career focus, work history, and professional interests. In other words, you'll want to rev up your personal branding efforts.

It's easy to buy into the false notion that you can have one brand for your personal life and one business brand for your professional life, but that's not the way personal brands work. Your brand is, quoting from *Branding For Dummies,* "whatever people believe about who you are and what you stand for, based on what they've personally experienced, what they've heard from others, or what they've seen online. Through personal branding . . . you help them see how you fit into their hierarchy of interests and needs. You enhance how they view you as an asset, a leader, and a star in your field. As a result, you improve how they react when they encounter you or your name and as they decide whether or not to involve you in their lives."

Because people are likely to either encounter you in both personal and professional situations or to come across online information that reveals both your personal and professional lives, it's important to keep your presentation in

The Internet's long memory

The Internet has countless stories about companies who considered hiring someone until they found and read their public social networking content. Thousands of people have learned this bitter lesson, and you should not have to follow in their footsteps.

The best approach for preventing the potentially embarrassing consequences of social networking is to change your understanding of how the Internet works. Anytime you post something online through a social networking site or a blog, or as a comment on another site, you should consider that action permanent and irreversible. Even if you can later remove an article, a photo, or a comment, it may still be discoverable by someone at any time in the future.

Similarly, you should consider any and every communication, whether by email, chat, instant message, or photo, as public information and discoverable by others. For example, many recent scandals entailed famous people taking and sending private photographs to others, but that content was later revealed to the entire Internet, much to their embarrassment. Even online apps that promise to immediately delete text and images should not be considered safe.

Be clear about the reputation you want to develop and keep all communications — personal or professional — consistent with that brand image.

both arenas complementary and segregated. In the same way that you likely act and communicate differently in the rec room than in the conference room, you can act and communicate differently in personal and professional arenas. But you need to stand for the same values and traits in both places.

Your professional brand communications are intentionally accessible to the entire Internet — to anyone who cares to seek information you've published. But to the degree possible, your personal social networking should remain separate and restricted to your personal connections. The primary reasons for this follow:

- ✔ **Details of your personal life are not relevant to your professional audience.** Although it's nice that you (may) have a family, we don't need to see their Halloween costumes, school play photos, or that great sushi dinner you had last week. Save those for personal social networking.

- ✔ **Details of your personal life should not be accessible to the general public.** These details include photographs and names of family members, their schools or workplaces, and their friends.

On Facebook, for instance, you probably should be cautious about who you connect to, because you may be sharing intimate details of your life. But you might readily accept connection requests on LinkedIn from professional associates with whom you would not want to share details about your personal life, no matter how interesting.

If you're heavily into personal social networking on Facebook or similar sites, and if you want to use Facebook as a part of your professional brand, you should build a separate Facebook page and keep your professional information and connections restricted to that page. The same is true for Twitter, Pinterest, LinkedIn, your blog, and any other social networking site that you want to use for both personal and professional purposes.

You need to decide what degree of transparency you want in your public profile, for both your professional and personal social networking. Also consider your privacy and personal safety, as well as that of your family members and other significant people in your life.

Search for yourself

A great way to see what others might discover about you online is to undertake several detailed searches on yourself. Example of ways you might search include by

- ✔ Your full name
- ✔ Your email address
- ✔ Your residence address (try different combinations, such as 123 Elm St. and 123 Elm Street)
- ✔ Your date of birth together with your name (you'll need to try a lot of different combinations)
- ✔ Your social security number
- ✔ Your work address
- ✔ Your work email address
- ✔ Any other details that are uniquely you

Because most search engines personalize results based on your location and past searches, obtain an unbiased look at your online image by signing out of your Google account, if you have one, or going to the right edge of the Google screen, pulling down the menu, and clicking New Incognito Window to hide your location, IP, address, past search activity, and other identifiers. On Safari, Bing, or Internet Explorer, select Private Browsing. On Firefox, select New Private Window from the File menu. Then study the results, including the results for images linked to your name.

Before you begin your next big job search, it's a good idea to spend a few hours searching for yourself, because any prospective employer is likely to conduct online searches about you as well. When you know what can be discovered about you online, you can take steps to get content altered or removed (or change your social networking privacy settings so that a future employer won't find those beer-binging photos from college). At the very least, you can ramp up efforts to develop strong, well-linked positive content that will push unflattering or off-brand links further down the search results.

 You can set up alert notifications with search services such as Google and Giga Alert to periodically email you regarding newly published pages with your specific keywords. These periodic searches can be a good way to discover new information that has been posted about you.

Working with Recruiters

Recruiters come in two flavors: Some are employees of a company looking to fill its own open positions, and others work for search firms that are looking to fill open positions for their corporate clients. In this section, we're looking primarily at the latter.

Think of a recruiter as your business agent, who will go to bat for you and pitch you as an ideal candidate for their corporate clients. In this regard, you need to make sure that your recruiter knows you, your knowledge and skills, and the kind of job you are looking for.

If possible, meet with your recruiter in person. That way, you can better understand the recruiter and he or she can better understand you. Explain your strengths, background, and the kind of job and company you are interested in. Give them confidence that you are a solid candidate with skills and professional integrity. When recruiters present you to one or more of their clients, they are putting their reputation on the line: If a recruiter's corporate client thinks you misrepresented yourself, the recruiter's relationship with that client could be in jeopardy.

 A recruiter who is familiar with you and who believes you're a solid performer is more likely to think of you instead of other candidates and is more likely to propose you to more companies.

Chapter 12

Creating a Winning Resume

A resume is usually the first thing that a typical employer will view about an employment candidate. Often, as little as ten seconds is spent scanning a resume before making an initial "keep or toss" decision, so it's vital that the appearance, structure, and words in your resume give it the best chance of landing in the "keep" list instead of the trash.

The Basics of a Great Resume

Your resume is a written statement that describes your work experience, education, and short-term career goals. Your resume is your most important marketing tool. Often, recruiters and hiring managers form their first impression of you based on your resume.

Prospective employers are looking for skills, but they are focused on reading about your past accomplishments. How have you saved your employer money, improved security, solved serious issues, or improved efficiency? Tangible results are effective and capture a hiring manager's attention. You need to emphasize positive results in your work experience.

In this section, you look at the various elements of a great resume. The later section, "Different Types of Resumes," describes variations in a resume's arrangement.

Heading

The top of the first page of your resume is the heading, and it contains your name and contact information. If you have prominent certifications, they may appear here as well. Figure 12-1 contains a few sample headings.

John A. Smith, CISSP, CISA

123 Elm St., Reno, NV 89509   johnasmith@gmail.com
linkedin.com/jasmith

Figure 12-1:
Sample
resume
headings.

John A. Smith

CISSP, CISA

123 Elm St., Reno, NV 89509 | johnasmith@gmail.com

Summary

Many resumes include a sentence or a short paragraph describing the candidate's mission or goals, or a statement about a desired position. Typically, this statement is about your experience and the position you want right now, not a position you want in the future. Your summary should tie directly into the position you are applying for and include a powerful statement regarding your experience, abilities, and meaningful accomplishments.

Example summary statements follow:

- Technology manager with eight years experience seeking a position in online financial services in software development or software QA.

- Security and compliance manager with experience managing successful PCI, SSAE16, and ISO27001 audits seeking a security leadership position in a SaaS company. Part-time university instructor and InfraGard board member.

The second example emphasizes accomplishments, in this case, successful audits.

Employment history

The employment history section describes each job that you've had, along with relevant details. If you're writing a chronological resume, each job will include a summary of responsibilities and accomplishments, as shown in Figure 12-2.

Figure 12-2:
Sample employment history entry in a chrono-logical resume.

> **Security Manager**
>
> Employer.com, Seattle, Washington, 1994-1999
>
> - Improved external audit results through key process improvements
> - Reduced number of vulnerabilities in online web application through vulnerability management process changes
> - Developed security awareness program and delivered training to headquarters and branch office employees

If you're writing a functional resume, each entry will include the company, position, and timeframe; the details will appear elsewhere in the resume. Figure 12-3 depicts employment history entries in a functional resume.

Figure 12-3:
Sample employment history entry in a functional resume.

> **Security Manager**. Employer.com, Seattle, WA. 1994-1999
>
> **Security Analyst**. Company.com, Bellevue, WA. 1990-1994

Whether you are creating a chronological resume or a functional resume, make sure you list accomplishments and not merely responsibilities and skills.

For a description of chronological and functional resumes, see the "Different Types of Resumes" section, later in this chapter.

Education

The education section describes your formal education, such as the college, university, vocational school, or technical school you attended. Typically, this section is short and may appear before or after the employment history section.

If you have little higher education and work experience, you may need to include your high school education. However, professionals with a college degree probably don't need to list their high school. If you do not have a college degree, list certifications and professional training.

Figure 12-4 contains a sample education section for a professional with more than ten years' experience.

Figure 12-4:
Sample
education
entries in a
resume.

> **BS Computer Science**. University of Washington, Seattle. GPA 3.25.
>
> **MS Information Assurance**. University of Washington, Seattle. GPA 3.9

Training and certifications

Training and certifications may appear together in one section or separately. Or you might put training information in the education section. As you can see, no single right way to put this information together exists, as long as it is readable and accurate.

Someone with just a few training courses may want to list them individually. However, if you have 20–40 years of IT work experience, you'll likely have more training courses than can fit in several pages of text! In such a situation, a short narrative for training might appear as shown in Figure 12-5.

Figure 12-5:
Training
summary in
a resume.

> **Training**
>
> Numerous courses in TCP/IP, network architecture, network routing, firewall configuration, systems administration, and database administration from organizations including SANS, Usenix, and Cisco.

Skills

People in a technology field learn a lot on the job, often without formal training, so be sure to include relevant skills on your resume. If you have a lot of skills in technology, you may want to group them in categories. Figure 12-6 includes a good example.

Skills
Programming Languages: C, C#, C++, Java, PHP, Ruby on Rails
Databases: MS-SQL, MySQL, Oracle 11i
Operating Systems: Windows 7/8, Ubuntu, RHEL
Networking: TCP/IP v4/v6, routing, Cisco firewalls, Tipping Point IPS

Figure 12-6:
Skills
summary in
a resume.

If you have too many skills to list, include relevant and up-to-date skills and discard the rest. For example, if you are applying for a Java developer job and your past experience includes Cobol and RPG, listing those skills may not be relevant. Look at what the company is seeking and highlight your related skills.

If you have a lot of skills but are light on employment history, you might place your skills section before your employment history section, so that someone reviewing your resume will see your skills first.

Other sections

Depending on your background, you might want to include additional sections on your resume. Whether to include each depends on several factors, such as the following:

- ✔ **Company culture:** Your research needs to include the company's culture — how the company behaves in the community and what it values. Tie yourself into that culture somehow, so that you look like a good fit. For instance, if a company you're targeting emphasizes its volunteer work, include a volunteer work section in your resume.

- ✔ **Rounding out your profile:** If you believe that you need to emphasize that you are more than just a programming machine, you may want to include a section listing your outside interests and involvements.

Some of the sections you might include in your resume are described next.

Interests

Some professionals include an "interests" section to demonstrate that they are not all work and no play. Outside interests can show that you are gregarious, have varied interests, and have a life outside work. If you know that you have a connection to your hiring manager (or someone higher up in the company) through an outside interest, list it so that you become more familiar.

You could list interests in a short, bulleted list or in a few lines of text, such as "Interests include landscape photography, scuba diving, and RC airplanes."

Industry associations

You can list your industry association memberships, including any positions beyond that of a general member. Figure 12-7 shows a typical industry associations section.

Industry Associations

InfraGard, 1998-2015. Board Member, 2010-2013.

(ISC)^2, 2000-2015.

ISACA, 2002-2015. Contributor to CRISC exam, 2014.

Figure 12-7: Industry associations section in a resume.

Volunteer work

Often, professionals like to include a short section on volunteer work. It's often not required, but it does demonstrate selflessness and a desire to help others. Employers usually appreciate someone who makes time for others, and volunteerism is a good indicator of someone who is comfortable in a variety of situations.

When filling in employment gaps, show that you kept busy.

References

Customarily, references are not included in a resume. In the past, including a general statement, such as "Professional and personal references available upon request," was common. Now this statement is unnecessary; an employer is going to ask for references whether or not you include this statement.

Resumes For Dummies, 6th Edition is a valuable resource if you want to read more on the topic of resumes and how they can help you find your dream job.

ANECDOTE

What I look for in a security resume

Whenever I am reviewing resumes for security positions in my organization, I look for the following things:

✔ Certifications: Which ones, and how long the candidates have had them (the longer, the better)

✔ Technology skills: Which technologies, including products and how they were used

✔ Soft skills: How the candidate worked with people in their companies to solve problems and finish projects

A really long list of certifications might indicate too much emphasis on technology skills at the expense of vital people skills. I'd rather see three or four certifications than ten or more.

Problem solving, working on project teams, and completing complex projects mean more to me than a long list of technology skills. I find that you can train someone on new technologies but not on people skills. Those with the wrong people skills usually remain in that state throughout their careers.

Peter H. Gregory, Seattle

Formatting Your Resume

The format of your resume is as important as its content. If it's cluttered and hard to read, a resume for the best candidate will be discarded as quickly as a well-written resume for an unqualified candidate.

A well-formatted resume has the following characteristics:

✔ **Plenty of whitespace:** Text should not crowd the top, bottom, or side margins. There should be room between sections and paragraphs.

✔ **Absence of colors:** Keep everything in one color — black.

✔ **Single, readable font:** The entire resume should be in one easily read font such as Times Roman, Helvetica, or Arial, with the following exceptions: The heading with your name can be slightly larger and in a different font, and the limited use of boldface and underline is acceptable.

✔ **Visual simplicity:** A good resume is beautiful in its simple elegance. In a good resume, less is better.

✔ **No graphics:** So many of today's applicant tracking and application systems parse and populate data from your resume. Graphics will cause problems and cause fields to be populated inaccurately. Avoid cool graphics and complicated formatting techniques with your resume. Unless you're a graphic designer or a marketing campaign designer, hiring managers don't care about the graphics and may consider them distracting. Recruiters definitely don't like graphics, because they often must edit your resume, to, say, add a heading.

In short, a well-formatted resume is minimalist in its visual style.

Soft copy

When working with soft copy resumes that you're sending via email or uploading to an employer's website, a job search site, or a recruiter, it's best to send the resume in Word or PDF format. If you're working with an outside recruiter who will be presenting your resume to one or more employers, send your resume in Word format, with the document unlocked, because the recruiter might need to transform your resume into a particular format.

Although Acrobat's cool features include prohibiting printing or copying text from a document, it's better not to use these features in a resume you upload or email. An employer's screening process might include the need to extract text from your resume, and you don't want to do anything to interfere with that. Best to send your resume as a plain, unprotected PDF.

In most cases, RTF (Rich Text Format) is acceptable format for your resume. Based on the rules of simplicity, your resume probably wouldn't need anything other than RTF in the first place.

Hard copy

For organizations that want hard copy resumes, print them on good quality white copier paper. Printing on colored paper (even the slightest off-white), textured paper such as linen, or paper with a lot of flecks can be harmful. (However, you might consider recycled paper if the company is committed to recycling.) Yes, in many ways you need to stand out, but using a brightly colored or textured resume is risky.

You might consider printing your resume double-sided, to give your potential employer the impression that you know how to be a good steward of resources.

Cleaning up metadata

Before you send a soft copy resume, you need to be sure it's free of metadata and other extraneous data that could cast you in a bad light. Check for the following:

✔ **Document properties:** Be sure that the document author and reviewers state your name or are blank. Check the description and also make sure that it contains your name or is blank.

✔ **Check for tracked changes:** If you have been using a Track Changes feature, be sure you have performed an "Accept All Changes" operation so that you are sending a completely clean resume free of any prior edits.

✔ **Hidden and deleted data:** When customizing resumes, you might mark some content as hidden. Sometimes, deleted content is still in the document. Make sure you have all that cleaned up. One technique is to start with a new, blank document and copy the text from a clean resume into the new empty document.

For more on hard copy resumes, see Chapter 13, which details the contents of a cover letter, and Chapter 14, which describes the interview process.

Tailoring Your Resume

You need to create a targeted resume for each position you seek. Word processing programs make this task fairly easy. However, be sure to develop a system to track each resume you send out.

Organizing your resumes

In this age of word processing programs, every resume should be customized for each particular job and company you're targeting. The method you use to create your customized versions is up to you. Some suggested techniques follow:

✔ **Super-sized resume (remove the parts you don't need):** Start with a master resume that includes lengthy descriptions of each job, education, and so on — perhaps even multiple separate descriptions. Make a copy of the resume, and then remove the parts you don't need. The result, those component parts that are just right for the position you are targeting.

✔ **Franken-resume (build from different parts):** From your collection of headings, summaries, employment positions, education, and more, pull together the pieces you want, in the order you want, to create that perfect, targeted resume.

✔ **Modify the last resume you used:** From the resume you most recently sent to another company, make all needed changes, so that your new resume is just right for the position you're targeting.

Content that you removed for a prior application may be relevant for a later one. Remember to restore content that you may need later.

Whichever method you use is up to you. Perhaps you have a system different from these that works for you. As long as you can keep your records organized and know which resume you sent to which company (and still have copies of each), you should be all right.

You should also consider keeping a worksheet that lists the resumes you used for each job. You might create a little database that includes a lot of different details about each position you targeted, who you spoke with, which resume you sent and to whom, and so on.

Customizing resume content

Every prospective job is different from every other. Even two jobs with the same job title are different. Every company has its own style and way of doing things. These considerations should compel you to take the time

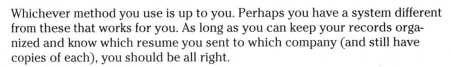

Using keywords to grab attention

Innovations in automated job posting sites such as Monster.com and Indeed.com have resulted in companies getting hundreds, and sometimes thousands, of resumes for each advertised job. As a result, companies have invested in software that electronically evaluates resumes, based in part on the presence of certain keywords. Too few keywords, and your resume will be routed to the bit bucket.

But just including a lot of keywords in your resume is not enough. If your resume gets through the first layer of screening, someone will be reading your resume to see if you sound like a candidate worth a phone screen. At this point, not so much what you say but how you say it gets you to the next level. Remember, though, that you'll never get to that second level without the right keywords.

to customize your resume for each job you apply for. Following are some pointers that will guide this work:

- **Match applicable skills and duties:** Read through the job description carefully, and make sure that each skill and knowledge required appears in your resume when applicable. In other words, if a job description requires Active Directory administration and you have that skill, make sure you include it in each job where you performed this task.

- **Emphasize company similarities:** Employers like to hire people who are familiar with their industry. If you have work experience in the right industries, make sure your resume includes this information.

- **Include required education:** If an education level is cited in the job description, and you have the proper education, make sure you include it clearly in your resume.

To make sure your resume stands out from others, you may want to read other position postings from the same company to get a broader view of the desired skills. Also, find out what you can about the company. Search for articles (good or bad) in local press and trade publications to get an even better idea of their recent history.

Plagiarizing

Although looking at other people's resumes is common, you should not borrow more than a phrase or two. Borrowing attractive styles and formats is okay. There is a tale of an employer who did an Internet search of a sentence in an applicant's resume, and found that exact text (and more) on a sample resume found online. If you have someone else's resume (or a sample) and you like the way something was said, seriously consider rewording it.

Types of Resumes

Every professional has a unique work history, education, skills, and career path, with different strengths and weaknesses. Because of this, no single resume structure will ideally highlight everyone's strengths. For some, showing a progression of employment is ideal. For others, the best approach is to showcase skills and experience. In this section, you look at the two primary types of resumes and a type that's a combination of the two.

Finding and using good examples

A good way to figure out how to structure your own resume is to view many other resumes and borrow what you like from each. Because resumes typically don't contain overly sensitive information such as compensation, it's usually appropriate to ask others for a copy of their resume. As long as you have a reputation of being trustworthy, most other professionals will consider your resume request a compliment. As you progress in your career, you might consider returning the favor to those who ask you for a copy of yours.

Chronological

A *chronological resume* lists work experience, typically in reverse chronological order (with the most recent position first). A chronological resume is the most common resume type because it's the easiest to build and maintain and because potential employers like to see a candidate's recent positions, responsibilities, and accomplishments first.

You'll want to use a chronological resume if you have continuous work experience and your most recent positions are relevant to the company and position you're targeting.

The typical order of sections in a chronological resume is

- ✔ Heading
- ✔ Summary
- ✔ Employment history, including detailed descriptions of each position and notable accomplishments
- ✔ Education
- ✔ Accomplishments, skills, training, interests, associations, volunteer work, and so on

Functional

A *functional resume* highlights your skills and work experience as your resume's primary theme. You'll use this type of resume if your recent work history doesn't adequately show that you have recent, relevant work experience. For instance, if you're seeking a programming job but your last position was something different, a functional resume can emphasize your programming skills even if they aren't as current as you'd like.

Following are some reasons why you might want to use a functional resume include:

- A need to emphasize skills
- Little work experience
- Gaps in employment history
- Work in various industry sectors
- Employment history that doesn't show a steady progression of job titles or responsibilities
- Employment history with a long work history in one position

Following is the typical order of sections in a functional resume:

- Heading
- Summary
- Accomplishments and skills
- Education
- Training
- Employment history, listing only employers, positions, and dates, with no other details
- Interests, associations, volunteer work, and so on

Note that in a functional resume, like a chronological resume, you put your best material early in the resume. In a functional resume, you emphasize your accomplishments, skills, and experience, whereas in a chronological resume you emphasize your employment positions.

Combination

A *hybrid resume* is a combination of chronological and functional resumes. A hybrid resume depicts both skills and employment history, and either one may appear first.

Resume or CV?

Is a CV (curriculum vitae) just a fancy term for resume, or is there a difference?

In some countries, a CV is a complete listing of all employment positions, education, and other relevant information, such as publications, whereas a resume is a summary of employment and education. Sometimes, however, the two are nearly identical.

A CV can be considered a long-form resume that may consist of many pages, whereas a resume is usually limited to two pages the front and back of A4 or letter-sized paper.

The typical order of sections in a hybrid resume follows:

- ✔ Heading
- ✔ Summary
- ✔ Skills, education, training
- ✔ Employment history, listing only employers, positions, and dates, with no other details
- ✔ Interests, associations, volunteer work, and so on

As mentioned, employment history could appear before the skills, education, and training sections.

No exact resume format exists. The types of resumes discussed in this chapter should serve as a starting point for you to build the resume that perfectly and succinctly describes your skills and work experience.

What Not to Put in Your Resume

Although various countries have local practices on resume structure and content, in most locations you would never include certain items in a resume, such as the following:

- ✔ **Compensation:** You should keep records of your pay, but your resume is not the place to include this information.
- ✔ **Date of birth:** Because you already have your name and contact information, including your date of birth might be excessive. A potential employer will ask for your date of birth on an employment application form.

Padding your resume

It's a popular notion that everyone embellishes his or her resume to some extent. Yes, that statement probably contains some truth. Now and then we hear news stories about people padding their resumes and having to resign.

Your resume should be truthful. In the information security profession, the nature of our responsibilities and our codes of ethics require a high standard of professional integrity. More than in many other professions, we should not even stretch the truth in our resume or in any other written statements about ourselves. Not even a little bit.

✔ **References:** Usually, you supply references in a separate document.

✔ **Opinion:** Your opinion of an employer, good or bad, is best left off a resume.

✔ **Work samples:** Including samples of your work could make your resume too long and might violate confidentiality agreements.

Examples of Winning Resumes

This section provides a complete chronological resume, shown in Figure 12-8, and a complete functional resume, shown in Figure 12-9. Both resumes describe the same fictitious individual whose background makes each type of resume ideal for that person.

The chronological resume shows a typical progression of work experience and accomplishments, whereas the functional resume portrays skills, accomplishments, and experience unrelated to the positions in which they occurred.

John A. Smith, CISSP, CISA

123 Elm St., Reno, NV 89509   johnasmith@gmail.com   linkedin.com/jasmith

SUMMARY

Security and compliance manager with experience leading SSAE16 and ISO27001 audits seeking a security leadership position in a SaaS company. Part time university instructor and InfraGard board member.

WORK EXPERIENCE

Security Manager. Employer.com, Seattle, Washington, 2010-2015

- Improved external audit results through key process improvements

- Reduced number of vulnerabilities in online web application through vulnerability management process changes

- Developed security awareness program and delivered training to headquarters and branch office employees

Security Analyst. Company.com, Bellevue, Washington, 2005-2009

- Updated internal audit procedures to improve recordkeeping, resulting in reduction of errors and audit findings

- Improved internal audit results three years in a row

- President's Club Award, 2008 and 2009

System Administrator. Workplace.com, Bellevue, Washington, 2002-2005

- Responsible for management of production and test servers for company business applications, external websites, and internal services

- Incorporated hardening guidelines from Center for Internet Security, resulting in improved results in vulnerability scans

- Developed written procedures for the creation and management of virtual machines

- New Employee of the Year, 2002

Figure 12-8:
Chronological resume example.

EDUCATION

BS Computer Science. University of Washington, Seattle. GPA 3.25.

MS Information Assurance, University of Washington, Seattle. GPA 3.9

TRAINING

Numerous courses in TCP/IP, network architecture, network routing, firewall configuration, systems administration, and database administration from organizations including SANS, Usenix, and Cisco.

SKILLS

Programming Languages: C, C#, C++, Java, PHP, Ruby on Rails

Databases: MS-SQL, MySQL, Oracle 11i

Operating Systems: Windows 7/8, Ubuntu, RHEL

Networking: TCP/IP v4/v6, routing, Cisco firewalls, Tipping Point IPS

INDUSTRY ASSOCIATIONS

InfraGard, 1998-2015. Board Member, 2010-2013.

$(ISC)^2$, 2000-2015.

ISACA, 2002-2015. Contributor to CRISC exam, 2014.

REFERENCES, SALARY HISTORY

References and salary history are available upon request.

Figure 12-8
(continued)

John A. Smith, CISSP, CISA

123 Elm St., Reno, NV 89509   johnasmith@gmail.com   linkedin.com/jasmith

SUMMARY

Security and compliance manager with experience leading SSAE16 and ISO27001 audits seeking a security leadership position in a SaaS company. Part time university instructor and InfraGard board member.

EDUCATION

BS Computer Science. University of Washington, Seattle. GPA 3.25.

MS Information Assurance, University of Washington, Seattle. GPA 3.9

AWARDS

- President's Club Award, 2008 and 2009

- New Employee of the Year, 2002

TRAINING

Numerous courses in TCP/IP, network architecture, network routing, firewall configuration, systems administration, and database administration from organizations including SANS, Usenix, and Cisco.

Figure 12-9:
Functional
resume
example.

SKILLS

Business: creation of procedural documentation, monthly executive reports, business process improvements

Programming Languages: C, C#, C++, Java, PHP, Ruby on Rails

Databases: MS-SQL, MySQL, Oracle 11i

Operating Systems: Windows 7/8, Ubuntu, RHEL

Networking: TCP/IP v4/v6, routing, Cisco firewalls, Tipping Point IPS

Security: system hardening, security procedures development

WORK EXPERIENCE

Security Manager. Employer.com, Seattle, Washington, 2010-2015

Independent consultant, Bellevue, Washington, 2007-2010

Security Analyst. Company.com, Bellevue, Washington, 2005-2007

Office Manager, City Realty, Kennewick, Washington, 2003-2005

System Administrator. Workplace.com, Bellevue, Washington, 1998-2002

INDUSTRY ASSOCIATIONS

InfraGard, 1998-2015. Board Member, 2010-2013.

(ISC)^2, 2006-2015.

ISACA, 2007-2015. Contributor to CRISC exam, 2014.

REFERENCES, SALARY HISTORY

Figure 12-9
(continued)

References and salary history are available upon request.

Chapter 13

Getting Attention with Your Cover Letter

In This Chapter

▶ Understanding the purpose of a cover letter

▶ Learning the key elements of a cover letter

▶ Making your cover letter effective in today's digital HR systems

Your cover letter is (probably) the first thing the hiring manager is going to see about you, so you want to make a good first impression.

A great deal of rumor, myth, and legend exists about what makes a good resume and how to construct one to maximize your success in getting an information security job. For some reason, the cover letter is often ignored in this process. Effective cover letters present the link between the job's requirements and your background and aspirations. Although a resume states what you have done, the cover letter cuts to the chase and addresses why you are the right person for the job.

The cover letter has the following logic: "Here is what you said you want. Here is what I have done. Here is how it relates. Here's my number, so call me, maybe." (Apologies to Carly Rae Jepsen.)

The goal is to get the cover letter and resume into the hands of the hiring manager. In a perfect world, your resume would tell the screener in HR, be it an internal or external recruiter or the applicant-tracking system, how good a fit you are. In the real world, the cover letter is your opportunity to spell it out for them.

Cover Letter Scenarios

At the highest conceptual level, your resume is fixed and you use the cover letter to express your interest to explain why you should be considered. In reality, with digital resumes, you can customize, or at least tune, your resume for each job opportunity. However, it is generally more expedient and effective to use the cover letter to answer the questions of how and why you are a fit.

You would write a cover letter in response to the following four scenarios:

- ✔ **Response to a job posting:** You see a job description that interests you in the careers section of a company website or on a job board, such as monster.com or indeed.com.

- ✔ **Follow-up letter of introduction:** Let's say your friend has a friend who needs someone with your skills and asks to see your resume. When you respond to this request, you had better include a cover letter that at least reminds the reader why you've sent your resume. A resume without context is likely to end up in the bit bucket.

- ✔ **Letter to a recruiter:** Recruiters offer an invaluable service in connecting employers with prescreened candidates. The goal of this cover letter is to get you from the unscreened category to the prescreened category.

- ✔ **Generic application:** You can send your resume to a company to keep on file in case they have a need for someone like you.

The cover letter differs for each scenario. In general, you'll spend most of your time writing cover letters in response to job postings. However, follow-up letters of introduction are more effective. Figure 13-1 shows the source of new jobs of all types, not specifically information security jobs.

This figure implies that you should focus on personal networking to get a job in information security. However, responses to job postings are something you can work on while you wait to hear back from your contacts. The next sections explore ways to make your responses to job postings as effective as possible.

For more about creating and improving your brand, see Chapter 11. Find out how to create a winning resume in Chapter 12.

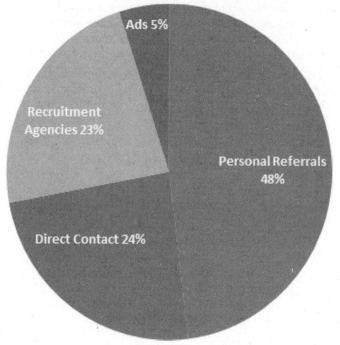

Figure 13-1:
The sources
of new jobs.

Source: U.S. Department of Labor

Essential Elements of the Cover Letter

Regardless of the scenario described in the preceding section, all cover letters have the following common elements:

- ✔ **Greeting:** Say "hello" in some manner.

- ✔ **Reason for the cover letter:** Before you start writing about how good a fit you are, give the reader some context. The reader of your cover letter doesn't necessarily know why he or she is reading it. Clarify who you are and the job you're seeking.

- ✔ **Logic of how you fit:** In this element, which is the body of the letter, you tie their needs to your skills and experience, point by point. Don't go down the list of every skill or experience stated in the job posting. Choose the two to four most critical requirements and focus a paragraph, maybe two, on those. You don't want a cover letter to be too long.

✔ **Call to action:** Now that you've laid out your logic, tell them what to do. Cover letters without a call to action, even one as minimal as asking for a return call, leave the reader feeling flat. The letter leaves the impression that you are interested only in talking about yourself.

✔ **Closing:** At this point, your goal is to get an interview. In the closing, sound excited and mention that you are looking forward to hearing from them.

The traditional cover letter

Readers of a certain age will recall a formal process associated with sending prospective employers a cover letter and resume. You'd take the draft of your resume to a printer, who would print your order of 250 to 500 copies (without typos, you hoped).

Next, you'd write your cover letter to respond to a particular job or one of the other scenarios described previously. If you were cool, your resume, cover letter, and envelope would use the same high rag content paper, preferably ecru. Off they would go in the mailbox to the intended recipient. A sample cover letter of this type is shown in Figure 13-2.

Sending a traditional cover letter by post is now as outmoded as rotary phones and CRT monitors. Their use says that the user is stuck in the old ways.

Cover letters with applicant-tracking systems

These days, the vast majority of job posting ads are on the Internet. Applying to them involves creating an identity on the applicant-tracking system of the hiring company (or the recruiter). After you create a user name (often your email address) and establish a password, the system will typically import your resume to populate what it can.

It would be convenient if applicant-tracking system could perfectly populate all routine data fields from a resume. But often, it does not. You as the job seeker get to spend your time both uploading your resume and then copying much of the same information into the fields. Although there are some efforts to improve this process, it is still painfully tedious.

Errors in cover letters are unacceptable.

William D. Boyce
1325 Walnut Hill Ln
Ottawa, IL 89049

March 16, 2015

Mr. John Hireme
Initec Widgets
742 Evergreen Terrace
Arlen, TX 90120

Dear John,

I have read your posting for the position of security analyst at Initec Widgets. Based upon your description, I have the skills and experience that you are seeking. I have seven years of security analyst experience at a number of leading firms.

I have learned many of the basic skills of security operations and security management while at the Bre-X Mining Corporation. I later applied and refined my skills at the sub-prime mortgage unit of the Washington Mutual Bank of Seattle, as well as the Bernard L. Madoff Investment Securities, LLC in New York.

Your job description calls for a security professional with extensive experience in risk analysis and risk management. I am proud to say that my work has stood up to intense scrutiny and has not been found lacking.

I have attached my resume to more fully describe my background. I would like to explore your needs for this role at your convenience.

Sincerely,

William D. Boyce

Figure 13-2:
A formal
cover letter.

William D. Boyce
Encl.: Resume for William D Boyce

Many companies enable you to upload or copy-and-paste a cover letter. The image is Figure 13-3 is a typical example.

The following sections offer helpful guidelines when writing a cover letter.

Greeting

A formal greeting is "Dear Sir or Madam" or "To whom it may concern." Some may find this type of greeting formal or stilted. With all due affection, get over it, unless you know that the company you're applying to would be put off with formality. A more casual option is "Greetings" or "Hello." You might be able to get away with "Hey there" if you're applying to a company stuck in 1960s counterculture. Otherwise, err on the side of formality.

Reason for the cover letter

The first sentences of the body of the cover letter give the reader some context as to why you're contacting them. Do not assume that the reason is readily apparent. Be helpful and tell the hiring manager which job you are seeking.

A formal start might look like this: "I have read your posting about the position of Security Analyst at Hughes Aircraft Company. Based on your job description for this role, I have the skills and experience that you are seeking."

* State	Washington ▼
County	
	Add More (Addresses)
(Optional) Desired Salary	USD $ ▼ 80000 Yr. ▼
* How did you initially hear about this job opportunity? (please choose one from the drop down list)	Online Job Board ▼
*Please specify	Indeed.com ▼

Figure 13-3:
A cover letter form in a typical applicant-tracking system.

(Optional) Copy/paste a cover letter here:

I have read your posting for the position of security analyst at Initec Widgets. Based upon your description, I have the skills and experience that you are seeking. I have seven years of security analyst experience at a number of leading firms.

I have learned many of the basic skills of security operations and security management while at the Bre-X Mining Corporation. I later applied and refined my skills at the sub-prime mortgage unit of the Washington Mutual Bank of Seattle, as well as the Bernard L. Madoff Investment Securities, LLC in

Finish Later   Submit My Profile

Adding the job number in this introduction is always appreciated and sends a signal that you know what you are doing and are organized. Managers want to hire people who are more organized than they.

Again, don't worry if the introduction sounds formal. You can restructure it to fit your own voice, but don't delete any information.

In your cover letter, don't include phrases like "as you can see from my resume."

Logic of how you fit

Next, explain from the company's perspective why your skills and experience match what they need. These paragraphs need to be *short and compelling*, ideally highlighting the most relevant aspects of your background.

So how do you know what is compelling? You don't. The best you can do is make inferences from the job description, and hope you get it right.

In any case, you need to tie your background to their needs. For example, if one of the first bullets in the job description refers to experience in risk analysis, by all means, talk about your experience in risk analysis.

A typical paragraph may begin with "The job description emphasizes experience in risk analysis. While a security analyst at Target Stores, I developed the risk analysis process and provided ongoing reports to management on risk-related issues."

Unsuccessful cover letters share these characteristics:

- ✔ **Exclusive focus on what you have done:** Tie your experience to the requirements in the job description. For example, having a great education is not enough; you must state how your education applies to the job.

- ✔ **Hubris:** If you give the impression that you are the best candidate in the entire world, the recruiter will think your ego is far too large for the organization.

- ✔ **Poor grammar:** Errors in the cover letter are showstoppers for many companies. If in doubt, ask someone to read your cover letter before you click Submit. Automated spell checking and grammar checking are not enough to catch every error.

Recognize that you must have experiences that relate in some way to the job. If not, applying is a waste of your time.

Many of these fields have a spell checker. Do not rely on spell checkers. Write your cover letter using your computer's word processor and save it along with the job description in a file. In this way, you are more likely to catch typos, which can kill an opportunity, and you'll have a copy of your cover letter if you get the interview.

Call to action

When applying to a job through an applicant-tracking system, about the only thing you can write for your call to action is "I look forward to hearing from you about this opportunity." This one sentence communicates that you want something to happen and sends the message that you are a doer.

Closing

End your cover letter as you would if it were a hard copy. Write "Sincerely," or "Sincerely yours," and then put your name below it. Done.

When you have your letter prepared, copy and paste it into the cover letter box or upload it to the applicant-tracking system.

Your cover letter (as well as your resume) will be digitally uploaded, and the applicant-tracking system will search it using keywords. It is critically important that a search on relevant keywords will show multiple hits for your cover letter and resume.

As mentioned, most companies allow you to enter a cover letter. Some notable exceptions are Microsoft, Amazon.com, and Verizon. These organizations believe that they can discern what they need strictly from your resume. This approach saves applicants time and encourages them to submit many applications, without much discernment as to whether there is a good fit.

Persistence

Paula Abdul, now a famous celebrity, got her start as a cheerleader for the Los Angeles Lakers, but she was not immediately selected for the squad. In an interview with Arsenio Hall, miss Abdul confessed that she was cut. She reregistered, and tried out again. Again she was in a group that was cut, but she got in line with the group that was not. Then she was selected and started her career.

The message here is persistence. Do not give up on a position until they send you a letter stating that you are no longer under consideration. Until you get that letter, feel free to keep on trying for similar jobs at that company or the same job if the position posting is updated. The folks in HR and hiring managers might change their mind. Even if the job description stays the same, they may realize that they were too selective. You may just have the skills that they now realize they need.

Cover letters for referrals and recruiters

When you send a cover letter to a referral or a recruiter, compose it in an email message. However, the cover letter is not an email to an old friend. You should come across as a professional. The elements of the cover letter are the same, but the content is adjusted to suit the context.

Greeting

The good news is that you have the person's name. Use it. In an email message, it is okay to write "Dear Miles" or just "Miles." (Assuming the person's name is Miles. Otherwise, it would be awkward.) Email is a casual medium, so there is no need to write, say, "Mr. Raymond."

Reason for the cover letter

When you state the reason for the email, just lay it out there. "I was told by our mutual friend, Maya Randall, that you are seeking a security analyst and that you requested that I send my resume." Similarly, a recruiter will want to know why you are sending the email. "I understand that you recruit security professionals for organizations in which I am interested" is sufficient.

Logic of how you fit

When you describe the logic of how your skills fit the requirements, be short and sweet. For example, "I have recently completed my Certified Information Systems Security Professional (CISSP), as Maya may have mentioned. I am now seeking the opportunity to use this certification at a firm such as yours." For recruiters, you would write, "I have recently completed my Certified Information Systems Security Professional (CISSP). I understand that placing information security professionals like myself is your area of expertise."

Call to action

Because you know the person's name and contact information, you have the opportunity to follow up. Your call to action should be polite and should give the person a chance to contact you. For example, you might write, "I have attached my resume to more fully describe my background. Please let me know if you have any questions. I will follow up with you in a week."

You need to be precise in your follow-ups. If you say you will follow up in a week, follow up in a week — not sooner, not later.

Closing

In the closing, write "Sincerely," on one line and your full name on the next. Some people omit the closing. This may be appropriate in correspondence with people you know, but it does not work here.

Generic replies to cover letters

When you get a response from a company that has reviewed your resume and cover letter but is not interested, they reassure you that they will keep your resume on file should another opportunity that better matches your background becomes available. It could happen. And the Cubs could win the World Series.

Although the chances that the employer will contact you in the future are slim, they are better than if you do nothing.

Your resume and cover letter will go into the applicant-tracking system and be available should the hiring manager need someone with your qualifications. This aspect of an applicant-tracking system works best when you have a unique skill.

Chapter 14

The Interview: Bringing Your Resume to Life

*T*he words on your resume and in your correspondence have taken you this far. The job interview is your opportunity to present your case on why you are the best candidate for the job.

At the same time, job interviews can be stressful. Regardless of whether you are introverted or extroverted, being on your A game for an extended period can take its toll. You can reduce your stress by being prepared.

The goal of this chapter is to give you the information you need to be as prepared as possible for an interview. You explore the purpose of the job interview, the types of interview questions you might face, and ways to appear as confident as possible. You also find out what *you* should get out of the interview so you can determine whether the job is right for you.

Knowing Why Interviews Are Important

First things first. You are not an interchangeable cog in a wheel. Similarly, the job responsibilities of a security analyst differ depending on whether you work at the National Security Agency, a local school district, a white shoe law firm, or a dot.com start-up. The technology is related, but the temperament of the users, the topology of the offices, the security requirements, and the corporate culture differ. All these factors contribute to the issue of whether a job is a good fit in terms of your technical competence and personality.

Your training, experiences, skills, flaws, ambitions, blind spots, strengths, and weaknesses define you. Your prospective employers also have training, experiences, skills, flaws, ambitions, blind spots, strengths, and weaknesses that define them. The interview is a chance to see whether the job and the company are a good fit for you and whether you are a good fit for them. Can we all just get along?

Being Prepared for the Interview

Preparation is critical for a successful interview. Sun Tzu, the author of the definitive book on military strategy and tactics, said, "Every battle is won before it's ever fought." The implication is that the side that is best prepared wins a battle.

Your goal is to get a job offer, so you must be as prepared as possible. You need to do a number of things to succeed: be prepared psychologically, know the prospective employer's environment, make a great first impression, and know what to say and what to ask.

Preparing yourself psychologically

The interview process is necessary but not natural. To be successful, it helps to put yourself in the right frame of mind:

- ✔ **Be on time.** Getting there right on time creates stress, which you do not need, so arrive five to ten minutes early. If you arrive more than 15 minutes early, just sit in your car or wait outside until you're within 15 minutes of your scheduled interview.

- ✔ **Allow them to take control.** If you are a take-charge kind of person, let that go. You are on their turf now, so do as you're told. Sit and go where they take you — with a smile on your face.

- ✔ **Turn off your phone.** Really. Do it. If it so much as vibrates, it can be interpreted as disrespectful to the interviewer. Do whatever you need to do to ensure that you give your interviewers your undivided attention.

- ✔ **Take notes.** Your memory is never as good as you think, in case you've forgotten. Bring a pad of paper. Ask your interviewers if it's okay to take notes. If it is, write their name and some highlights. This information will come in handy when you write thank-you notes. It may seem ironic to take notes on a pad of paper during an interview for a technology job, but using your computer, tablet, or smartphone instead would be distracting.

Investigating the corporate culture

Before the interview, investigate the company. Employers like to see interviewees who have done their homework and are serious about this opportunity. A lack of basic understanding of what the company does is a big red flag for many managers. Do not fall into the trap that information security is a support function so knowing the company's business is not that important. It is important to the management team who might want to hire you.

So how do you find out about the company? Following are your primary options:

- ✔ **Read the company's website.** Read the website thoroughly. Look at other jobs they are advertising. You can learn more about the organization by reading its other open position descriptions. You can learn about the technologies in play, internal initiatives, and maybe a thing or two about new products or services they're working on. Become familiar with their solutions and their customers. Know their founders and their board members.

- ✔ **Find a contact at the target company via LinkedIn.** If you're not already on LinkedIn, put down this book right now and sign up. Come back to this page when you are finished and have linked with at least a few of your work friends. Not having a LinkedIn account when you are job hunting is like not being on a social media site when you are an adolescent and want to have social contacts. For more on LinkedIn, see Chapter 11.

  After you have a stable of contacts, you can enter the name of the target company and see how well you are connected. When you find a contact inside your target company, ask them if you can meet or at least talk on the phone. I have never found a company where I learn more from the website than talking to an employee for five minutes.

- ✔ **Find a contact at the target company via alumni networks.** The same logic as described in the preceding point applies to using your alumni network. Talk to someone within the company. Only a stick-in-the-mud will ignore a request for a brief call.

- ✔ **Look up reviews on Glassdoor.com.** If you can't find a contact, look at company reviews on Glassdoor.com. After you log in, you can see how other employees rate your prospective employer. As long as you understand that this site tends to be over-represented with disgruntled former employees, you can find some interesting perspectives on what working at this firm is like.

✔ **Study the company financials.** If the target firm is publicly traded, check its profitability. If you have no idea what you are looking for, read some of the financial expert analyses of the firm. Your main concern is to know whether this position is open because they are growing like gangbusters and need help, or they are a sinking ship and the staff is leaving in droves.

✔ **Poke around on the Internet.** A good ol' Internet search will uncover some interesting tidbits of information. Give it a try. You have nothing to lose!

Setting up for the first impression

Depending on the expert, it takes between one-tenth of a second and seven seconds for a person to develop a first impression. Regardless of whether this is fair or not, it is human nature.

Remember two facts. One, that impression may be positive. In a moment, you learn about some ways to make a good impression (feel free to use these tips in other situations).

Two, you may never know what the interviewer is seeking. For example, in many cases, facial tattoos are problematic. However, when I worked with the hiring manager of a call center, he told me that as long as the candidate was polite on the phone and otherwise technically competent, facial ink was a plus. Too many employees from this call center were learning their skills and then leaving to work in retail. There's nothing like a pentagram tattoo on the forehead to make for a loyal call center employee.

Be yourself. It does everyone a disservice if you pretend to be someone you are not. That said, you can be yourself and help your chances of creating a good first impression as follows:

✔ **Wear clothes that are one step nicer than is worn in the office.** So how do you know what they wear in the office? Unless you know that the interviewer wants you to dress business casual or even casual, you should wear a dark conservative suit, a white shirt (and for men, a tie). In most cases, it doesn't hurt to be overdressed, but being underdressed can be devastating.

✔ **Don't smell.** Don't smell either good *or* bad. You don't want to hit the interviewer with too much of your best perfume or cologne or the onions from your Big Mac. Good grooming is also essential.

✔ **Show good posture.** Good posture conveys confidence. Don't sit back in your seat. Sit toward the front edge of your chair with your back tall and straight.

✔ **Make eye contact and smile.** Making eye contact is important in the majority of North America businesses, and a smile conveys confidence. Work on these skills to avoid making the interviewer feel awkward. However, these gestures can be a significant challenge to someone from a different culture. Native Americans, Latin Americans, and Asians, for example, may consider it rude to look someone directly in the eyes, particularly when introduced to a person in a superior position. Know with whom you are interviewing.

The basic strategy is to make the interviewers feel at ease so that they can focus on your qualifications, not the spinach stuck in your teeth.

Most hiring managers are well trained in Equal Opportunity rules. If you are a member of a protected minority, do not make this an issue. Most companies actively want underrepresented minorities. Ideally, they want to give a person a chance, but some may only want to enhance their status with the bosses who are seeking to comply with nondiscrimination laws. Whatever the underlying cause, this requirement works best when you, the candidate, come across as competent in your area of expertise and not as a militant promoting minority rights. Just be a good team player.

If, in spite of training the interviewing managers received, you are openly discriminated against, immediately document the offence. Relay your experience of discrimination to the HR department. If you're certain that you've been asked an illegal question about your protected status, you probably don't want to work in the organization anyway.

Preparing to say what interviewers want to hear

Beyond all the preparation, ultimately the interview will determine whether you have the technical chops to perform the job and the personal skills to mesh with the company's culture. They want to find out if you are a better blend of technical skills and temperament than the other folks they are interviewing.

It costs an organization a lot of time and effort to fire a person, so companies want to make sure that they are making the right decision when they bring you on in the first place.

Regardless of the interview style, you can improve your chances of getting an offer by doing the following:

- **Bring several hardcopies of your resume.** If your interviewer does not have a copy (or, more likely, did not have time to read your resume before interviewing you), you can offer a hardcopy. It is not a total waste of your time if the interviewer does not have a resume on which to take notes, but it is close. A softcopy doesn't work as well in the interview environment.

- **Bring a hardcopy of the job description.** This copy is for your reference during the interview. It is bad form for you to have your laptop open during an interview.

- **Directly connect what is in the job description to the skills found on your resume.** Citing examples of work experience and training in comparison to the words in the job posting makes a powerful case. Before the interview, put together a cheat sheet with the words in the job description on your left and your qualification on the right. The conversation will flow better as you use your cheat sheet to link their requirements to your experience.

- **Answer in the positive.** If they ask if you have done something you have not done, respond with a related effort. For example, if they ask, "Have you performed an organization-wide risk assessment?" you might say "I have performed risk analyses on our subsidiary companies and larger suppliers." This would be factually correct and communicate that you are ready for the larger task. This advice takes some work, and you have to be on your toes to be a good spin-doctor.

- **Work your soft skills into the conversation.** Add unsolicited details about how you anticipated problems and took appropriate action to help your employer avoid or solve them. Employers want to hire employees who prevent problems. They will hire a lower skilled employee who gets along well with people and can keep the distractions down. You win if you bring these up first.

- **Discuss how you can add value to the company.** A common frustration managers have is that employees think narrowly about doing their job and don't think about how their job makes the company successful. Working in your past value contributions during the conversation will demonstrate an understanding of your job in the larger context.

Value is a key word in today's business world. You should always speak of your contributions in terms of value.

Following are some things that you should *not* to do during an interview:

- **Speak negatively about previous or current employers.** You may work at the worst company in the world and for the worst boss in the universe. You may be desperate to get out of your current situation. Resist the temptation to say anything bad. This is an interview, not a therapy session. Do whatever it takes to stay positive. Talk about how you have grown and are now seeking greater challenges.

- **Reveal confidential information**. During the interview, never divulge details about your current company that could be considered confidential. If they want to obtain the experience that their competitor has paid for, let them make you an offer. Even after you are hired, it is poor form to traffic in confidential information. Your new company may appreciate it, but they will also know that you lack professional integrity.

- **Misrepresent your skills, work history, training, or education.** You will be found out, and being found out is cause for immediate dismissal in all 50 states and the District of Columbia. If you get through the interview process and are hired under false pretenses, you will get to keep your paycheck during the two weeks in which they figure out the truth. You will then need to spend the rest of your career explaining why you were employed for such a short time. It's just not worth it.

- **Talk too long.** Perhaps you enjoy interviews. You may find it fun to have the undivided attention of someone so you can talk about yourself. Avoid this trap.

Preparing to hear what you want to hear

As mentioned, the interview process is an excellent time to find out if this company is going to give you the fulfillment you are seeking. Assuming you are meeting multiple managers and prospective coworkers, you have the opportunity to find out if this company will give you the professional experience that moves you forward in life as well as the work/life balance that you need at this point in your journey.

Chapter 19 offers ten questions you can ask to find out whether this company will be a good fit for you. The assumption in these questions is that you know what you want beyond a big fat paycheck.

Consulting firms and startups are known for being demanding on your schedule. More established firms, particularly ones in stable industries, do have their moments when all hands must be on deck, but these late-night scenarios are few and far between. It is best to consider where you want trade-offs.

In addition, Part III discusses various types of organizations and their demands on your work-life balance.

Types of Interviews and Tips for Each

In general, you won't know what kind of interview you are going to experience. Beyond the start time, perhaps the end time, and directions to the facility, you will typically have no idea if you are going to one long interview or a series of short interviews. You won't know whether you are interviewing with one person at a time, or a panel of interviewers. You won't know if the focus will be on technical skills or other relevant characteristics. You will need to be prepared for any of these scenarios and roll with the punches as the day goes on. If you have a friendly contact on the inside, he or she may be able to provide you with insight.

The following are the most common forms of interviews you'll encounter.

Open-ended interview

An open-ended interview is the simplest and most common type of interview. The interviewer comes in and asks you to be taken through your work history. It is usually in your discretion whether you go from your earliest education to present day or the other way around. In either case, you should practice describing your professional journey. (I find it logical to start at the beginning.) Find a sympathetic friend or relative and practice before your first interview.

Be careful. If the interviewer asks for a summary of your job history, give them a brief summary. Let the interviewer ask for more details. Being long-winded on your first interview question is a fatal mistake!

The painful reality is that the interviewer may not have read your resume. Although this might seem discouraging, it is an opportunity because you can take the interviewer through your resume and highlight the technical and leadership areas that relate to the job description.

You can also let the interviewer see how you have grown professionally. By the end of the day, you may have repeated this story four or five times. Just remember that this is a new story for each person you meet. It is okay to enthusiastically emphasize the same points.

It will help to have some practice interviews. Few are smooth talkers the first time we talk about a subject, even if the subject is ourselves. Work with someone who does interview coaching professionally so you can get feedback. College and technical schools where you are an alumnus or have some affiliation often offer interview-coaching service. Your state's department of employment often offers interview-coaching service to unemployed citizens.

Technical interview

The technical interview format tests your technical skills. Usually, a technical professional gives you a test consisting of true/false questions, multiple choice, open-answer questions, or hands-on problem solving. The questions help the company determine whether you can perform the tasks required in the position.

Technical interviews tend to go one of four ways. One, the interview is straightforward and you pass with no problem. Two, you are familiar with the questions but are a little rusty. Three, the questions are unfamiliar, and you come to realize that you don't have the skills that they are seeking. Four, the questions have nothing to with the job as described.

The first scenario, or course, is the ideal. The second scenario is under your control but only before interview day. If you have any indication that there will be a technical interview, brush up on your certifications. How deeply you dive into refreshing depends on your motivation and available time. The trade-off is that you have the chance to refresh your memory with manuals and other resources when you have the job. This is the challenge with technical interviews. As with so many other things in interviews, you can't anticipate every question in every challenge you face. Being as prepared as possible is your only approach.

What if you find yourself in the third situation, where the questions look legitimate but you don't have a clue where to start? This embarrassing situation will be made worse if you do not speak up to say that there must have been some misunderstanding about your qualifications. It takes courage to admit that you are not qualified, but your honesty may pay dividends later.

In the last situation, when you are asked questions that are not relevant for the job as described, perhaps the left hand in this company doesn't know what the right hand is asking. The only saving grace in the situation is that the hiring process probably involves nontechnical interviews. That would be your opportunity to clarify that you are eager to take a technical test closer suited to the kind of work that you expect to be doing. It is risky, but the only thing you can do to save this opportunity.

Another more recent version of the technical interview involves white boarding a technical challenge. The interviewer might present a scenario and then draw something on the whiteboard. You are then asked to add details and explain your logic. Or the interviewer might verbally describe a problem and ask you to whiteboard the problem and its solution.

Chances are, the interviewer is describing a current or recent issue, or something memorable from the past. Remember, this is an interview, so you need to treat the problem as theoretical. It is not a good idea to ask whether this is an actual problem that the business is facing right now.

If you are venturing into uncharted territory, don't be afraid to say so, but keep talking through the problem and do the best you can. Unless the interviewer tells you, you might not know whether the topic you've been asked to discuss is part of your job or something more advanced that you would not be expected to work on right away.

Behavioral interview

A recent trend in interviewing circles is to make the interview process more meaningful than one where the candidate repeatedly reviews his or her resume for a series of interviewers. In behavioral interviews, HR asks each interviewer to ask candidates about how they handled a situation or two.

At least in theory, HR collects the notes from the interviewers and shares them with the team. You can tell that this is the kind of interview when you get asked a questions that starts "Describe a situation where you." For example, describe a situation where you

- Had a difficult coworker and how you handled it
- Encountered a technical obstacle and how you overcame it.
- Set your sights too high
- Set your sights too low
- Were able to use persuasion to convince someone to see things your way
- Used good judgment and logic when solving a problem
- Had too many things to do and were required to prioritize your tasks
- Set a goal and were able to meet or exceed it
- Had to use your presentation skills to influence someone's opinion
- Had to go above and beyond the call of duty to get a job done

> ✔ Showed initiative and took the lead
>
> ✔ Used your fact-finding skills to solve a problem
>
> ✔ Anticipated potential problems and developed preventive measures
>
> ✔ Had to discipline or terminate an employee

You should have ready answers to these questions even if you do not have a behavioral interview. If you dig back through your experiences, you'll probably come up with good answers even if they do not relate to a work situation. Your answers will show that you are competent and can think on your own.

Panel interview

Panel interviews are arguably more efficient than single interviews because you don't have to repeat yourself multiple times covering the same background and qualifications. In this scenario, you walk into a room with a group of interviewers. Usually the more senior person will lead the questions, but everyone gets to ask questions and form their own impressions.

Many people find panel interviews to be more stressful than the other interview types. If you fit this description, it might help to consider that you need to be truly on for only one interview.

Confrontational interview

In a confrontational interview, the interviewer comes in angry and challenges every statement you make. The interviewer challenges you when you are

---

How deep is your knowledge?

I was interviewed for a consulting job in a small company. One of the company partners interviewed me and asked technical question after technical question. I couldn't answer many of them, and I politely told him so each time. I figured I was not going to get the job. But at the end of the interview, he said, "I knew you wouldn't be able to answer every question.

I ask hard questions to see how people respond to difficult situations, and because I want to know just how deep your knowledge goes."

I was instantly relieved (and it probably showed), and I got the job!

Peter H. Gregory, Seattle

Videoconferencing interviews

Many companies now perform videoconferencing interviews, for a variety of reasons. With more of the workforce working out of their homes, some of the people who may be interviewing you may not live in the city where the company is located. Or perhaps you are interviewing for a national company with people scattered all over. You might also be interviewing for a job in a city where you are considering relocating.

If you are in a videoconferencing interview (for example, Skype with video), you need to be prepared:

✔ Find a quiet place free of distracting sights or sounds.

✔ Make sure your Internet connection is reliable and fast enough for high-quality video and audio.

✔ Check what the interviewer will see behind you.

✔ Check that the lighting on your face and background results in a good image.

✔ Test your technology with a friend to make sure your hardware and software work properly. Nothing is worse than experiencing technical problems during a video interview.

The rules for making a good first impression during in-person interviews apply also to videoconferencing interviews.

right, when you are wrong, and when you voice an opinion. You may as well be a new recruit for the Marine Corps during your first week on Parris Island.

Thankfully, this kind of interview has gone out of vogue. Perhaps this interview technique weeds out candidates who would struggle under the stressful situation of working at the company. If you come across this kind of interview technique, take it with a grain of salt and try your best not to become flustered.

Your Turn to Ask Questions

In almost every interview, the interviewer will ask if you have any questions. Like other aspects of the interview, you need to prepare. Blurting out, "How do you like working here?" is not a good first response. This shallow question will almost always get a positive answer, whether the interviewer likes the job or not.

Before your interviews, write down some questions based on your research on the company or when reading other job descriptions or reviews from Glassdoor.com. Some examples follow:

✔ Ask whether the open position is new, or would you be replacing someone who left the company? (Don't pry too much on the reason your predecessor left.)

✔ Ask questions about management above the hiring manager.

✔ Ask about current or upcoming projects that you may be a part of.

✔ Ask a follow-up question on a topic discussed in this interview or a prior interview.

✔ Ask about recent events described in the company's press releases.

If the company has had a security breach, be careful. It would be okay to acknowledge the breach and commiserate with them, but don't ask for details. You don't work there — yet.

Chapter 19 contains more ideas for questions you can ask in your interview.

Focusing on the Goal

To get an interview, at least someone in the company has read your resume and perhaps done a phone screen. You have followed the guidelines, aced the technical questions, and assured them that you are cool (or at least cool enough for this role). Now you want to end the interview with a strong close.

If you were an interviewer and had two equally qualified candidates, would you hire a person who is eager for the job or one who seems indifferent? The clear answer is that the one with energy and enthusiasm has the advantage. Be that person!

Offering the following information shows that you are ready, without being too pushy:

✔ **Tell them when you could start.** Don't be shy about this. State it as a fact that you would need to give two weeks' notice. Tell them if you need longer because of a project you are completing. In practice, companies struggle to move fast anyway. You will come across as a person who is positive and has integrity — and integrity is highly valued in the information security profession.

✔ **Ask for their contact information.** You want the opportunity to follow up. Ask them if you may follow up if you haven't heard from them in a certain timeframe, depending on when they tell you that you can expect to hear something.

✔ **Mention any special circumstances.** Assuming that things are looking good, tell them now if you have a non-disclosure agreement (NDA) or a non-compete clause. These can usually be managed. Telling them now is better than after you have an offer and they need to rescind it.

Chapter 15

After the Interview

*E*ven after a great interview, your job-hunting tasks aren't over. From writing thank-you notes to negotiating your job offer, in this chapter you look at what you need to do to seal the deal.

Writing a Thank-You Letter

Thank-you letters are one of the easiest — and most overlooked — ways to stand out as a job candidate. Think about it. You've no doubt spent many hours creating your resume, writing cover letters, applying for jobs, and preparing for and going to interviews. What's another ten minutes of your time to write a short note of gratitude? A thank-you note helps the interviewer remember who you are (which is helpful if the interviewer has talked to several candidates over an extended period of time) and could be the icing on the cake that gets you the job!

You thought you were buying "Information Security Jobs For Dummies," not "Business Etiquette For Dummies." Actually, you bought both, because getting and keeping any job requires proper business etiquette. And writing a thank-you note is essential if you want to stand out as a candidate who is interested in working for the new organization.

In the last chapter, I mentioned that you should ask each interviewer for a business card. If you followed my advice, you know the full name, title, email address, and snail-mail address of each interviewer.

If you don't have all this information, check the company's website to glean as much as you can. Then contact the HR department or the recruiter you worked with to provide the rest.

Within 24 hours of your interview, write a thank-you letter to each person. This effort says a lot about who you are, your enthusiasm for the position, and how you would conduct yourself when employed. If nothing else, it sets you apart from the other schlubs who interviewed for this position and did not write a thank-you note.

However, don't write a hastily penned, canned note in the parking lot immediately after your interview. Spend the time to write a professional, meaningful, and personalized letter of gratitude.

Handwritten thank-you notes are a nice touch, but if your penmanship isn't neat and legible, stick with a typed letter or an email.

Thank you notes should be brief — typically no more than two or three *short* paragraphs. As with all written correspondence, use a business letter format and proofread your letter for proper grammar and spelling.

You might start your note with "Thank you for taking the time to meet today. I enjoyed our discussion about the opportunity, particularly the part where we found that we both took our Basic Networking class from Dr. Skolnick! Now that I have met many people from your team, I am even more excited about working at the law firm of Dewey, Cheatham, and Howe."

In addition to expressing appreciation for your interviewer's time and consideration, each thank-you letter should include specific details from the interview and then highlight something in your background that was relevant. (This is another reason why you should take notes in your interviews.) These people may have interviewed dozens of people, and it will help if you can stick out. For example:

- Emphasize specific qualifications or discussion points in which that particular interviewer seemed to show interest.

- If the interviewer asked you a question that you didn't answer as well as you would have liked, use the thank-you letter as an opportunity to refine your answer.

- If you forgot to mention something important during the interview that may help their decision, bring it up.

- Summarize the two or three most important points that you want them to remember about you.

Finally, close your thank-you letter by expressing your continued interest and enthusiasm for the company and the position.

Write a different thank-you note for every person you meet at your interview and address each note by name. Be sure to include the receptionist and any assistants you met at the start of your interview (believe it or not, these are often some of the most important — and overlooked — people in the decision process. Always treat them professionally and courteously).

Following Up

As you wrap up your interview, you should clearly establish when, how, and with whom you should follow up regarding the status of your application (see Chapter 13). Then do it! If you agreed in the interview that you would follow up after one week via email, don't call the interviewer three days later!

When you do follow up, be polite, courteous, and professional. Recognize that hiring decisions are important, so your interviewer will want to get it right. Also, the selection process doesn't always move according to the hiring manager's desired timetable, so if you follow up according to what was agreed in your interview only to be told "we're still evaluating candidates," don't get impatient or press for more information than the organization is prepared to give at that time. Politely thank them, and ask when you should follow up next.

The follow-up is different than the thank-you letter. You write the thank-you letter and send it the day after the interview. You do a follow-up as stated during the interview.

Other Sources of Information about You

In addition to information collected in your application, resume, and interview, employers use other sources of information to help them in the selection process. These include

- ✔ Professional and personal references
- ✔ Past employer verification
- ✔ Criminal background checks
- ✔ Pre-employment tests

✔ Credit checks

✔ Records verification

✔ Social media (such as Facebook, LinkedIn, Twitter, and Pinterest)

You can read more about branding yourself with social media in Chapter 11.

Employers look at social media and networking profiles on Facebook, LinkedIn, and Twitter. Check that the information there is consistent with the information on your resume. Also make sure your social media accounts do not contain inappropriate information or pictures.

Professional and personal references

You should have at least three professional references to list on your employment application. Ideally, your references should be former managers or coworkers who have firsthand knowledge of your work experience. If possible, at least two of your references should be a former manager or supervisor who you worked for directly. However, for legal reasons, many companies have policies that limit the information that current employees can provide about former employees. Your best bet in these cases is to reference a former manager or coworker who is also no longer at the company where you previously worked together.

If you are just starting your career, include the names of one or two professors whose classes you took (and in which you received a good grade). It's best to choose professors whose classes are related to the job you're applying for.

Some applications require references other than former employers or managers! Be sure to read the application instructions carefully and have both professional and personal references ready.

Other sources for references (both professional and personal) include classmates, consultants, or other business associates who may have worked with you closely on a temporary basis (for example, a specific project), and people who have worked with you outside a business setting (for example, in a volunteer activity or a charitable organization). As a last resort, you might include long-time friends who work in the same industry as you and can vouch for your professional knowledge and character.

Never list relatives or casual acquaintances as references.

Before listing references on an application, contact them to ask for specific permission to list them as a reference. If it has been more than a few months since you've spoken to your references, spend some time filling in that reference on what you've been doing in your career and what type of job you are pursuing now. You should also send a copy of your resume to your references so that they can recall some of your specific accomplishments during the reference call. It's also a great opportunity for you to invite your references to pass your resume along to other companies or contacts for a possible job lead!

You should be sending customized resumes to each prospective employer (see Chapter 11), so if you're listing someone as a reference for more than one company, you'll need to send them each of those resumes and make sure they can easily tell which is which.

Prepare a list of references before going to your interview and have several copies available to provide to the interviewer in lieu of listing this information on an application, if appropriate. In fact, prepare your list of references (including contacting your potential references) as early as possible in your job search. For each reference, list his or her name, title, address, phone, and e-mail address, and a brief note about how you know the person and for how long you've known him or her.

Employers are aware that you aren't going to knowingly provide them with bad or weak references. However, reference checks are still valuable to prospective employers because they provide an opportunity to verify the information you've provided during the interview. Also, a good human resources professional will ask open-ended questions that may lead to the revelation of additional nuggets of information about you. Finally, prospective employers don't have to limit their reference checks to the names you provide. A glance at your LinkedIn profile will quickly identify any connections you may have in common. Such a reference could either be a tremendous asset (a prospective employer will trust the information received from this person more than from someone they don't know) or an embarrassing liability (a prospective employer will trust the information received from this person more than from someone they don't know)!

You should have a list of six to eight references. Employers typically only ask for three references, but having additional references available is helpful when

- ✔ A prospective employer has difficulty contacting one of your references and is holding up your job offer because they are required to contact a minimum of three references.

- ✔ An employment application stipulates that previous employers cannot be listed as references.

- ✔ An opportunity exists for you to cherry-pick your references. For example, you discover during your interview that the interviewer knows one of your other references.

Beyond asking for permission to list someone as a reference, you should also contact your references when a reference check is imminent.

Contacting your references after your interview is also a great opportunity to provide feedback about the interview itself. For example, if the interviewer focused on specific areas of interest and character traits, your references might be able to reinforce what you discussed in your interview. However, don't be too specific — you don't want your reference to sound coached.

Perhaps the most important call for you to make to your references is a thank-you call or an appropriate gift after you get the job. Showing gratitude recognizes their part in helping you get your new job and helps ensure their willingness to help again in the future.

Past employer verification

Almost all employers will contact the human resources department of your past employers to verify the information you provide in your application and resume. For legal reasons, many employers are hesitant to provide any more information than whether or not you worked there and your dates of employment. Some will go a step further and may provide salary information, job title, and whether or not you are eligible for rehire (whether you left on good or bad terms). In a few increasingly rare instances, a past employer is forthright in answering any questions your potential future employer may ask.

Despite the limited information that is generally provided by past employers, a prospective employer will do their due diligence and perform these verification checks. Be certain that the information you provide in your application and resume is 100 percent accurate. Even the smallest error or omission (such as mistaking the date you left a job three years earlier by one month) can cost you your next job!

Professional integrity is more important in information security than in other types of work. Don't burn your bridges with any employer or even one person you work with. You never know whether disparaging information about you may find its way to your next prospective employer.

Criminal background checks

Local and national police record checks are inexpensive, and almost all employers routinely request these checks as part of the employment screening process. You'll be required to sign an authorization and provide any other names you may have used in the past as well as your date of birth.

If you have any prior convictions, be sure to disclose this information in your employment application. If appropriate, discuss the circumstances of the conviction with the employer. Some employers automatically disqualify candidates with any type of arrest or conviction. Almost all employers, however, automatically disqualify candidates who fail to disclose this information. A criminal background check will reveal any information you may have omitted from your application.

If you think that an employer might discover something about your past, you may want to run a background check on yourself, to see what information will be revealed. In some states, you are entitled to a copy of your background check (possibly for a fee).

Pre-employment tests

Employers are increasingly using various types of pre-employment tests to create a more complete profile of their job candidates. These tests may be administered at any point in the selection process: before scheduling an interview, during or after an interview, or before an offer is made.

Pre-employment tests may include technical tests to validate your technical knowledge, skills tests to assess your ability to perform certain tasks or functions, and personality tests to determine your fit in the company or team.

You can study for a technical test and practice for a skills test, but you can't prepare for a personality test. You simply need to be honest — technically, there are no wrong answers. If your personality isn't a good fit, you won't be happy working at that company or on that team anyway!

The Myers-Briggs Type Indicator (MBTI) is one of the more popular personality tests that employers use to determine whether a candidate for a particular job would be a good fit. Myers-Briggs has 16 classifications based on different combinations of personality traits: extroverted or introverted, sensitive or intuitive, thinking or feeling, and judging or perceiving, as shown in Table 14-1. You can find out more about the Myers-Briggs test at www.myersbriggs.org/my-mbti-personality-type.

Table 14-1	Myers-Briggs Personality Pairs (or Dichotomies)		
E	**S**	**T**	**J**
Extroverted	Sensing	Thinking	Judging
I	**N**	**F**	**P**
Introverted	Intuitive	Feeling	Perceiving

Credit checks

A credit check may be required for certain leadership positions or in jobs with access to sensitive information (such as customer or financial data). Most companies in the financial industry require a credit check.

You will need to provide authorization for a credit check, as well as your social security number. For the most part, employers are primarily interested in bankruptcies, collections, and foreclosures. You should disclose bankruptcies or foreclosures on your job application (if that information is requested) and be prepared to discuss them in your interview.

In some cases, your credit score may come into consideration as well. If you have concerns about your credit history, discuss those concerns during your interview. A credit score is a number — it doesn't necessarily paint a complete picture of a candidate. A costly divorce or a medical emergency can hurt your credit score, but doesn't (legally) reflect negatively on your suitability for a job.

If you have concerns about your credit history, being honest and forthright is generally the best policy. But be aware that some employers will be uncomfortable discussing these issues with you. For example, it is illegal for an interviewer to ask you about divorces and medical conditions issues. And if you volunteer this information, it can create a legal problem for the interviewer. If you are asked to give authorization for a full credit check, you should ask how that information will be used in the decision process and explain that extenuating circumstances have affected your credit score and you are willing to discuss them if necessary.

Records verification

In some instances, a potential employer may verify your educational and military records, as well as any technical or professional certifications you hold.

An employer can easily verify that you attended a specific college or university, but additional information about your academic record (such as specific grades) is next to impossible to obtain unless the employer requests a copy of your transcript.

Verification of military service usually involves requesting a copy of your DD Form 214, which includes dates of service, rank, awards, wars or campaigns in which you served, and the nature of your discharge (honorable, dishonorable, other than honorable).

Professional and technical certifications can generally be verified online for organizations that manage certifications.

Negotiating the Offer

If you were dreading the interview process, you're in for a real treat now! After successfully impressing your interviewers and passing all their other pre-employment screenings, your reward is the opportunity to negotiate the terms for your new job! Many people rank negotiating as a major phobia somewhere between public speaking and spiders.

However, you're probably better at negotiating than you think. After all, you negotiate with people every day! Whether you're asking for a day off from work, deciding which movie to see with your significant other, or figuring out what to eat for dinner, life is full of negotiations!

Never bring up the subject of compensation during your interview. Always let the interviewer start this discussion. If the interviewer tries to bring the subject up before you've had an adequate opportunity to discuss your qualifications, try to shift the discussion back to what you can offer the company. For example, you might say, "I'd like to know a little more about the company and position before discussing my compensation, so that we both understand the value I can bring to your organization."

Interviewers will sometimes ask your salary requirements on your employment application or during a prescreening telephone interview. The purpose of the question at this time is to quickly eliminate candidates who are too far out of the position's salary range (too high or too low). In these situations, try to shift the question back to the interviewer by asking their range for the position. Or present your salary history and a broad range of your own, while making it clear that you are open to negotiation and would like to learn more about the position and how you can benefit the company before giving a more specific answer.

Approach the negotiation seeking a win-win outcome. Ultimately, you want to be paid what you know you are worth, and your employer wants to compensate you fairly and appropriately for the value you contribute to the organization. Use the following strategies to negotiate your offer successfully:

✔ **Be prepared.** Offers are rarely made in the interview itself, but stranger things have happened. At a minimum, be prepared to discuss your salary requirements in the interview. This will often set the stage for later negotiations. And don't get caught off guard if an offer does come through in the interview! Be ready to hammer out the details if the employer is ready to move forward.

✔ **Do your homework.** Know your market value and do appropriate research. If you're looking at salary surveys, be sure to compare several surveys and use a median salary rather than an average (extremely high and low salaries will skew your results). Try to find surveys that target your job title, city or region, and industry. Also, talk to similar companies in your area (possibly even a few competitors) and to peers in your industry.

✔ **Know what you want and what you need.** Have a realistic salary in mind for what you *want*. This number should be the high end of your range. (If your number is too high, you could be immediately disqualified.) Keep in mind that if you're changing careers, you may have to take a temporary cut from your current salary. Also be careful not to price yourself out of a job (proper research will help you avoid this pitfall). At the low end of your range is the salary you *need* to cover your living expenses, relocation costs (if applicable), and transportation; maintain your desired lifestyle; and be happy! The difference between these two numbers should provide ample room for negotiation (at least $10,000). Make sure the organization knows that you are flexible on compensation.

✔ **Discuss details before numbers.** Get the total compensation package on the table before discussing specific numbers, and then *mentally* adjust your number up or down accordingly. Important factors to consider in the compensation package include

- Health benefits (including eligibility, coverage, and cost of premiums)

- Other insurance (such as life insurance, short-term disability, and long-term disability)

- Retirement plans (including eligibility, options, vesting, and matching contributions)

- Flexible work arrangements (for example, telecommuting options and flex hours or days)

- Vacation and other paid time off (PTO)

- Performance bonuses (based on company, team, and individual performance)

- Performance evaluations and salary reviews (frequency and average rates)

- Cost-of-living adjustments

- Stock options

- Career development opportunities such as continuing education, training, and certifications (including reimbursement, programs, and work schedule flexibility)

- On-site facilities such as cafeterias, daycare, fitness clubs, and medical clinics

- Other tangible benefits (such as company cars, cell phone and Internet reimbursement, and product or service discounts)

✔ If your interviewer wants you to commit to a compensation figure (or range) before you fully understand the benefits, try to negotiate a meeting with a benefits specialist, so that you can get to a final number that will work for you.

✔ **Strengthen your position.** Focus on your qualifications and the benefits you'll bring to the company. Refer to your research about the industry, similar jobs in other companies, the cost of living, and any other factors, so the interviewer will know that you've done your homework and can understand how you objectively came up with your requirement.

✔ **Don't discuss expenses or other sources of income.** Don't try to rationalize your salary requirement by complaining about your student loans, medical bills, car payments, or any other personal issues. Conversely, telling the interviewer about any other sources of income you have will weaken your position.

✔ **Pay attention to the other negotiating party.** Watch for nonverbal cues, such as facial expression, hand or arm gestures, and changes in tone, posture, or demeanor. Don't let the negotiation become adversarial. Know when the negotiation is over and it's time to put forth your final offer or (figuratively) walk away.

It is far better to negotiate in person than over the telephone or by letter or email. If you receive an offer by phone, letter, or email and the terms aren't what you had hoped for, try to schedule a meeting to discuss the offer in person.

If your compensation needs are higher than the employer's range, you may be able to make it work for you in other ways. For example, you might ask for additional time off, a signing bonus, or a vehicle allowance.

Be aware that most offers must be accepted within a certain time period (usually a few days). Many offer letters state that the offer will expire on a given date. If not, ask the employer if you can have some time to consider the offer. This should prompt the employer to provide you with a reasonable deadline. If not, let the employer know when you will give them a decision and ask if your timeline is acceptable. Regardless of your initial reaction to the offer, always express your gratitude for the offer, continued interest in the company, and enthusiasm for the job.

Finally, remember that an offer isn't an offer unless you get it in writing! Be sure the written offer letter includes everything that has been negotiated and agreed to, including your title, supervisor's name, salary and benefits, and starting date. If anything needs to be corrected in the offer letter, let them know *immediately*.

Likewise, your acceptance of an offer isn't an acceptance unless you give it to them in writing. Re-state the pertinent information from the offer letter so that there is no confusion about the details of your offer, and express your gratitude and enthusiasm.

Breaking Up Is Hard to Do

After you have a written offer in hand and have accepted your new position (and not a moment before), it's time to break the news to your current employer. And no matter how excited you are about your new job or how badly you may want to leave your current job ("I can't wait to see the look on so-and-so's face when I quit!"), submitting your resignation is never easy, because resigning signals an end to the business relationship and possibly to some personal relationships at work.

Under no circumstances should you ever resign from your current job until you have a firm *written* offer that you have formally accepted *in writing*. No matter how excited you are about your new opportunity and how trivial such a formality may seem, far too often a job candidate will resign from a current position only to have some sort of issue or misunderstanding arise that causes a "soft" job offer to be rescinded. Make sure that you both get the offer and accept it in writing (a formal letter or a simple email).

You can't predict how your current employer will react. Will he or she be devastated or tell you "not to let the door hit you in the gluteus maximus?" Will your employer try to entice you to stay by making a counteroffer or a promotion? Or will he or she turn down your two weeks' notice and have you immediately escorted out of the building? Regardless of your employer's reaction, remain professional and courteous when submitting your resignation.

Counteroffer

If a current employer offers to match an offer or promote you in response to your resignation, be skeptical. Ask yourself why you weren't worth the increase in pay or responsibility before your resignation. Not all counteroffers are bad, but you were probably seeking a new position due to more than just your pay, so don't lose sight of that.

Written resignation

Submit your resignation in writing. Your letter of resignation should be professionally formatted, like any other business letter, and addressed to your immediate supervisor. The letter should be brief — three or four sentences. State that you are resigning your position and the effective date of your resignation (or your expected last day), and include a brief statement of gratitude. It isn't necessary to state where you are going, your reasons for resigning, or any other details. You should sign your letter of resignation and (ideally) submit it to your boss in a private meeting. Your letter of resignation will become part of your personnel record at that company.

Do not discuss your resignation with anyone until after you officially submit your written resignation to your boss. Then discuss it with others only if your boss does not ask you to keep the news of your resignation private (some companies do not announce personnel resignations). Ask your boss who you should transition your responsibilities to and if he or she has any specific areas of concern that you need to clarify, focus your efforts on, or document before your departure (such as your daily responsibilities, critical processes you perform, or a special project).

 People will realize something's up when you begin transitioning duties. If nothing is mentioned about keeping your resignation confidential or announcing it to your team, ask your boss how he or she would like you to address any questions that arise from your peers.

Giving notice

As a professional courtesy, give a minimum of two weeks' notice. If you anticipate that your current employer will ask for a longer transition period (perhaps you're involved in a critical project that will be completed in three weeks), discuss this with your new employer after you've accepted your written offer (so that you don't jeopardize your offer or weaken your negotiating position). If your new employer is unwilling to wait more than two weeks, you should provide your current employer with only the standard two weeks (unless you're legally obligated to provide a longer period of notice in, for example, an employment contract).

If your current employer requests more than two weeks' notice but your new employer needs you to start in two weeks, you may be able to work out an alternative arrangement with your current employer, such as a limited (paid or unpaid) consulting engagement.

If your new employer is unwilling to wait the standard two weeks, think carefully about whether or not you want to work at that company. Not providing two weeks' notice is unprofessional and will burn bridges for you. An employer that doesn't respect that norm probably engages in other unsavory business practices that you may later find disagreeable.

The purpose of giving two weeks' notice is to ensure that your company can continue functioning smoothly after you leave. Of course, some people secretly hope that everything will fall apart when they're gone so that the company will realize how valuable they were. This attitude is wrong. A better testament to your legacy is that the company doesn't miss a beat when you leave because you've trained your successor thoroughly and documented your day-to-day responsibilities. Your company, your boss, and your coworkers will all appreciate your effort.

Immediate termination

When companies immediately terminate an employee who attempts to resign, some do it out of spite but most do it to protect the company—and the employee, particularly IT employees. Terminating employment immediately protects the company from an unscrupulous employee who may attempt to steal data or sabotage systems. Although such occurrences are rare, the potential liability far outweighs the benefits of a smooth transition, so immediate termination is the policy. For the employee, immediately terminating your employment, and thus any access to sensitive systems or data, eliminates you as a suspect should a security breach or other major incident occur shortly after you resign. Most companies with such policies will often pay you for the two weeks you offered as notice, so you can think of it as a paid vacation!

Transitioning out

During your transition period, it's important to work every day as if it were your first. Put forth your best effort until the end of your last day. You'll be remembered for your professionalism during this time, which is important. (At the very least, a future employer will contact your past employers for reference checks.) You might also work with a former coworker again someday, perhaps at another company or if you return to your previous company in a new position.

Finally, as you're saying your goodbyes, take the opportunity to update contact information and build your professional network. Ask for letters of recommendation from your managers and coworkers, if appropriate. Collect copies of your performance evaluations, commendations, awards, or laudatory e-mails you may have received, and past work samples (if permitted). You might want to showcase these elements in your professional work portfolio.

Welcome Aboard!

Congratulations, you got the job! That was the easy part. Now it's time to start planning your success in your new career.

Your first day will no doubt be filled with anticipation and excitement. You'll meet lots of new people and start learning about your new job. Be sure to get off to a good start by being prepared and knowing what to expect.

After you accept your job offer, your new employer should provide you with some additional details, such as what time to show up on your first day (this may not be your normal starting time going forward), where to park, the dress code, and who you'll be meeting with to start your day.

Even if you're not normally a breakfast person, have a good breakfast. There's no telling when you'll get a lunch break or where you'll eat on your first day.

Getting to work

Be sure you leave for work early on your first day and know how to get there! Being late is a terrible way to start a new job, and getting lost or stuck in traffic is an equally terrible excuse! Even if you've traveled there before, you might have done so in the middle of the day, when traffic conditions were different than in the early morning hours.

If you aren't sure where to park, arrive early, park in a visitor space, and then ask the receptionist, security, human resources, or your new boss where you should move your car.

Wearing the right attire

Dress appropriately for your first day. Business casual (slacks and a dress shirt for men, or a dress or skirt and blouse for women) is always a safe bet. A business suit is also a good idea —particularly if you're going to work in a professional office. If you find out later that you're overdressed, you can always leave your jacket and tie at your desk. Don't assume that casual attire is appropriate, even if everyone in the office was wearing jeans and t-shirts during your interview. Were you interviewing on a Friday? Perhaps Fridays are casual days, but every other day of the week is more formal.

You'll most likely start your day at the human resources department. They'll have plenty of forms for you to complete (including the Employment Eligibility Verification Form I-9 if you're working in the U.S.) and policies to sign. Be sure you have two acceptable forms of identification and know your social security or tax identification number.

Go to www.uscis.gov for more information about the Employment Eligibility Verification Form I-9 and acceptable forms of identification.

Most companies have an onboarding or orientation process that could last anywhere from a half day to several weeks. Always carry a notepad and pen so you can take notes and write down names of the people you meet.

Drug testing

Finally, be prepared for one more test when you begin your new job: a drug-screening test. Not all companies do a drug screening, but it's still fairly common. You can't study for this test, but you can definitely prepare for it by not taking any illegal drugs before starting your new job (or during your employment, for that matter).

Some employers make a job offer contingent on a successful drug screening. Make sure you know this well before your first day of work.

Although marijuana use is now legal in several states, employers may still have and enforce a zero-tolerance drug policy. Employers have a right to enact a drug-free workplace policy even for substances that are otherwise legal.

The next 89 days

Your first 90 days in any new job are usually considered a probationary period, in which an employer can dismiss you without cause or warning and without fear of reprisal. But that shouldn't be your primary motivation for doing a great job during your first 90 days.

Your success in the first 90 days will largely lay the groundwork for your ongoing success at your new company for many years to come. During this important transition period, you'll get to know your new boss and team members, build strategic relationships, become acclimated to the corporate culture, and start making positive contributions.

Create a plan for what you need to accomplish in your first 90 days in your new job, with specific, measurable goals for you to achieve. This plan can be private — or even better, one that you work on with your new boss. Many companies provide new employees with a 90-day performance review, and some consider giving you a small salary increase to accompany your successful review!

Read Michael Watkins' bestseller *The First 90 Days: Proven Strategies for Getting Up to Speed Faster and Smarter* to help you make the most of the first 90 days in your new job!

Part V

The Part of Tens

 Find ten tips for success for InfoSec professionals, audit professionals, and security executives at www.dummies.com/extras/gettinganinformationsecurityjob.

In this part . . .

- ✔ Discover ten organizations for information security professionals.

- ✔ Get ten resources for staying current in information security.

- ✔ Find ten security references that every security professional should know.

- ✔ End your interview on a high note by asking the interviewer excellent questions.

Chapter 16

Ten Organizations for InfoSec Professionals

*P*rofessional organizations are a great resource for information security professionals just starting out in their career as well as those who have been in security for decades. The ten best organizations are described in this chapter.

These organizations provide fresh, relevant, and usable content as well as many services, such as training, conferences, standards, magazines, ezines, and certifications. With this wide variety of organizations, certainly a few will appeal to your interests and needs.

ASIS International

www.asisonline.org

Formerly known as the American Society for Industrial Security, ASIS International is a membership organization with a rich variety of resources for information security professionals. ASIS publishes standards and guidelines, hosts conferences, and publishes newsletters and the *Security Management* magazine.

ASIS administers the following professional certifications:

- Certified Protection Professional (CPP)
- Professional Certified Investigator (PCI)
- Physical Security Professional (PSP)

Center for Internet Security (CIS)

www.cisecurity.org

The Center for Internet Security (CIS) is an organization devoted to the enhancement of security readiness for public and private sector organizations.

CIS is known for the following published resources:

- **CIS Benchmarks:** Provides detailed plans for improving the security of well-known computing hardware and software
- **Multi-State Information Sharing & Analysis Center (MS-ISAC):** Issues security advisories and newsletters
- **Trusted Purchasing Alliance (TPA):** Serves government and nonprofit agencies through trusted expert guidance and procurement of security tools and services

CERT Coordination Center (CERT/CC)

www.cert.org

The CERT Coordination Center (CERT/CC) is an organization that facilitates effective response to information security incidents through research, education, and conferences.

Cloud Security Alliance (CSA)

www.cloudsecurityalliance.org

The Cloud Security Alliance (CSA) is an organization best known for developing security standards for cloud computing services. CSA developed these standards in response to concerns raised early in the history of cloud computing regarding the need for standard security controls used by cloud service providers.

These standards also help organizations evaluate cloud-based services and controls that should be established in the client organization to ensure proper management of cloud-based services.

CSA also administers the Cloud Computing Security Knowledge (CCSK) professional certification, which demonstrates knowledge of cloud technology and security controls.

Resources available from CSA include the following:

- ✔ **Cloud Controls Matrix (CCM):** Framework of controls for cloud service providers

- ✔ **Consensus Assessments Initiative Questionnaire (CAIQ):** Questionnaire for client organizations to submit to cloud service providers to understand their security controls

- ✔ **Enterprise Architecture:** Methodology and set of tools to assess internal and cloud-based security needs

- ✔ **Security Guidance for Critical Areas of Focus in Cloud Computing:** Guidance for organizations considering cloud computing

- ✔ **Security Guidance for Critical Areas of Mobile Computing:** Guidance for organizations considering mobile computing

International Council of Electronic Commerce Consultants (EC-Council)

www.eccouncil.org

The International Council of Electronic Commerce Consultants (EC-Council) is a membership organization that is primarily a certification body for information security professionals. Two of many certifications offered by EC-Council are Certified Ethical Hacker (CEH) and Certified Chief Information Security Officer (CCISO).

EC-Council also holds a number of information security conferences, including the following:

- ✔ Hacker Halted
- ✔ TakedownCon
- ✔ CISO Forum

EC-Council also offers a Masters Degree in Security Science and a Masters Degree in Business Administration in eBusiness.

Information Systems Security Association (ISSA)

www.issa.org

The Information Systems Security Association (ISSA) is a global organization for information security professionals. Volunteers organize and run more than 100 local chapters around the world that run local meetings and educational events for local members and others in the community.

ISSA hosts international conferences and seminars, and publishes newsletters and the *ISSA Journal*.

InfraGard

www.infragard.net

InfraGard is a membership organization dedicated to the partnership between private industry and the U.S. Federal Bureau of Investigation (FBI). InfraGard chapters exist across all 50 states and offer training, education, and volunteer opportunities in public service. Membership is open to U.S. citizens and is free of charge.

International Information Systems Security Certification Consortium [(ISC)²]

www.isc2.org

The International Information Systems Security Certification Consortium, or (ISC)², is an organization well known for its CISSP certification. (ISC)² also offers conferences for information security professionals, as well as the *InfoSecurity Professional* ezine.

Certifications offered by (ISC)² include the following:

- ✔ Systems Security Certified Practitioner (SSCP)
- ✔ Certified Authorization Professional (CAP)
- ✔ Certified Secure Software Lifecycle Professional (CSSLP)
- ✔ Certified Information Systems Security Professional (CISSP), plus three concentrations (ISSAP, ISSEP, and ISSMP)
- ✔ Certified Cyber Forensics Professional (CCFP)
- ✔ HealthCare Information Security and Privacy Practitioner (HCISPP)

ISACA

www.isaca.org

Formerly known as Information Systems Audit and Control Association, ISACA is a risk-, audit-, and governance-oriented organization with active chapters worldwide. ISACA sponsors several global conferences each year and publishes the magazine *Control*.

ISACA develops and maintains the COBIT (Control Objectives for Information and Related Technology) framework of IT controls, which was first released in 1996.

ISACA offers the following certifications:

- ✔ Certified Information Systems Auditor (CISA)
- ✔ Certified Information Security Manager (CISM)

✔ Certified in the Governance of Enterprise IT (CGEIT)

✔ Certified in Risk and Information Systems Control (CRISC)

SANS (System Administration, Networking, and Security) Institute

www.sans.org

The SANS (System Administration, Networking, and Security) Institute is dedicated to the education of system administrators, network engineers, and security professionals through numerous online and local training events, conferences, and certifications. For a complete list, see Chapter 4.

Chapter 17

Ten Security Resources to Help You Stay Current

*I*t seems as though the information security field moves at light-speed, with daily new developments on several fronts. This chapter contains ten general-purpose resources that will satisfy the insatiable hunger of most information security professionals.

Center for Education and Research in Information Assurance and Security (CERIAS)

www.cerias.org or www.cerias.purdue.edu

Center for Education and Research in Information Assurance and Security (CERIAS) was founded by one of the pioneers in information security, Gene Spafford. This site is rich with resources, including security seminars, news, research reports, books, blogs, and security tools.

CERIAS is home to the Cassandra tool, which is used to inform subscribers about new vulnerabilities in the products of each subscriber's choice.

Dark Reading

www.darkreading.com

Dark Reading is an online security news website with daily and weekly newsletters called Dark Reading Daily and Dark Reading Weekly. Dark Reading is an excellent source of security events, which information security professionals need to stay up to date.

Department of Homeland Security (DHS) Daily Open Source Infrastructure Report

www.dhs.gov/dhs-daily-open-source-infrastructure-report

The DHS Daily Open Source Infrastructure Report is a daily email newsletter containing news stories on U.S. critical infrastructure. Read the newsletter to stay informed on the latest news, threats, and vulnerabilities of significance to information security professionals.

Computer Security Resource Center: NIST Special Publications

csrc.nist.gov

Computer Security Resource Center is the home of special publications and standards from the National Institute of Standards and Technology (NIST). Some of the most well-known publications follow:

- ✓ **NIST SP800-37, Guide for Applying the Risk Management Framework to Federal Information Systems: A Security Life Cycle Approach:** A seminal guide to risk management used by many public agencies and private organizations

- ✓ **NIST SP800-53, Security and Privacy Controls for Federal Information Systems and Organizations:** Required for all U.S. federal information systems and organizations, and adopted by many other government agencies and private organizations

- ✓ **NIST SP800-144, Guidelines on Security and Privacy in Public Cloud Computing:** A good resource for enacting security and privacy controls when using public cloud computing resources

- ✓ **FIPS-197, Advanced Encryption Standard.** A technical description of AES, which is based on the Rijndael algorithm

- ✓ **FIPS-199, Standards for Security Categorization of Federal Information and Information Systems:** A great model for data and systems classification

- ✓ **FIPS-200, Minimum Security Requirements for Federal Information and Information Systems:** A companion to NIST 800-53 and adopted by many agencies and private organizations

Hakin9

www.hakin9.org

Hakin9 is a print and online magazine devoted to the discussion of offensive and defensive security techniques. *Hakin9* includes a blog, discussion forums, and online training courses.

Information Security Magazine

searchsecurity.techtarget.com/ezine/Information-Security-magazine

Information Security Magazine, for years a print magazine but now online, has lost none of its quality. This magazine is a great resource for security technologists as well as those in security management.

ISACA Journal

www.isaca.org/journal

The *ISACA Journal* is a print and online news resource for information security professionals, particularly those interested in governance and risk management. The ISACA Journal is free for all members of ISACA. Membership information is available at www.isaca.org/membership.

Risks Digest

www.risks.org

Formally known as the Forum on Risks to the Public in Computers and Related Systems, the *Risks Digest* is a semiregular newsletter comprised of security news and opinion. The Committee on Computers and Public Policy of the Association for Computing Machinery has published *Risks Digest* since 1985.

SANS Reading Room

www.sans.org/reading-room/

Founded in 1989, the SANS (Systems Administration, Network, and Security) Institute is an organization primarily devoted to training information technology and information security professionals. The SANS Reading Room is a trove of resources for security professionals.

SANS created the GIAC (Global Information Assurance Certification) program, which manages dozens of certifications for information security professionals. GIAC is located at www.giac.org.

SANS also sponsors the Internet Storm Center, located at https://isc.sans.edu.

Hacker's Quarterly

www.2600.com

The *Hacker's Quarterly*, also known as *2600*, is a magazine devoted to offensive and defensive security techniques and discussions. A must for all information security technologists, *2600* was first published in 1984.

Chapter 18

Ten Essential Security References

*I*nformation security professionals are successful not because of what they can memorize but because they can find good information quickly. This chapter contains ten essential security references, plus a bonus reference that will help you find almost anything.

Framework for Improving Critical Infrastructure Cybersecurity

www.nist.gov/cyberframework/

The U.S. Cybersecurity Framework is a voluntary framework based on existing standards, guidelines, and practices for reducing cyberrisks to critical infrastructure in the U.S. and elsewhere.

Cloud Controls Matrix (CCM)

cloudsecurityalliance.org/research/ccm/

Published and maintained by Cloud Security Alliance, Cloud Controls Matrix (CCM) is a framework of controls for cloud service providers and of great value to organizations using services from cloud providers.

Unified Compliance Framework (UCF)

www.unifiedcompliance.com

Unified Compliance Framework (UCF) is a spreadsheet that maps the world's information security standards, information security laws, and privacy laws to each other. UCF is a gigantic spreadsheet and a little unwieldy to use at first, but it's a great resource for any organization that needs to reduce its patchwork of controls into a single unified set.

ISO27001

www.iso.org/iso/home/standards/management-standards/
iso27001.htm

ISO27001:2013 — Information Technology Security Techniques and Information Security Management Systems Requirements is the latest version of the well-known international standard for information security management. ISO27001 is divided into two parts. The first part describes the structure for an effective ISMS (Information Security Management System), which is the set of processes used to manage security in an organization. The second part is an initial set of security controls that an organization can use until it has determined what additional controls are needed.

Open Web Application Security Project (OWASP)

```
www.owasp.org
```

Open Web Application Security Project (OWASP) is an organization dedicated to the education of software developers so that they will write more secure code. The most popular resource at OWASP is the Top 10 Most Critical Application Security Risks list.

Center for Internet Security (CIS)

```
www.cisecurity.org
```

Center for Internet Security (CIS) publishes a rich library of benchmarks, which are documents that explain how to configure systems to be as secure as possible.

Common Vulnerabilities and Exposures (CVE)

```
www.cve.mitre.org
```

Common Vulnerabilities and Exposures (CVE) is the authoritative repository of publicly known information security vulnerabilities and exposures. CVE is used in many tools, processes, and services, including US-CERT bulletins, intrusion prevention system (IPS) products, and the U.S. National Vulnerability Database (NVD).

COBIT 5 Toolkit

```
www.isaca.org/COBIT/Pages/COBIT-5-Implementation-product-
page.aspx
```

COBIT 5 Toolkit contains the COBIT standard, plus implementation guides, PowerPoints, and other materials to educate and guide organizations that want to implement the COBIT framework.

COBIT is a complete IT controls framework for IT management and IT governance. Why is this included in a list of resources for information security professionals? Simple: Without a solid foundation of IT controls, any effort to implement security controls is futile.

You need to be an ISACA member to obtain the COBIT Toolkit and other COBIT materials.

U.S. and International Technology Laws

www.hg.org

The HG.org website is a great jumping-off point for information on U.S. and international computer security and privacy laws. Grouped by topic, links from this site point to other legal portals that drill deeper into different types, categories, and jurisdictions of laws. Check out the following:

- www.hg.org/compute.html
- www.hg.org/data-protection.html
- www.hg.org/encryption-law.html
- www.hg.org/internet-law.html
- www.hg.org/telecommunication.html

Top 125 Network Security Tools

www.sectools.org

For more than ten years, the Top 125 Network Security Tools list has showcased the best security tools in several categories: network security scanners, password crackers, network sniffers, web application vulnerability scanners, forensics, secure communications, cryptography, debuggers, and more. Each tool is reviewed and rated, and many are available at no charge.

Bonus Resource: InfoSysSec

www.infosyssec.com

One of the most complete information security portals, InfoSysSec has more categories and links than you can imagine. You'll find information on everything you can think of in information systems security, and far more.

Chapter 19

Ten Great Questions to Ask Your Interviewer

Congratulations! You've just completed a grueling interview in which you answered some of the most probing and thought-provoking questions about yourself that anyone has ever asked. But your answer to one final, seemingly innocuous question could blow it all.

Interviewer: "Do you have any questions for me?"

You: "Uh, no. I believe you've answered any questions. Thank you."

At best, this answer is a polite way to end the interview. At worst (and more likely), this answer may be construed as a cop-out that demonstrates a lack of intellectual curiosity, preparation, and interest in the company or the job!

Always be prepared with a few questions to ask at the end of the interview. It's likely that the interviewer may have answered many of your questions during the interview without you even having to ask them. And ideally, you've had several opportunities to ask questions and engage in meaningful dialogue during the interview. This chapter provides ten questions you might want ask.

You should always go into an interview with at least five or six questions written down. Be prepared to ask these questions during and at the end of the interview.

How Has Your Department Contributed to the Success of the Company?

You should include specific details about the company when you ask, "How has your department contributed to the success of the company?" Your goal is to show the interviewer that you researched the company. This question is also a great way to showcase your business acumen and demonstrate your understanding of what the company does. Far too many IT professionals get caught up in the cool technology and forget that IT supports the business — not the other way around (unless you happen to be applying for a job at an IT company)!

Everyone applying for the job will have some level of knowledge and experience in IT. Make yourself stand out as a candidate by demonstrating a keen understanding of the company's core business.

If the company is publicly traded, their annual 10-K Securities and Exchange Commission (SEC) shareholders report is available on the company's website. This report contains a wealth of information about who's who in the company, the overall strategic direction, and detailed financial data. Let the interviewer know that you've studied this report by asking questions that begin along the lines of "I see in your latest 10-K filing that the company's price-to-earnings ratio has increased to 28 times earnings over the past three quarters."

Getting information about private companies is more difficult because these companies tend to keep their financial performance data, well, private. However, you can still get a wealth of information from the company's website, press releases, and other sources. Both public and private companies love to tout their successes in the local media. Look for news interviews with company officers in local business journals and special interest stories such as a charitable cause the company supports, a recent community outreach project, a new diversity initiative, or a recent expansion or new client that the company is excited to talk or write about.

Complete your question by asking how the interviewer's department or team has contributed to that success. People usually enjoy talking about their accomplishments, so this question should lead to an engaging discussion and will also give you some insight on your potential new boss. Does the person speak with humility and downplay the team's contributions? Or does he or she burst with pride while offering specific examples and calling attention to key individuals on the team? After the interviewer answers this question, make it personal by explaining how you would help the team continue to succeed and contribute to the company's success.

Do your homework! If the company has had some recent struggles or setbacks, you don't want to ask about their recent success! In such cases, you may not want to ask this type of question at all.

What Are Some of the Biggest Challenges Your Department Is Facing?

To learn more about the company overall and some of the specific projects you may be working on if you get hired, ask "What are some of the biggest challenges your department is facing?" Your interviewer may not be comfortable giving you specifics, but you can still glean a lot of information from the answers you do get.

For example, your interviewer is unlikely to tell you "We're really short-handed since a lot of people have quit because of the long hours we work." But you might gain some helpful insight from an answer such as "We've had some turnover recently."

And it's unlikely that you'll hear, "Well, we've been behind the eight ball since that huge security breach last month, so we're scrambling to shore up the network infrastructure." But you might learn about a new initiative to build out a hybrid cloud infrastructure and that the executive team has concerns around security in the public cloud. There's your opportunity to talk about how your experience at your last company can help them address those challenges!

The answers to this question may also give you some idea of how urgently the company needs to fill the position and could strengthen your negotiating position when you get the job offer!

What Keeps You Excited About Coming to Work Every Day?

Cultural fit is at least as important as your skills and experience. If your personality isn't in sync and your values aren't aligned with the company, you don't want the job. Period. You won't be happy, your new employer won't be happy, and you'll inevitably part ways on terms that leave neither of you happy.

Some people thrive in large organizations; others prefer a small company. Some people enjoy working in a loud, chaotic environment. Others prefer order and solitude. Some people need clear direction; others need autonomy. Understand who you are and what values are most important to you.

Listen carefully to your interviewer's answer to the question, "How would you describe the company's culture?" The answer will give you an idea of how happy people are working for the company. Does the interviewer describe the culture with passion and enthusiasm? Do you get specific examples? Does the interviewer explain how the culture affects him or her personally? Or does the person just recite the company's mission and values statement? It's hard to be passionate about a company's culture if the truth is that your interviewer can't stand his or her job and dreads coming to work every day. If that's the case, do you really want to work there?

Ask open-ended questions that enable follow-on questions and further discussion. After the interviewer answers your question, thank him or her and continue by explaining how you fit in or can contribute to the company based on the answer. For example, "Thank you for giving me that insight into your company's culture. Cultural fit is very important. XYZ company has a similar culture and when I worked there I believe I was an integral part of that culture because. . ."

What Do You Like About Working Here?

If you want to know what you might find rewarding about the job, ask "What do you like about working here?" You want to get answers at different levels, so that you can get several perspectives.

Next, you want to find out about the organization as a whole. Are people proud to be working there? The mood and the tone in the organization will affect you. Again, if people are unhappy, you'll hear this more in what they don't say than in what they do say.

If everyone is all smiles, you may have found the ideal organization where everyone is happy, or maybe they're putting happy dust in the coffee every morning. Somehow, you'll want to get to the bottom of everyone's bliss if it feels superficial.

Can You Describe How We Would Be Working Together?

Because a large part of your work satisfaction depends on your relationship with your boss, you need to ask, "Can you describe how we would be working together?"

There is no good or bad answer, because individual work habits drive how people work by themselves and with each other. However, you need to be able to determine whether you will find your manager's style compatible. You want the working relationship to be harmonious from day one.

There may be better ways to ask this question, such as:

- "What sort of daily, weekly, or monthly status reporting will you require of me?"
- "How much freedom will I have in the regular tasks that I'll be expected to perform?"

What Is the Makeup of the Team or Organization?

If someone hasn't already described the team's makeup, you might ask, "What is the makeup of the team or organization?" You are not looking for actual names, but instead you're trying to understand how the team or organization is structured.

You can ask about the position titles for others on the team, and to understand what their responsibilities are. Chances are you will be working closely with most of them, and that you'll be asked to fill in for some of them while they are out sick or on vacation. In fact, this is another good line of questioning that will tell you more about team dynamics.

What Are the Key Traits of Your Most Successful Employees?

By asking, "What are the key traits of your most successful employees?" you're asking about the traits the interviewer is looking for in you.

Expend some effort interpreting the answers you get to this question. The interviewer might be telling you what is expected of everyone on the team and, if so, his or her answer might reflect a team dynamic or insight into the company's definition of success.

If you can, find out whether the company has published a set of guiding principles. If you're lucky, they'll be framed and hanging on the wall in the conference room where you're being interviewed. See whether or not interviewers describe traits straight from the guiding principles.

Interviewers might be telling you about the successful employees on the team and how they got that way. That may, or may not, mean that you need to have those same traits. But as team dynamics go, you might have different traits that could help the team be even more successful. Often, a diversity of skills makes a team more successful than a team in which everyone has the same strengths and weaknesses. Ask a follow-up question or two to see which is the case.

How Would You Define Success During the First 90 Days?

The question "How would you define success during the first 90 days?" will tell you a lot about the level of maturity and organization in the team you're considering joining. If the team (or the hiring manager) is not well organized, they might not have a good answer for this question. They may be frantically working to put out fires with no time for even short-term planning; they just need another set of hands to pass buckets of water along the bucket brigade! If this is the case, think long and hard about whether this is the kind of position you want. Perhaps the company is looking to hire someone to replace one or more burnouts. Or maybe they want help to move the organization to the next level, which would be an extraordinary opportunity.

If you interview with a more organized team (or manager), they will be more likely to know what success looks like. And you'll have an idea of what will be expected of you in the first few months.

Honestly assess whether you are up to the job (or *almost* up to the job). Ask any follow-up questions, such as what resources will be available to you right away. Discuss tools that are available as well as the company's plans for future tools and technology.

Just as the company will put new hires on a 90-day probation, you should do the same with your employer. After 90 days, reassess whether this is the company you thought you were joining and whether they have met or exceeded your expectations.

Do You Have Any Concerns About Me That I Can Address Now?

You'll want to appear as the ideal, near-perfect candidate to your interviewers. But every employee has some imperfection, large or small. It takes a bit of courage to ask, "Do you have any concerns about me that I can address now?" The interviewer may answer with a gap in your skills or knowledge that is a shortcoming.

Do not despair and keep your good attitude. Consider the interviewer's point of view and tell him that you agree with his observation. If you can do so realistically, tell the interviewer what, if anything, you can do about the shortcoming. Every candidate has shortcomings, and the company may be willing to take you as-is.

What Is Your Next Step in the Selection Process?

"What is your next step in the selection process?" is a great question at the end of the interview. The answer helps clarify the next steps to expect, such as when and how you should follow up with the interviewer, whether or not there will be additional interviews (perhaps with human resources or other team members), and how long you should expect to wait before a hiring decision is made. Following are some variations of this question:

- ✔ "When should I expect to hear from you?"
- ✔ "When and how should I follow up with you?"
- ✔ "How soon do you expect to make a hiring decision?"

Be specific during your follow-up at the end of the interview. After asking, "When can I expect to hear from you?" follow up with "If I haven't heard from you by that date, may I follow up on [date]?"

After the interviewer answers this question, be sure to thank her for her answer and for taking the time to meet with you. Then restate the next steps so the interviewer knows that you understand her answer and knows what to expect from you. Finally, and most importantly, close with a crisp summary statement that asserts your enthusiasm for the position and the value you will bring to the table! If you are truly enthusiastic about the position and want the job, let the interviewer know. "I am excited about the opportunity to work at Dewey, Cheatham, and Howe and look forward to hearing from you soon."

The answer to this question may also provide insight into how well you did in the interview. For example, the interviewer may tell you she'd like to go ahead and schedule you to meet the rest of her team. A vague answer, such as "Well, we still have several other candidates to interview but we'll be in touch" might indicate some concerns or a lack of interest in you as a candidate.

Glossary

access matrix. An access model in which a two-dimensional matrix defines the persons or groups who are permitted to access specific data or systems.

access review. An examination of user access rights to determine whether any access rights need to be changed or discontinued.

accreditation. The process of formally approving the use of a system.

accumulation of privileges. The process whereby a person accumulates access rights to systems over a long period of time.

Advanced Persistent Threat (APT). A party with the tools, knowledge, and patience to successfully attack a target system.

adversary. An individual, an organization, or a force that opposes or attacks.

agent. A small program that runs on a local system with some type of connection to a master program or console elsewhere.

antimalware. Software designed to detect and prevent the installation and execution of malware.

antivirus. See *antimalware*.

applet. A program that operates within the context of another program.

applicant-tracking system. An information system used to accept, manage, and screen resumes and cover letters from employment candidates.

application whitelisting. A method of preventing malware by permitting only known, registered programs to execute.

authentication. The process of asserting one's identity (a user ID, a value assigned to a person or machine), including required proof such as a password, token, or biometric to a system.

authentication bypass. An attack on a system in which the attacker attempts to bypass authentication controls.

availability. The concept in information security related to measures taken to ensure that systems and information can be accessed on demand.

back door. A feature in a program that gives someone covert access to the program.

background check. The process of investigating an individual's criminal, financial, education, and work history.

backup. The process of making copies of sensitive data.

barbed wire. A continuous heavy wire with sharp points along its length, placed at the top of a fence or wall to deter others from climbing over it.

beacon. An invisible image or other object on a web page for the purposes of tracking who accesses the page.

Bell LaPadula. A security model in which people can read documents at or below their level of security, and write documents at or above their level of security.

Biba. A security model in which people can read documents only at their level of security, and write documents at or above their level of security.

biometrics. The science of measuring the physical properties of people to verify their identity.

block cipher. An encryption algorithm used to encrypt and decrypt data in batches, or blocks.

blog. A website consisting of articles and other information.

Bluetooth. A wireless protocol for data transmission using devices in close proximity.

bot. A system controlled by an unauthorized external party.

botnet. A collection of bots. See also *bot*.

break-in. Unauthorized access to a system.

buffer overflow. An attack on a system in which the attacker provides data in an input field, and the software program requesting data is not performing input validation or boundary checking.

bus. The component in a computer where data and instructions flow between and among the CPU, main storage, and secondary storage, and externally through peripheral devices and communications adaptors.

business continuity planning (BCP). Activities that facilitate an organization's capability to continue business operations using alternate facilities, equipment, or personnel in a disaster scenario.

business impact assessment (BIA). A risk assessment used to identify an organization's critical business processes and their dependencies.

CAT-6 cable. Copper cabling capable of transmitting Ethernet at speeds up to 10Gbps.

central processing unit (CPU). The component in a computer where computer instructions are executed and calculations performed.

certificate authority (CA). A trusted party that issues digital certificates to other parties after confirming their identity.

certification. The process of examining a system to determine its compliance to a set of requirements.

chain of custody. A part of forensic procedures to ensure the integrity of collected evidence.

change management. An IT operations process that is concerned with the management and control of changes that are made in IT systems.

CIA triad. The depiction of the three pillars of information security: confidentiality, integrity, and availability.

ciphertext. A message that has been transformed (encrypted) into a scrambled message that is unintelligible.

Clark-Wilson. A security model that is a scheme for creating and protecting sensitive information.

client-server. An application architecture in which some of the application resides on a workstation (usually having to do with data display and data input), and some resides on a central server (usually having to do with data storage and retrieval).

cloud computing. The practice of utilizing remote resources for the processing of information, or storage of information, or both.

COBIT (Control Objectives for Information and Related Technology).
A control framework for business processes related to information
technology (IT).

**Committee of Sponsoring Organizations of the Treadway Commission
(COSO).** An IT controls framework applied to financial systems.

Common Criteria (CC). A framework for the specification, implementation,
and evaluation of a system against a set of security requirements.

compiler. A program that converts a program in source code form into
machine-readable form.

compromise. The act of impairing a system to incapacitate it or steal its
contents.

confidentiality. The concept in information security related to measures
designed to protect information from access by unauthorized parties.

consulting. A business activity in which an expert party issues advice or
guidance to another party.

control. Any specific instance of a policy, standard, or key step in a business
process or procedure that management has determined is essential for
the proper operation and security of business processes and information
systems.

cookie. An identifier sent from a website and stored in a browser.

cover letter. A personalized introductory letter, usually accompanying a
resume, sent to a prospective employer, containing a description of qualifications as they relate to the posted job description.

covert channel attack. An attack on a system by using a hidden communications channel.

curriculum vitae (CV). A complete listing of employment positions, education, publications, and so forth. See also _resume_.

cybercrime. Illegal activities related to information and information systems.

cryptanalysis. An attack on a cryptosystem with the intention of discovering
the encryption key or encrypted messages.

cryptography. The science of encrypting and decrypting information.

cryptosystem. An implementation of encryption.

cutover test. A test of business continuity plans in which production systems are shut down or disconnected, and recovery systems are activated to manage live workload.

dark fiber. Unused optical fiber available for voice or data communications.

data classification. The process of defining levels of sensitivity and handling procedures for information.

data destruction. The process of safely discarding information when it is no longer needed.

data loss prevention (DLP). Tools used to detect and prevent unwanted movement of sensitive data.

Data Over Cable Service Interface Specification (DOCSIS). A family of technologies used to transport TCP/IP over cable television service.

data retention. The process of defining minimum and maximum intervals for the retention of different types of information.

database. A structured collection of information.

database management system (DBMS). A software program used to facilitate the storage and retrieval of information from a database.

decryption. The process of transforming ciphertext back into plaintext.

decryption key. See *encryption key*.

defense in depth. The strategy for protecting important assets by surrounding them with layered defenses.

denial of service (DoS). An attack on a target system designed to incapacitate the system.

Department of Defense Information Assurance Certification and Accreditation (DIACAP). A process framework used to certify and accredit military systems.

digital certificate. An electronic document that consists of a personal or corporate identifier and a public encryption key, and is signed by a certificate authority (CA).

digital signature. The result of a hashing operation carried out on a file, used to verify the integrity of a file.

digital subscriber line (DSL). A family of protocols delivered over copper telephone network cabling to homes and businesses.

digital video recorder (DVR). A device that records images from one or more video surveillance cameras.

Director of Central Intelligence Directive (DCID 6/3). A framework used to certify and accredit systems in use by the Central Intelligence Agency (CIA).

disaster. An unexpected event that directly or indirectly disrupts ongoing business operations.

disaster recovery planning (DRP). Activities that facilitate the salvage of facilities and equipment in a disaster scenario.

discretionary access control. A security model in which the owners of individual documents or folders manage access to information.

distributed application. An application architecture consisting of several components residing on different systems.

distributed denial of service (DDoS). A denial of service (DoS) attack that originates from many points.

document review. The process of reviewing process or procedure documentation to assess its viability.

dropper. The portion of malware that installs malicious code onto a target system.

DS-1. A family of multiplexed telecommunications technologies that have carried voice and data for decades in the United States and Europe.

E-1. See *DS-1*.

electric generator. A device powered by gasoline, diesel fuel, natural gas, or propane that can generate electric power for hours, days, or more.

electronic protected health information (EPHI). Information related to the health and medical care of an individual.

encapsulation. The process of inserting messages of one protocol into messages of another protocol.

encryption. The process of transforming plaintext into ciphertext through the use of an encryption algorithm.

encryption algorithm. A mathematical technique used to transform plaintext into ciphertext.

encryption key. A set of characters used with an encryption algorithm to encrypt or decrypt a message.

Ethernet. A family of technologies for transmitting messages over a wired network.

exfiltration. The process of transferring data out of an organization. Typically considered a theft.

expert system. A system that accumulates knowledge of a particular subject in past events, used to predict future events.

exploit. The portion of malware that is designed to take advantage of a known weakness, thereby relinquishing control to the malware.

exterior lighting. Illumination of areas where an intruder would otherwise be able to work in darkness.

Facebook. A social networking service with some business networking features.

fail closed. The result of a control in the event of its failure, where the control prevents all access or activity.

fail open. The result of a control in the event of its failure, where the control allows all access or activity.

Federal Energy Regulatory Commission (FERC). The U.S. agency that regulates public utilities.

Federal Risk and Authorization Management Program (FEDRAMP). A framework for security assessments, authorization, and continuous monitoring for cloud-based security providers.

Federal Trade Commission (FTC). The U.S. agency that regulates all businesses.

fence. A structure used to prevent persons from accessing an area.

file integrity monitoring (FIM). A tool used to detect authorized and unauthorized changes to files on a system.

FIPS 200: Minimum Security Requirements for Federal Information and Information Systems. A U.S. set of security requirements for federal information systems.

fire extinguisher. A portable device used to suppress a fire.

firewall. An inline device placed between networks to control the traffic that is allowed to pass between those networks.

firmware. Software stored in persistent memory in a computer, generally used to store initial instructions that are executed when the computer is switched on.

Food and Drug Administration (FDA). The U.S. agency that regulates the food, pharmaceutical, and medical devices industries.

Forensics. The set of tools and procedures used to investigate an event and preserve evidence.

fraud. An act of deception carried out for unfair, undeserved, or unlawful gain.

governance. The set of activities performed by management to exert control over the organization.

Gramm-Leach-Bliley Act (GLBA). A U.S. law that requires the protection of personal information in financial services organizations.

guard. A person with duties to protect facilities and personnel

guard dog. A trained canine used to protect facilities and personnel.

guideline. A statement that provides ideas on the implementation of policies and standards.

hacker. A hobbyist or enthusiast who seeks to understand complex systems and be able to make modifications to them.

hacktivist. A hacker-activist who attacks a system for political or ideological reasons.

hashing. A cryptographic operation used to produce a short, fixed-length message (known as a *message digest*) from a file or block of data.

Health Insurance Portability and Accountability Act (HIPAA). A U.S. law that defines requirements for the protection of health related information.

heating, ventilation, and air conditioning (HVAC). Equipment that regulates temperature and humidity in buildings containing personnel, computers, or both.

identity theft. The process of obtaining personal information that facilitates the capability to access resources in the name of the victim.

implementation. The process of installing hardware, software, or a business process.

incident management. An IT process or security operations process or both used to properly respond to operational and security incidents.

incident response. Activities performed as a result of an incident.

inert gas fire suppression. A fire suppression system in which inert gas is discharged into an area to displace oxygen.

information flow. An access model in which information at specific levels of security are permitted to flow to specific systems or locations.

injection attack. An attack on a system in which an attacker injects commands into input fields.

integrity. The concept in information security related to the protection of information and systems from unauthorized alteration.

internal audit. A process of self-examination of controls to determine their effectiveness.

interview. A discussion between an employer and an employment candidate, for each to assess the other for suitability of employment.

intrusion prevention system (IPS). An inline device that examines incoming and outgoing network traffic, looking for signs of intrusions; when any intrusion is detected, the device will block such traffic.

IP address. A unique identifier assigned to a node on a network.

ISO 27001. An international standard for the management of security in an organization.

job rotation. The practice of periodically moving personnel from role to role.

key card. A plastic card with a magnetic stripe, an RFID circuit, or an embedded processor and memory that is assigned to an individual worker and used to activate door locks to permit entry into a room or building.

key logger. A hardware or software mechanism used to intercept keystrokes, especially login credentials.

key management. Procedures for the creation, use, protection, and disposal of encryption keys.

keylength. The length of an encryption key.

least privilege. The principle that people (and machines) should have the lowest possible level of privilege required to complete required tasks.

line conditioner. A device that absorbs noise present in utility power, such as spikes and surges.

LinkedIn. A business networking site used to establish business relationships.

logic bomb. Code placed in an application that performs some malicious action, such as deleting or altering data.

main storage. The component in a computer where information is stored temporarily.

malicious software. Software designed to steal or alter data, steal login credentials, or permit a takeover of the target system for a malicious purpose.

malware. See *malicious software*.

man-in-the-middle attack. An attack in which the attacker intercepts and alters communications between two parties.

managed security service provider (MSSP). An organization that performs operational security tasks for one or more client organizations.

mandatory access control. A security model in which an access manager manages access to information.

mantrap. A set of two interlocked doors with a short passage between to control movement of personnel.

maximum tolerable downtime (MTD). The theoretical period of time that a business process is incapacitated, after which the organization may fail to survive.

message digest. See *hashing*.

multifactor authentication. The presentation of a user ID, together with a token or biometric.

multilevel. An access model in which a system will contain information at more than one security level. People can read information at or below their security level.

multiprotocol label switching (MPLS). A packet-switched technology used to transport a variety of protocols, such as TCP/IP, Ethernet, ATM, or VoIP, over long distances.

National Information Assurance Certification and Accreditation Process (NIACAP). A process framework used to certify and accredit U.S. national security systems.

near field communications (NFC). A protocol for wireless communications over short distances (up to 6cm).

need to know. The principle that people should have access to only the information (and systems) they need to perform their job.

netflow. A tool used to create a record of all network communications between systems.

neural network. A system used to solve a particular problem, given a large collection of relevant situations and outcomes.

NIST 800-53: Security and Privacy Controls for Federal Information Systems and Organizations. A U.S. standard for the protection of information systems and supporting processes.

nondisclosure agreement. A legal agreement in which one or more parties agrees not to disclose the secrets of one or more other parties.

noninterference. An access model in which activities performed by people at a higher level of security will not interfere with activities performed at lower levels of security.

nonprofit. A private organization that retains its surplus revenues to further its goals.

nonrepudiation. A property of a system in which a person would be unable to deny having performed a transaction.

North American Electric Reliability Corp (NERC). The U.S. organization that creates standards for the protection of public utility control systems.

offer letter. A formal written offer of employment, written by an employer and given to an employment candidate.

object. In access control, a system or data record that someone or something wants to access. See also *subject*.

object oriented. A hierarchical system that consist of classes (software libraries), objects, methods, and logical construction that includes encapsulation, inheritance, and polymorphism.

operating system. A set of programs that facilitate the use of computer hardware, including storage, memory, and peripheral devices.

parallel test. A test of business continuity plans in which recovery systems are activated and process live data, but do so in isolation so as not to disturb production systems that are still running.

password. A secret word, phrase, or random characters used as a part of authentication.

password quality. A measure of a password based on its complexity and resistance to attack.

password recovery. The process of assisting a user who has forgotten his or her password.

Payment Card Industry Data Security Standard (PCI-DSS). A standard for the protection of credit card data that is stored, processed, and transmitted.

phishing. A social engineering attack in which fraudulent messages are sent to targeted individuals in an attempt to trick them into performing unauthorized actions.

PIN pad. A keypad with numbers or letters, generally used with key cards.

plain old telephone service (POTS). See *public-switched telephone network*.

plaintext. A message in its original, readable format (as opposed to *ciphertext*).

policy. A formal statement that describes what actions and behaviors are required or forbidden in an organization.

pre-sales. Activities between a vendor and a client organization in which the vendor is exchanging information with the client.

privacy. The concept and practice of protecting sensitive information about people.

private sector. The portion of an economy that consists of all organizations owned and operated by private individuals or groups.

procedure. Step-by-step instructions for carrying out a task.

process. A set of one or more procedures used to carry out a business activity.

proof of concept (POC). The implementation of a system for a limited period of time to determine its long-term viability.

pseudorandom number generator (PRNG). A technique for deriving a random number for use during encryption and decryption.

public sector. The portion of an economy that consists of all organizations owned and operated by governments.

public-switched telephone network (PSTN). The worldwide network of telephones, cabling, and switches to facilitate voice communications.

quotation. A statement of cost for a particular product or service.

race condition. See *state attack*.

razor wire. A continuous mesh of metal strips with sharp edges along its length, placed at the top of a fence or wall to deter others from climbing over it.

recovery capacity objective (RCapO). The capacity of temporary processing systems compared to production systems.

recovery consistency objective (RCO). The measure of integrity and consistency in data in the emergency operations system compared to the original production system.

recovery point objective (RPO). The period of maximum data loss after a disaster strikes.

recovery time objective (RTO). The period of time from disaster onset until the process or system is operational.

recruiter. An individual who searches for employment candidates for one or more organizations.

reference. An individual who agrees to independently verify an employment candidate's background.

remote access. The process and technique of facilitating an employee's ability to remotely access information systems that are not accessible from the Internet.

replay attack. An attack on a system in which an attacker intercepts and then replays login credentials.

resignation. A written or verbal statement of intent to discontinue employment with an organization.

resume. A document that summarizes skills, education, and employment history. See also *curriculum vitae (CV)*.

risk assessment. An examination of risks present in specific systems, processes, suppliers, or the entire organization.

risk ledger. A listing of risks identified in a risk assessment or by other means.

risk management. Formal activities to identify and appropriately respond to risk.

risk treatment. The formal acceptance, mitigation, transfer, or avoidance of identified risks.

role-based access control (RBAC). An access model in which access is assigned to groups of users instead of individual users.

router. A device that forwards TCP/IP packets toward their destination.

routing table. A list of networks that permits the router to correctly route packets.

salting. The practice of inserting a set of characters into a hashing operation to thwart cryptanalysis.

Sarbanes-Oxley Act. The U.S. law that requires publicly held organizations to enact business and IT controls to ensure the integrity of their financial systems and financial statements.

secondary storage. The component in a computer where information is stored permanently.

security awareness training. Formal training for employees regarding an organization's security policies and procedures.

segregation of duties. See *separation of duties.*

separation of duties. The practice of designing a critical task so that two or more people are required to complete it.

session hijacking. An attack on a system in which an attacker intercepts session tokens and attempts to take over the session.

side channel attack. A technique of observing a system's running states to make inferences about activities in the system.

simulation. A review of procedures in business continuity planning or disaster recovery planning in which a realistic scenario is defined and exercised.

single-factor authentication. The presentation of login credentials using a single method.

single point of failure. A component, system, or individual without an alternative resource.

smoke detector. A device that alerts personnel when smoke is detected. A smoke detector is considered an early warning device in the event of a fire.

social engineering. The practice of tricking individuals into performing unauthorized actions.

software development life cycle (SDLC). The business process used to develop and maintain software programs.

Software Engineering Institute — Capability Maturity Model Integration (SEI-CMMI). A model for assessing the maturity of an organization's security practices.

source code. The human readable form of a computer program.

spam. Unwanted email, generally sent from an unknown party.

sprinkler system. A fire suppression system in which water is sprayed into an area.

standard. A formal statement that describes how security policy will be carried out.

state attack. A technique of exploiting a timing flaw in a system. Also known as a *race condition,* a state attack can be used to gain access to a resource used by another process.

steganography. A technique used to hide a message in a larger file such as an image file, a video, or a sound file.

subject. In access control, a person or system that wants to access something. See also *object.*

stream cipher. An encryption algorithm used to encrypt or decrypt a stream of data, one character at a time.

Synchronous optical network (SONET). A family of protocols for carrying voice and data traffic over copper and fiber telecommunications networks.

Systems Security Engineering Capability Maturity Model (SSE-CMM). A model for evaluating an organization's capability to implement security in a system.

T-1. See *DS-1.*

tailgating. The practice of closely following an authorized person through a security door to gain unauthorized entry.

take-grant. An access model used to establish or disprove the safety of a given computer system.

TCP/IP (Transmission Control Protocol/Internet Protocol). A family of data communications protocols for the transmission of data over networks.

threat. The capability and intent to carry out a harmful act.

token. A hardware device used to facilitate authentication to a system.

Trojan horse. A program with a stated purpose as well as an unstated, malicious purpose.

trusted platform module (TPM). A hardware device used to store encryption keys.

Twitter. A microblogging site used to share information.

uninterruptible power supply (UPS). A device equipped with backup batteries that can supply power to computing equipment from several minutes to an hour or more.

user ID. A personal identifier issued to the user of a system.

video surveillance. A system of one or more cameras plus monitors, or recording equipment, or both that monitor key locations inside or outside a facility.

virtual private network (VPN). A technique used to encapsulate network traffic flowing between two systems, between a system and a network, or between two networks.

virus. Malicious code that attaches itself to a file.

visitor log. A written or an electronic record of visitors to a building.

vulnerability management. An IT operations process that is concerned with the identification and mitigation of vulnerabilities in IT systems.

walkthrough. A review of a process or procedure document in a group setting.

wall. A building structure used to prevent persons from accessing an area.

watering hole attack. An attack on an organization in which an attacker compromises a system that users are known to access.

watermarking. A technique used to implant a visible (or audible) imprint onto a document, an image, a sound recording, or a video recording.

web access filter. A device that examines the websites that users want to visit and then blocks or permits such access based on policy rules.

web application. An application consisting of a web browser on a user's workstation (or mobile device), a web server, and often an application server and a database management system.

Wi-Fi. A family of protocols for wireless communications over a distance of up to 100 meters.

wired equivalency protocol (WEP). An obsolete standard for encrypting data over Wi-Fi.

wireless protected access (WPA). A standard for encrypting data over Wi-Fi.

wireless protected access 2 (WPA2). A standard for encrypting data over Wi-Fi.

worm. Malicious software that can self-propagate.

Worldwide Interoperability for Microwave Access (WiMAX). A wireless telecommunications standard for voice and data communications.

zero-day. An exploit that has not been observed in the wild. See also *exploit*.

Index

N

O

About the Author

Peter H. Gregory, CISA, CISSP, CRISC, C I CISO, QSA, is the author of forty books on security and technology, including *Solaris Security* (Prentice Hall), *CISSP For Dummies* (Wiley), *IT Disaster Recovery Planning For Dummies* (Wiley), and *CISA Certified Information Systems Auditor All-In-One Study Guide* (McGraw-Hill/Osborne Media Group).

Peter is a 30-year career technologist and is currently Director of Strategic Services at Fishnet Security, a national information security professional services firm. He has had tactical and strategic security jobs in SAAS, retail, and large wireless telecommunications organizations. He has also held development and operations posts in casino management systems, banking, government, nonprofit organizations, and academia. He is the lead instructor and advisory board member for the University of Washington certificate program in information systems security and a graduate of the FBI Citizens' Academy.

Peter can be found at www.peterhgregory.com.

Dedication

To Rebekah, Shannon, and Nathan, and to the memory of my other children.

Author's Acknowledgments

Peter H. Gregory would like to thank Amy Fandrei, Acquisitions Editor at Wiley, for her vision and guidance. Thank you to Susan Pink for her expert copyediting and for keeping this project organized, and to subject matter experts Wendell Tankersley and Tim Heagarty for their productive and valuable feedback.

Heartfelt thanks to several contributors, including Dave Matthews (the Seattle InfoSec pro, not the band leader), Brian Haller, Marc Gordon, Richard N., Todd Plesco, and Glen Sorenson for their anecdotal descriptions of life as an information security professional.

Next, I would like to thank the information security professionals I've had the pleasure of knowing and working with over the past twenty-plus years. You have enriched my professional life through assistance, large and small. We need many more like you, which is the primary motivation for writing this book.

My contribution to this book would not have been possible without support of my wife and business manager, Rebekah Gregory. Thanks also to Carole Jelen, my literary agent, with whom I've had the pleasure of knowing and working with for over fifteen years.

Publisher's Acknowledgments

Acquisitions Editor: Amy Fandrei

Copy Editor: Susan Pink

Technical Editors: Wendell Tankersley, Tim Heagarty

Editorial Assistant: Claire Brock

Sr. Editorial Assistant: Cherie Case

Project Coordinator: Melissa Cossell

Cover Image: ©iStockphoto.com/Courtney Keating